In cooperation with

D1432470

NorthStar

Building Skills for the TOEFL® iBT

Advanced

Linda Robinson Fellag

Series Editors
Frances Boyd
Carol Numrich

PEARSON
Longman

NorthStar: Building Skills for the TOEFL iBT, Advanced

Pearson Education, 10 Bank Street, White Plains, NY 10606

Vice president, multimedia and skills: Sherry Preiss
Project manager: Debbie Sistino
Development editor: Mykan White
Production coordinator: Melissa Leyva
Senior production editor: Robert Ruvo
Director of manufacturing: Patrice Fraccio
Senior manufacturing buyer: Dave Dickey
Photo research: Shana McGuire
Cover design: Rhea Banker
Cover art: Der Rhein bei Duisburg, 1937, 145(R 5) Rhine near Duisburg
    19 × 27.5 cm; water-based on cardboard; The Metropolitan Museum of
    Art, N.Y. The Berggruen Klee Collection, 1984. (1984.315.56)
    Photograph © 1985 The Metropolitan Museum of Art. © 2003 Artists
    Rights Society (ARS), New York / VG Bild-Kunst, Bonn
Text composition: Anthology, Inc.
Text font: 11/13 Sabon
Credits: see pages xii–xiii

Library of Congress Cataloging-in-Publication Data

Fellag, Linda Robinson.
    NorthStar : building skills for the TOEFL iBT Advanced / Linda
Robinson Fellag.
        p. cm.
        ISBN 0-13-193709-X (pbk.) — ISBN 0-13-198577-9 (pbk. w/audio CD)
        1. English language—Textbooks for foreign speakers. 2. Test of
English as a foreign language—Study guides. 3. English language
—Examinations—Study guides.   I. Title. II. Title: Building skills for
the TOEFL iBT Advanced.
PE1128.F42425 2005
428'.0076—dc22

                                                                        2005023862

ISBN: 0-13-193709-X (Student Book)
           0-13-198577-9 (Student Book with Audio CDs)

ETS, the ETS logo, and TOEFL are registered
trademarks of Educational Testing Service (ETS),
used under license by Pearson Longman.

Printed in the United States of America
2 3 4 5 6 7 8 9 10—VHG—09 08 07 06

Contents

Welcome to *NorthStar Building Skills for the TOEFL® iBT*   iv

Preface   v

Part One: NorthStar Practice Units for the TOEFL® iBT

UNIT **1**   Addiction   1

UNIT **2**   Communities   19

UNIT **3**   Personality   39

UNIT **4**   Trends   57

UNIT **5**   Cross-Cultural Insights   77

UNIT **6**   Faith   97

UNIT **7**   The Workplace   117

UNIT **8**   Perspectives on War   137

UNIT **9**   The Arts   159

UNIT **10**   Freedom of Expression   179

Evaluation Forms for Integrated and Independent Tasks   203

Audioscript   205

Answer Key   223

Part Two: ETS Practice Sets for the TOEFL® iBT

Listening   242

Reading   247

Writing   256

Speaking   258

Audioscript   261

Answer Key   265

TOEFL® iBT Writing and Speaking Rubrics   267

CD Tracking Lists   271

Welcome to NorthStar

Building Skills for the TOEFL® iBT

In Cooperation with ETS®

Pearson Longman and *ETS* combine their expertise in language learning and test development to create an innovative approach to developing the skills assessed in the new TOEFL Internet-based test (iBT). *NorthStar Building Skills for the TOEFL iBT*, a new three-level series, links learning and assessment with a skill-building curriculum that incorporates authentic test material from the makers of the TOEFL iBT.

Each book in the series has 10 thematic units that are organized like the TOEFL iBT into listening, reading, speaking and writing sections. Each unit includes focused integrated skill practice to develop critical thinking and communicative competence. Authentic TOEFL iBT practice sets developed by ETS offer practice and further assessment.

Purpose

The TOEFL test has changed, so preparation for it must change, too. *NorthStar: Building Skills for the TOEFL iBT* takes a new approach—an instructional approach—to test preparation. In this approach, students develop academic skills in English, while building test-taking confidence.

The TOEFL iBT requires students to show their ability to use English in a variety of campus and academic situations such as listening to lectures on unfamiliar topics, orally paraphrasing and integrating information that they have just read and listened to, and writing a well-organized essay with detailed examples, correct grammar, and varied vocabulary. The speaking and writing tasks require clear and confident expression. With these books, students move progressively, sharpening language skills *and* test-taking abilities.

The three *Building Skills* texts are intended as stepping stones from classroom instruction in English to TOEFL and academic readiness. In language instruction, students will benefit most from an integrated-skills, content-based curriculum, with a focus on critical thinking. In instructional test preparation with these books, students will encounter the same content-rich material, tasks, and question types that appear on the test. Using these books in the classroom will improve students' communicative skills, keep their interest, sharpen awareness of their skills, and build their confidence.

Extensive Support to Build the Skills Assessed on the TOEFL iBT

The *Building Skills* books strengthen English language skills while they familiarize students with the type of content, questions and tasks on the *TOEFL iBT*. Practice and mastery of these skills can help learners build confidence to communicate successfully in an academic environment.

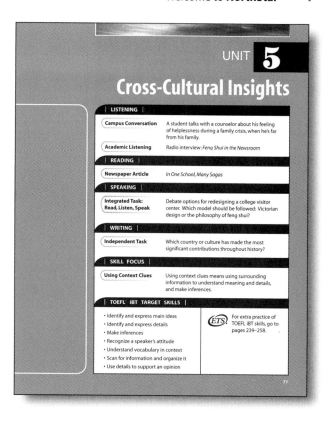

High-Interest Listening Selections

Campus conversations introduce students to practical vocabulary, conversations, and situations encountered in everyday life in a college or university.

Academic listenings present lectures, reports, and interviews, helping students understand a wide variety of styles and topics.

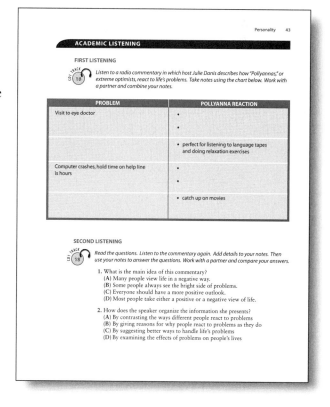

High-Interest Academic Reading Selections

Through engaging readings from many different academic disciplines, students sharpen critical reading skills such as categorizing, summarizing, and analyzing.

2 Reading

COCA-COLA THINKS INTERNATIONAL

PRE-READING

1 *Read the questions. Then quickly read the passage that follows to answer the questions. Write on the lines the number of the paragraph in which you found each answer. Work with a partner to compare your answers.*

_____ 1. In how many countries does Coca-Cola operate?

_____ 2. How many employees did Coca-Cola transfer in its leadership development program?

_____ 3. Who is the president of Coca-Cola, and where was he born?

_____ 4. Where does Coca-Cola earn the greater portion of its profits?

2 *Quickly read paragraph 1 of the passage. What is the general idea of the paragraph? Work with a partner to compare your answers.*

READING

Read the passage and answer the questions. Then work with a partner and compare your answers. When you disagree, go back to the text to find helpful information.

COCA-COLA THINKS INTERNATIONAL

1   Coca-Cola has been operating internationally for most of its 100-year history. Today the company has operations in 160 countries and employs over 400,000 people. The firm's human resource management (HRM) strategy helps to explain a great deal of its success. In one recent year Coca-Cola transferred more than 300 professional and managerial staff from one country to another under its leadership development program, and the number of international transferees is increasing annually. One senior-level HRM manager explained the company strategy by noting:

From *International Business: A Strategic Management Approach,* by Alan M. Rugman and Richard M. Hodgetts, McGraw-Hill, 1995, p. 323. Reproduced with permission of the McGraw-Hill Companies.

Extensive Note-taking Practice

Students practice structured and semi-structured note-taking. These kinds of activities not only enhance comprehension of both listening and reading selections, but they also teach students how to organize information for speaking and writing responses.

LISTENING

CD2 TRACK 25

Listen to a conversation. Use the outline to take notes as you listen.

Main Idea: Two students apply the psychological theory of music and intelligence to their own lives and conclude that music enhances their spatial and analytical skills.

Anna's case

•
•
•
•

Sean's case

•
•
•

Study of children

•

SPEAKING

Speak on the following topic. Follow the steps below to prepare.

Debate the merit of arts education. What are its benefits? What are its disadvantages?

Step 1

• Work with a partner. Skim the reading and your notes from the reading and listening tasks (pages 170–172) to answer the following questions.

1. What are the benefits of music and arts education?

2. What are the disadvantages of having arts programs in schools?

3. What counterarguments can arts opponents give for each argument in favor of arts education?

4. What counterarguments can arts proponents give for each argument against arts education?

• Work in a group to discuss the arguments for and against arts education, as well as the counterarguments that can be made in response to each. Use your answers to the questions above to help you. Take notes on your ideas.

New TOEFL-Type Items and Item Analysis

Extensive TOEFL-type practice items familiarize students with the kinds of questions and tasks they will encounter in the TOEFL iBT. Analysis activities help them understand the purpose of each item.

---

8. The word *this* in paragraph 6 refers to
   (A) Algeria
   (B) the grandfather
   (C) Algeria's war of independence
   (D) the grandfather's torture and death

9. The word *taboo* in paragraph 7 is closest in meaning to
   (A) forbidden
   (B) popular
   (C) unauthorized
   (D) uncommon

10. Which of the following information is NOT true of the family histories mentioned in paragraphs 6 and 7?
    (A) Both stories explained the death of a grandparent.
    (B) Both stories occurred during war-time periods.
    (C) Both stories were openly discussed in the students' homes.
    (D) Both stories told about violence in the students' homes.

11. Look at the four squares ☐ that indicate where the following sentence could be added to the passage. Where would the sentence best fit? Circle the letter that shows the point where you would insert this sentence.

    She thought they might be as uninformed about their family roots as she was at that age.

    The incident set the teacher thinking. A traditional role of French schools is to prepare children of immigrants to become French citizens. ☐A Yet Meak's reaction made Mrs. Contrepois realize that she knew nothing of the background of the young people of different races whom she faced every day. ☐B Clearly, some students' parents came to France simply to find work. Others came fleeing wars and dictatorships. ☐C Yet Mrs. Contrepois, who comes from an immigrant family herself, also wondered whether the teenagers themselves knew why they were in France. Did they know their own family history? ☐D

    A year ago, seeking answers, she gave the 120 students in her six classes a research project titled: "In what way has your family been touched by history?"

12. An introductory sentence for a brief summary of the passage is provided below. Complete the summary by circling the THREE answer choices that express the most important ideas in the passage. Some sentences do not belong in the summary because they express ideas that are not presented in the passage or are minor ideas in the passage.

    Students in a French school researched their immigrant families' histories for a class project.

    (A) The collection of stories was called "History, My History."
    (B) The project required the students to write a paper on the effects of history on their families.

    (continued on next page)

(C) The teacher hoped the project would help her students improve their language skills.
(D) Their stories told of the difficult experiences that led their families to immigrate.
(E) The project helped the students accept both their lives in France and their origins.
(F) The project required students to conduct their research on the Internet.

ANALYSIS

It is helpful to know the purpose of a test item. There are four types of questions in the reading section.

1. Basic Comprehension
- main ideas
- details
- the meaning of specific sentences

2. Organization
- the way information is structured in the text
- the way ideas are linked between sentences or between paragraphs

3. Inference
- ideas are not directly stated in the text
- author's intention, purpose, or attitude not explicitly stated in the text

4. Vocabulary and Reference
- the meaning of words
- the meaning of reference words such as *his*, *them*, *this*, or *none*

Go back to the reading questions and label each question with 1, 2, 3, or 4. Then work with a partner to see if you agree. Check the Answer Key for the correct answers. Which questions did you get right? Which did you get wrong? What skills do you need to practice?

3 Speaking

INTEGRATED TASK: READ, LISTEN, SPEAK

In this section, you will read a short passage and listen to an excerpt on a related topic. Then you will speak about the relationship between the two.

Guided Practice in Integrated and Independent Tasks

Integrated tasks require students to synthesize information from two sources and then speak or write a response. Students practice critical thinking, as well as note-taking and other practical steps for producing a quality response.

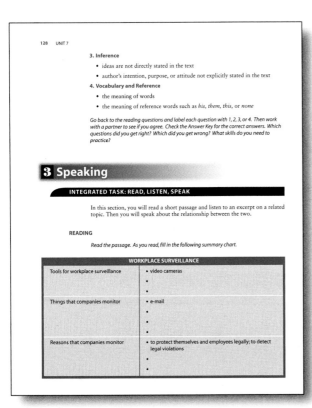

128   UNIT 7

3. Inference

- ideas are not directly stated in the text
- author's intention, purpose, or attitude not explicitly stated in the text

4. Vocabulary and Reference

- the meaning of words
- the meaning of reference words such as *his, them, this,* or *none*

Go back to the reading questions and label each question with 1, 2, 3, or 4. Then work with a partner to see if you agree. Check the Answer Key for the correct answers. Which questions did you get right? Which did you get wrong? What skills do you need to practice?

3 Speaking

INTEGRATED TASK: READ, LISTEN, SPEAK

In this section, you will read a short passage and listen to an excerpt on a related topic. Then you will speak about the relationship between the two.

READING

Read the passage. As you read, fill in the following summary chart.

WORKPLACE SURVEILLANCE	
Tools for workplace surveillance	• video cameras • •
Things that companies monitor	• e-mail • •
Reasons that companies monitor	• to protect themselves and employees legally; to detect legal violations •

Independent tasks help students build the skills they need to express and support opinions.

---

130   UNIT 7

SPEAKING

Speak on the following topic. Follow the steps below to prepare.

Imagine that your employer has asked you to help develop its employee monitoring program. How could you design a program that addresses both the company's security needs and its employees' concerns about privacy?

Step 1

- Work with a partner. Skim the reading and your notes from the reading and listening tasks (pages 128–129) to answer the following questions.

  1. How are employees monitored at work?

  2. Why do companies monitor employees?

  3. What are employees' concerns about monitoring?

  4. How could a monitoring program meet employers' needs while protecting employees' privacy?

- With your partner, discuss what employers/managers and employees want in a monitoring program. Discuss how each "side" can accommodate the other side's needs and concerns. In the box below, make a list of practices that might satisfy both groups. Use your answers to the questions above to help you.

Monitoring Practices to Satisfy Both Sides

Step 2

With your partner, practice a two-minute role play, acting as a manager and an employee who are working together to establish a company's monitoring program. Take turns stating and responding to key points. Discuss ways to satisfy both sides' needs and concerns. Then switch roles and repeat the role play. Be sure to use the information in your list to help you.

The Workplace   131

Step 3

Change partners. Take turns doing the two-minute role play again. Then switch roles and repeat the role play.

To evaluate your partner's response, use the Speaking Evaluation Form on page 204.

4 Writing

INDEPENDENT TASK

Write on the following topic. Follow the steps below to prepare.

Describe your ideal job. Discuss the work you would do, where you would work, your colleagues, and the salary and benefits you would receive.

Step 1

- Work in a group. Brainstorm ideas about appealing or interesting jobs. Share ideas about the following aspects of the jobs: duties, workplace and schedule, coworkers and managers, salary and benefits. Take notes on what you hear.

- On your own, evaluate what you have heard. What are the most appealing or interesting jobs that were mentioned? What are the characteristics of those jobs? Which ideas could you use in your own writing?

- Choose the job that you would most like to have. Organize your ideas by filling in the chart below with information about the job.

MY IDEAL JOB	
Description of job job title, type of work, duties	
Workplace inside/outside, atmosphere, hours, colleagues/managers	
Compensation salary, benefits	

Essential Academic Skills for TOEFL iBT Success

The Skill Focus section in each book raises students' awareness of a key academic language skill. At each level of the series, students deepen and broaden mastery of these ten essential skills:

- Skimming and Scanning

- Identifying and Using Main Ideas and Details

- Making Inferences

- Identifying and Using Rhetorical Structure

- Using Context Clues

- Paraphrasing

- Summarizing

- Using Detailed Examples

- Comparing and Contrasting

- Identifying and Using Cohesive Devices

---

14   UNIT 1

Step 2

Write for 20 minutes. Leave the last 5 minutes to edit your work.

To evaluate a partner's writing, use the Writing Evaluation Form on page 203.

5 Skill Focus

COMPARING AND CONTRASTING

EXAMINATION

1 Read the following excerpt from the unit. Work with a partner and answer the questions about the excerpt.

Item 1 (Campus Conversation, p. 3)

> **Professor:** Look, I'd like every student to know how to do research, but what really matters is this: Can you communicate the information you uncover—in a genuinely meaningful way? . . . Being able to describe the key points is a lot more important than knowing a bunch of facts and details.

- What is being contrasted in this statement?
- What words does the professor use to show contrast? Underline them.

2 Look at the following task from the unit. Work with a partner and answer the questions about the task.

Item 2 (Independent Task, p. 13)

Compare and contrast alcoholism with another, more recent addiction. What are the similarities and differences between the two? In your opinion, which is more severe? Support your opinions with examples from your own or other people's experiences.

- Review your written response to the topic. Which features (causes, effects, etc.) of the two addictions did you compare and contrast? Which examples did you use to help illustrate similarities or differences, and why did you choose them?
- How did you organize your response? Did you focus more on similarities or differences? If you focused more on one, why did you do so?
- Did you use any special words or phrases to signal your comparisons and contrasts? If so, circle them. Show them to your partner and discuss your choices.

Addiction   15

Tips

To do well on the TOEFL, it is essential to learn how to be aware of and use comparisons and contrasts in written and spoken English. Comparisons address similarities; contrasts address differences. Using and recognizing comparisons and contrasts can help you to analyze information and to explain and understand relationships and opinions.

Listening and Reading

- Pay attention to the balance between comparison and contrast. Writers and speakers use either more comparisons or more contrasts in order to show their point of view, or opinion.
- Look for words and phrases that signal comparison and contrast.

  Comparison signals: *also, both, similarly, like, comparable, the same, likewise,* and so on

  Contrast signals: *but, however, unlike, differences, in contrast, more/less . . . than,* and so on

- Notice examples used to support each point of view.

In **Item 1**, the professor contrasts the two activities because he believes that they are very different and that one of them is more important. To show contrast, he uses the word *but* and the phrase "more important than."

Speaking and Writing

- When expressing your opinion, use more comparisons to show that you think subjects are alike, or more contrasts to show that you think they are different. When you do not intend to express your opinion, use an equal balance of comparisons and contrasts.
- Give equal time or space to each of the subjects you are comparing and contrasting; compare and contrast the same features about each subject. Try to balance each point about one subject with a related point about the other subject(s).
- Use words or phrases to introduce comparison and contrast.
- Support ideas with detailed examples.

In your response to **Item 2**, you should have written about both addictions equally, including detailed examples to support your ideas about each one. Your response could have focused on the causes of both addictions or the effects of both addictions, but it should not have focused on the causes of one addiction and the effects of the other.

ETS Practice Section

Developed by ETS especially for this new series,
TOEFL iBT tasks offer authentic practice and
further assessment.

LISTENING

Listen to the conversations and lectures. Answer the questions based on what is stated or implied by the speakers. You may take notes while you listen. Use your notes to help you answer the questions. (Check the Answer Key on pages 265–266.)

CONVERSATION 1

1. What are the two speakers mainly discussing?
(**A**) How to use graphs effectively in a class presentation
(**B**) Where the professor posts class information on the Internet
(**C**) The way the student requests information from the professor
(**D**) What the student needs to do to meet a deadline for a paper

2. According to the professor, e-mail communication is useful in certain situations. What two examples does the professor mention? **Choose TWO answers.**
(**A**) Obtaining more details on class work with imminent deadlines
(**B**) Providing the professor with copies of student presentations
(**C**) Sharing information about research sources for class papers
(**D**) Asking follow-up questions about a lecture the professor has given

3. What does the professor imply about discussion groups on the Internet?
(**A**) They are not as effective as discussion groups that meet in person.
(**B**) They do not always provide accurate information for participants.
(**C**) They are not adequate substitutes for attending her seminar.
(**D**) They do not make use of the professor's lectures on the course material.

4. What does the professor ask the student to do?
(**A**) Take better notes
(**B**) Talk more in class
(**C**) Write longer papers
(**D**) Send more e-mails

Measuring Skills

To develop fluency and accuracy in English, students need practice and feedback. Students can complete Writing and Speaking Evaluation Forms to assess each other's written and spoken responses.

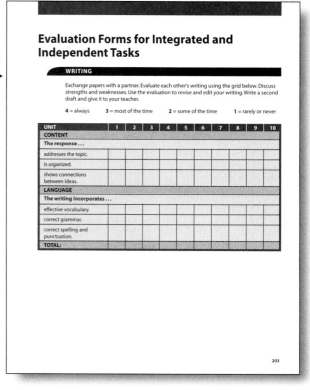

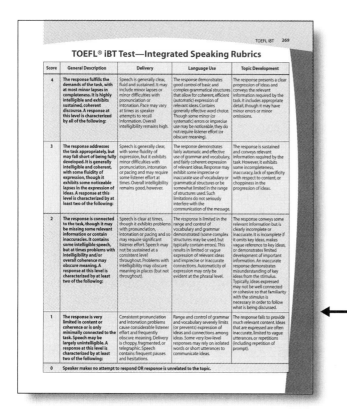

Teachers can use the authentic TOEFL iBT Scoring Rubrics developed by ETS to assess student responses to Integrated and Independent Tasks.

Teachers' Manuals

Teachers' Manuals for each level provide unit-by-unit suggestions as well as evaluation tools to track students' progress. The Teachers' Manuals also include actual student responses to speaking and writing tasks at all score levels. Provided by ETS, these authentic samples enable teachers to assess proficiency.

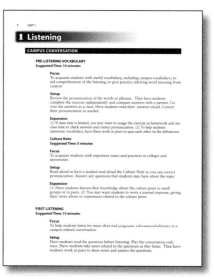

Acknowledgments

The author wishes to express her heartfelt thanks to the team of editors and authors who worked together to sustain the high standards of this series: Sherry Preiss, Frances Boyd, Carol Numrich, Debbie Sistino, Paula Van Ells, and Mykan White.

Many people at ETS contributed to this project, but Longman would especially like to thank Phil Everson, Matt Chametzky, Kate Kazin, Will Jared, and Frank Heron.

Credits

page 4 "Time to Do Everything but Think" "Next Frontiers 3-To What End" From Newsweek On Air, April 30, 2001. Copyright © 2001, Newsweek, Inc. and AP Network News. All rights reserved. Used with permission.; **page 6** "Mick's Toughest Inning" Reprinted with permission from the NEW YORK POST, 1995, Copyright © NYP Holdings, Inc.; **page 11** "Interview with an Internet Addiction Counselor" *Talk of the Nation: Science Friday*, interview with Jonathan Kandell, February 2, 1996. Reproduced with permission of Talk of the Nation; **page 23** "Living in Celebration" *Fresh Air with Terry Gross*, produced in Philadelphia by WHYY.; **page 25** "Making Ends Meet" Copyright © 2001 by The New York Times Co. Reprinted with permission.; **page 29** "Celebration Experiment" © ® 1996, 1999, Minnesota Public Radio. All rights reserved. Reproduced with permission of Minnesota Public Radio (www.mpr.org) and American Public Media. Marketplace® is the largest daily national business show and is heard on over 330 public radio stations. Visit Marketplace on the web at www.marketplace.org.; **page 43** "Pollyanna Syndrome" © ® 1996, 1999, Minnesota Public Radio. All rights reserved. Reproduced with permission of Minnesota Public Radio (www.mpr.org) and American Public Media. Marketplace® is the largest daily national business show and is heard on over 330 public radio stations. Visit Marketplace on the web at www.marketplace.org.; **page 45** "Keeping Your Confidence Up" from *Taking the Fear Out of Changing*, by Dr. Dennis O'Grady. Reprinted with permission from Bob Adams, Inc. Copyright © 1992, 1994.; **pages 49, 55** "Types of Shyness" "Americans are Generally Shy and Getting Shyer" The text and audio of a news interview by NPR's Alex Chadwick was originally broadcast on National Public Radio's *Morning Edition* on August 30, 1995, and is used with the permission of National Public Radio, Inc. Any unauthorized duplication is strictly prohibited.; **page 60** "Tipping Points in Fighting Crime" An interview with Malcolm Gladwell on the Todd Mundt Show, January 2, 2001. Reproduced with the permission of Michigan Radio, © Copyright, 2001.; **page 63** "The Story of Silent Spring" Reprinted with permission of Natural Resources Defense Council.; **page 80** "Feng Shui in the Newsroom" *West Coast Live*, interview with Kirsten Lagatree by Sedge Thomson, February 10, 1996.; **page 83** "In One School, Many Sagas" "Sad Voyages to France: One School, Many Sagas." Copyright © 1994 by the New York Times Co. Reprinted with permission.; **page 95** "Lost in Translation" (1) "Exile," from LOST IN TRANSLATION by Eva Hoffman, copyright © 1989 by Eva Hoffman. Used by permission of Dutton, a division of Penguin Group (USA) Inc. (2) From *Lost in Translation* by Eva Hoffman, published by William Heinemann. Reprinted by permission of The Random House Group Ltd.; **page 101** "Describing Monastic Life" From *Monks and Monasteries* broadcast on June 18, 2001 on Public Interest with Kojo Nnamdi. Used with permission from WAMU—American University Radio.; **page 104** "Religion" Reprinted with permission from *Encyclopaedia Britannica*, © 1993, 1994 by Encyclopaedia Britannica, Inc.; **page 108** "The Religious Tradition of Fasting" Copyright

Photo Credits

NorthStar Practice Units for the TOEFL® iBT

UNIT **1**

Addiction

| LISTENING |

Campus Conversation   A student and a professor discuss Internet research and addiction.

Academic Listening   Radio interview: *Time to Do Everything except Think*

| READING |

Newspaper Article   *Mick's Toughest Inning*

| SPEAKING |

Integrated Task: Compare and contrast the effects of Internet
Read, Listen, Speak   addiction with those of compulsive shopping.

| WRITING |

Independent Task   Compare and contrast alcoholism with another, more recent addiction.

| SKILL FOCUS |

Comparing and Contrasting   Comparing and contrasting means recognizing relationships, analyzing similarities and differences, and distinguishing two points of view.

| TOEFL® iBT TARGET SKILLS |

- Identify and express main ideas
- Identify and express details
- Make inferences
- Recognize comparison in a listening
- Organize information
- Use detailed examples to compare two ideas
- Complete an outline with topics and details

 For extra practice of TOEFL iBT skills, go to pages 242–259.

1 Listening

CAMPUS CONVERSATION

PRE-LISTENING VOCABULARY

Read the sentences. Guess the meaning of the boldfaced words and phrases. Then match each word or phrase with a definition or synonym from the list below. Work with a partner and compare your answers.

_____ 1. If you **leave out** an important source in a research paper, you should go back to add the information.

_____ 2. On the first class day, the professor usually gives an **overview** of the course, that is, a description of the goals, assignments, and requirements of the course.

_____ 3. You need to be **discriminating** in your use of the Internet, choosing sites carefully and evaluating whether or not the information is reliable.

_____ 4. If you don't keep up with your assignments, they will **accumulate**, and you will have to do a lot of work in a short time.

_____ 5. It is considered **unethical** to copy another person's words or ideas and claim those words or ideas as your own.

_____ 6. If you want ideas for weekend activities, look in your local newspaper. Some useful information is sure to **turn up**.

_____ 7. An academic reading may be difficult to **grasp** if students do not understand the basic concepts presented in the reading.

_____ 8. If you have additional questions about the homework, come to see me during my **office hours** from 2:00 to 4:00 P.M. today.

a. appear

b. build up

c. dishonest, immoral

d. do not include

e. selective

f. summary

g. time for meeting with students

h. understand

> **Culture Note:** College and university students often stop by their professors' offices to ask questions about or get help with assignments that they are working on. Professors generally keep office hours and announce at the beginning of the semester when they are available to students.

FIRST LISTENING

Read the questions. Listen to the conversation between a student and a professor. Take notes as you listen. Share your notes with a partner. Then use your notes to answer the questions.

1. What are the student and the professor discussing?

_____

_____

2. What does the student want?

_____

_____

3. What is the professor's main concern?

_____

_____

SECOND LISTENING

Read the questions. Listen to the conversation again. Add details to your notes. Then use your notes to answer the questions. Work with a partner and compare your answers.

1. Why does the student go to see her professor?
  (A) To ask where to find resources for researching addiction
  (B) To request that she be allowed to turn a paper in late
  (C) To ask permission to submit a longer paper
  (D) To talk about a website that she has developed for the class

2. What does the professor imply about using the Internet to do research?
 (A) It is unethical to do research that way.
 (B) It is a resource that does not cause a problem of addiction.
 (C) It is a resource that needs to be used with caution.
 (D) It is the most reliable way to find accurate information.

3. What does the professor consider an essential skill for his students to develop?
 (A) Mastering all the details associated with a topic
 (B) Delivering a memorable oral presentation
 (C) Using the Internet to complete assignments
 (D) Explaining the central ideas of a topic clearly

4. How does the professor suggest the student use her newly acquired knowledge?
 (A) By writing a longer paper for extra credit
 (B) By preparing a presentation for the class
 (C) By developing new research tools for the class
 (D) By helping other students finish their assignments

 Listen again to part of the conversation. Then answer question 5.

CD1 TRACK 03

5. What does the professor mean when he says, "Honestly."?
 (A) He is expressing polite criticism of the student's actions.
 (B) He is questioning whether the student really spent much time on the assignment.
 (C) He is reminding the student to use her own ideas when writing a paper.
 (D) He is defending his earlier statement in praise of the Internet.

ACADEMIC LISTENING

FIRST LISTENING

 Listen to an excerpt from a radio news interview with David Brooks, author of a book about life in the high-tech twenty-first century. Listen for the positive and negative ideas about the information we deal with in our world. Take notes using the chart below. Work with a partner and combine your notes.

CD1 TRACK 04

POSITIVE	NEGATIVE
• multi-tasking makes brain work faster	• bombarded & overwhelmed
•	•
•	•
•	•
•	

SECOND LISTENING

Read the questions. Listen to the interview again. Add details to your notes. Then use your notes to answer the questions. Work with a partner and compare your answers.

1. What is the conversation mainly about?
   (A) The fact that more and more people are using cell phones
   (B) The fact that we are becoming more dependent on computers
   (C) The fact that our thinking is changing because of communications
   (D) The fact that technology has made people less communicative

2. In this conversation, the men discuss
   (A) examples of technological devices
   (B) causes for technological advances
   (C) effects of technology and communications
   (D) ways to improve technology and communications

3. Which of these statements most accurately reflects David Brooks' response to the research study that David Alpern mentions?
   (A) Brooks thinks that taking in a great deal of information benefits the brain.
   (B) Brooks believes that too much information flow can be harmful to our brains.
   (C) Brooks does not express his opinion about the research study that Alpern mentions.
   (D) Brooks thinks that the brain is helped as much as hurt by so much information.

Listen again to part of the interview. Then answer question 4.

4. Why does David Alpern say, "Seriously though"?
   (A) To disagree with the information David Brooks gave
   (B) To make the conversation more serious
   (C) To change the focus of the discussion
   (D) To give an example of what David Brooks is saying

Listen again to part of the interview. Then answer question 5.

5. What does Brooks mean when he says, "I don't think we're becoming a race of global idiots."?
   (A) It is not a good idea to multi-task.
   (B) Multi-tasking is damaging our brains.
   (C) Multi-tasking is not such a terrible activity.
   (D) Multi-tasking is the best type of activity for us.

2 Reading

MICK'S TOUGHEST INNING

PRE-READING

The following article describes the illness of a famous U.S. baseball star, Mickey Mantle, who was an alcoholic. The article, written shortly before Mantle's death in 1995, presents the writer's opinion about health-care policies that determine who should receive certain medical services.

Read the question and write a short response. Work with a partner and compare your responses.

Should there be any differences between the type of medical treatment that a celebrity and an average citizen receive?

READING

Read the passage and answer the questions. Then work with a partner and compare your answers. When you disagree, go back to the text to find helpful information.

Mick's Toughest Inning

By Cathy Burke (from the *New York Post*)

1   Mickey Mantle played his way into the pantheon of baseball gods, and drank his way to the brink of death. So in today's cynical debate over health-care priorities, Mick's record drinking would drop him to the bottom of the list for a life-saving transplant. Chilling but true. He's over 60 and was an alcoholic for most of his life, a choice that helped make him as sick as he is today. Then there's his age and medical condition, which would put his chances at about 60 percent for surviving a liver transplant for five years or more. The cynics would say Mick is a poor risk indeed. They are wrong. Such a heartless and politicized point of view has gained strength ever since

1984, when former Colorado governor Richard Lamm made the famous declaration that the terminally ill have a "duty to die and get out of the way. Let the others in society, our children, build a reasonable life," he said. What kind of a reasonable life is it when politicians decide whether it is a good risk to save a human life? But Lamm had more to say on modern technology, exactly the kind that could save Mickey Mantle. "How many hearts should we give to a smoker . . . how many liver transplants can we afford to give to an alcoholic," he asked, implying that one was too many.

2   In Oregon, Lamm's legacy lives on in something called the Oregon Health Plan, a "medical rationing" welfare program started in February 1994. The plan prioritizes 565 diseases and their treatments based on how effective the treatments are and how much they cost. Transplants for liver cancer patients are not funded. Can we trust the politicians to do the right thing for the sickest and poorest among us? In Oregon, the health professionals decide what diseases and treatments go on the list and then a computer determines treatment priorities based on death rates and costs. But the politicians decide how much money is spent. No matter what the proponents say, the Oregon system rations people out of care simply by denying them medical services because some politician doesn't like the survival odds or costs. Fortunately, Mick won't have to worry about getting a chance at a liver transplant. Get well, Mick, before the most cynical of the health-care reformers do us all in.

1. What is the author's main point in the reading?
   (A) Mickey Mantle needs a liver transplant because of his alcoholism.
   (B) The chances of alcoholics like Mantle surviving a liver transplant are low.
   (C) Alcoholics are poor risks, so they should not receive medical treatment.
   (D) Some people wrongly argue that people like Mantle don't deserve medical treatment.

2. All of the following characteristics describe Mickey Mantle EXCEPT
   (A) too poor to afford medical care
   (B) over 60 years old
   (C) alcoholic most of his life
   (D) in need of a transplant to survive

3. The passage can be best described as
   (A) an objective report on a health-care plan
   (B) a criticism of Mickey Mantle's health care
   (C) an opinion piece condemning a health-care policy
   (D) a report outlining the best practices in U.S. health care

4. According to paragraph 1, which of the following is true about Richard Lamm's ideas about health care?
   (A) Smokers and alcoholics should receive the medical treatment they need.
   (B) Society should not waste money on medical care for the terminally ill.
   (C) The cost of health care is low enough to cover all citizens.
   (D) The next generation should be permitted to decide health-care priorities.

5. In paragraph 2, what is the author's attitude towards politicians?
   (A) They worry too much about welfare programs.
   (B) They have created a helpful health-care plan.
   (C) They can't be trusted to advocate for the sick and poor.
   (D) They are in the best position to make funding decisions.

6. The word *prioritizes* in paragraph 2 is closest in meaning to
   (A) explains
   (B) denies
   (C) ranks
   (D) defines

7. The word *one* in paragraph 1 refers to
   (A) Mickey Mantle
   (B) smoker
   (C) alcoholic
   (D) liver transplant

8. The word *odds* in paragraph 2 is closest in meaning to
   (A) impossibilities
   (B) chances
   (C) expenses
   (D) recommendations

9. Look at the four squares ☐ that indicate where the following sentence could be added to the passage. Where would the sentence best fit? Circle the letter that shows the point where you would insert this sentence.

   > The state's health department says this program serves more low-income people by using federal health-care funds and eliminating funding for certain costly procedures.

   In Oregon, Lamm's legacy lives on in something called the Oregon Health Plan, a "medical rationing" welfare program started in February 1994. [A] The plan prioritizes 565 diseases and their treatments based on how effective the treatments are and how much they cost. [B] Transplants for liver cancer patients are not funded. [C] Can we trust the politicians to do the right thing for the sickest and poorest among us? In Oregon, the health professionals decide what diseases and treatments go on the list and then a computer determines treatment priorities based on death rates and costs. But the politicians decide how much money is spent. [D] No matter what the proponents say, the Oregon system rations people out of care simply by denying them medical services because some politician doesn't like the survival odds or costs.

10. Which of the following best expresses the essential information in this sentence from the passage?

> So in today's cynical debate over health-care priorities, Mick's record drinking would drop him to the bottom of the list for a life-saving transplant.

(A) Nowadays, people would argue that alcoholics like Mantle should not receive transplants.

(B) Transplants must be made immediately available to save the lives of alcoholics like Mantle.

(C) Some argue that transplant surgery should be a low health-care priority today.

(D) Mantle's alcoholism is currently being debated among health-care professionals.

11. An introductory sentence for a brief summary of the passage is provided below. Complete the summary by circling the THREE answer choices that express the most important ideas in the passage. Some sentences do not belong in the summary because they express ideas that are not presented in the passage or are minor ideas in the passage.

> Deciding health-care priorities on the basis of survival odds or cost is lacking in compassion.

(A) Mickey Mantle has been an alcoholic most of his life.

(B) Oregon has established a rationing plan for funding health care.

(C) Transplants for liver cancer patients are not funded.

(D) The Oregon program started in 1994.

(E) In Oregon's plan, health-care professionals decide what services are funded.

(F) Politicians decide how much money is spent.

ANALYSIS

It is helpful to know the purpose of a test item. There are four types of questions in the reading section.

1. Basic Comprehension

- main ideas

- details

- the meaning of specific sentences

2. Organization

- the way information is structured in the text
- the way ideas are linked between sentences or between paragraphs

3. Inference

- ideas are not directly stated in the text
- author's intention, purpose, or attitude not explicitly stated in the text

4. Vocabulary and Reference

- the meaning of words
- the meaning of reference words such as *his, them, this,* or *none*

Go back to the reading questions and label each question with 1, 2, 3, or 4. Then work with a partner to see if you agree. Check the Answer Key for the correct answers. Which questions did you get right? Which did you get wrong? What skills do you need to practice?

3 Speaking

INTEGRATED TASK: READ, LISTEN, SPEAK

In this section, you will read a short passage and listen to an excerpt on a related topic. Then you will speak about the relationship between the two.

READING

Read the passage on the next page. As you read, fill in the following summary chart.

SIGNS OF INTERNET ADDICTION	
Lifestyle	• •
Relationships	• •
Feelings	• •

Interview with an Internet Addiction Counselor

Interviewer: What are the symptoms? How do I know when my Internet compulsiveness is turning into an Internet addiction?

Counselor: I'm not sure the exact amount of time is really the issue, but I think when it becomes something that really begins to affect other areas of your life—for instance, your work performance or your school performance or relationships with other people. One of the problems I see with the Internet, especially the chat rooms, is that people start developing relationships over the Net and they are very different from relationships that you have on a face-to-face basis, and you start losing some of the skills that make relationships successful. So that's certainly a warning signal. I think if people are beginning to say something to you like, "You seem to be spending a lot of time online," that's probably a good indicator as well.

But, I think, a real important thing is to examine what's going on with you when you are not on the Net. If you are beginning to feel anxious or depressed or feeling empty and lonely, and you know you really look forward to those times when you can be online to be connected with other people in that way, then, I think, a serious issue is starting to happen.

LISTENING

 CD1 TRACK 07

Listen to a conversation. Use the outline to take notes as you listen.

Main Idea: People become shopaholics for different reasons, and this condition affects their lives in many ways.

Reasons for compulsive shopping

-
-
-

Effects of compulsive shopping

- Lifestyle:
- Financial:
- Emotional:

SPEAKING

Speak on the following topic. Follow the steps below to prepare.

Compare and contrast the effects of Internet addiction with those of compulsive shopping. How are they similar and/or different?

Step 1

- Work with a partner. Skim the reading and your notes from the reading and listening tasks (pages 10–11) to answer the following questions.

    1. What is Internet addiction?

    2. What are some effects of Internet addiction?

    3. What is compulsive shopping?

    4. What are some effects of compulsive shopping?

- Fill in the chart below. Write the effects of the two addictions.

EFFECTS OF INTERNET ADDICTION	EFFECTS OF COMPULSIVE SHOPPING

- Identify the similarities and differences between the effects of the two types of addiction. In the chart below, list similarities and differences to discuss in your oral presentation.

SIMILARITIES	DIFFERENCES

Step 2

With your partner, take turns practicing a one-minute oral response to the topic. Be sure to use the information in your list to help you.

Step 3

Change partners. Take turns giving a one-minute response to the topic again.

To evaluate your partner's response, use the Speaking Evaluation Form on page 204.

4 Writing

INDEPENDENT TASK

Write on the following topic. Follow the steps below to prepare.

Compare and contrast alcoholism with another, more recent addiction. What are the similarities and differences between the two? In your opinion, which is more severe? Support your opinions with examples from your own or other people's experiences.

Step 1

- As a class, brainstorm a list of more recent types of addictions, such as Internet addiction, and write them on the board. Choose ONE addiction that you can compare and contrast with alcoholism.

- Work with a classmate or classmates who are interested in writing about the same addiction. Discuss the following questions.

   1. Why do people do this activity?

   2. How do they become addicted?

   3. What effects does the addiction have?

   4. How is this addiction similar to or different from alcoholism?

   5. Is this addiction more or less severe than alcoholism?

- On your own, evaluate what you have heard. Are the descriptions of alcoholism and the other addiction accurate and clear? Which ideas could you use in your own writing?

- Prepare for your writing by making a list of the similarities and differences that you will write about. For each one, take notes about the examples you will include. Refer to your list as you write.

Step 2

Write for 20 minutes. Leave the last 5 minutes to edit your work.

> To evaluate a partner's writing, use the Writing Evaluation Form on page 203.

5 Skill Focus

COMPARING AND CONTRASTING

EXAMINATION

1 *Read the following excerpt from the unit. Work with a partner and answer the questions about the excerpt.*

Item 1 (Campus Conversation, p. 3)

> **Professor:** Look, I'd like every student to know how to do research, but what really matters is this: Can you communicate the information you uncover—in a genuinely meaningful way? . . . Being able to describe the key points is a lot more important than knowing a bunch of facts and details.

- What is being contrasted in this statement?
- What words does the professor use to show contrast? Underline them.

2 *Look at the following task from the unit. Work with a partner and answer the questions about the task.*

Item 2 (Independent Task, p. 13)

Compare and contrast alcoholism with another, more recent addiction. What are the similarities and differences between the two? In your opinion, which is more severe? Support your opinions with examples from your own or other people's experiences.

- Review your written response to the topic. Which features (causes, effects, etc.) of the two addictions did you compare and contrast? Which examples did you use to help illustrate similarities or differences, and why did you choose them?
- How did you organize your response? Did you focus more on similarities or differences? If you focused more on one, why did you do so?
- Did you use any special words or phrases to signal your comparisons and contrasts? If so, circle them. Show them to your partner and discuss your choices.

Tips

To do well on the TOEFL, it is essential to learn how to be aware of and use comparisons and contrasts in written and spoken English. Comparisons address similarities; contrasts address differences. Using and recognizing comparisons and contrasts can help you to analyze information and to explain and understand relationships and opinions.

Listening and Reading

- Pay attention to the balance between comparison and contrast. Writers and speakers use either more comparisons or more contrasts in order to show their point of view, or opinion.

- Look for words and phrases that signal comparison and contrast.

  Comparison signals: *also, both, similarly, like, comparable, the same, likewise,* and so on

  Contrast signals: *but, however, unlike, differences, in contrast, more/less . . . than,* and so on

- Notice examples used to support each point of view.

In **Item 1,** the professor contrasts the two activities because he believes that they are very different and that one of them is more important. To show contrast, he uses the word *but* and the phrase "more important than."

Speaking and Writing

- When expressing your opinion, use more comparisons to show that you think subjects are alike, or more contrasts to show that you think they are different. When you do not intend to express your opinion, use an equal balance of comparisons and contrasts.

- Give equal time or space to each of the subjects you are comparing and contrasting; compare and contrast the same features about each subject. Try to balance each point about one subject with a related point about the other subject(s).

- Use words or phrases to introduce comparison and contrast.

- Support ideas with detailed examples.

In your response to **Item 2,** you should have written about both addictions equally, including detailed examples to support your ideas about each one. Your response could have focused on the causes of both addictions or the effects of both addictions, but it should not have focused on the causes of one addiction and the effects of the other.

PRACTICE

Read the passage. Use the tips from the previous section to help you answer the questions and complete the activities that follow. Work with a partner and compare your answers.

Mickey Mantle

1   Mickey Mantle was one of the greatest baseball players of all time. He played for the New York Yankees in their years of glory. From the time Mantle began to play professionally in 1951 to his last year in 1968, baseball was the most popular game in the United States. For many people, Mantle symbolized the hope, prosperity, and confidence of America at that time.

2   Mantle was a fast and powerful player, a "switch-hitter" who could bat both right-handed and left-handed. He won game after game, one World Series championship after another, for his team. He was a wonderful athlete, but this alone cannot explain America's fascination with him.

3   Perhaps it was because he was a handsome, red-haired country boy, the son of a poor miner from Oklahoma. His career, from the lead mines of the West to the heights of success and fame, was a fairy-tale version of the American dream. Or perhaps it was because America always loves a "natural": a person who wins without seeming to try, whose talent appears to come from an inner grace. That was Mickey Mantle.

4   But like many celebrities, Mickey Mantle had a private life that was full of problems. He played without complaint despite constant pain from injuries. He lived to fulfill his father's dreams and drank to forget his father's early death.

5   It was a terrible addiction that finally destroyed his body. It gave him cirrhosis of the liver and accelerated the advance of liver cancer. Even when Mickey Mantle had turned away from his old life and warned young people not to follow his example, the destructive process could not be stopped. Despite a liver transplant operation that had all those who loved and admired him hoping for a recovery, Mickey Mantle died of cancer at the age of 63.

1. a. What two topics related to Mantle's life are being compared or contrasted in this passage?
   b. Draw a line between the paragraphs where the division between the two topics occurs.
   c. Circle the key word that shows the change in topics.

2. Does this passage focus on comparison or contrast?

3. Fill in the outline to identify the main topics developed for this comparison/contrast. First write phrases or sentences to express the two topics. Then write the details used to support each topic.

Topic 1: _____

_____

Details: _*played for the Yankees in their years of glory*_

_____

_____

Topic 2: _____

_____

Details: _*constant pain from injuries*_

_____

_____

Communities

| LISTENING | |

Campus Conversation — Two students discuss a search for housing.

Academic Listening — Radio interview: *Living in Celebration*

| READING |

Book Review — *Making Ends Meet*

| WRITING |

Integrated Task: Read, Listen, Write — Explain how the principles of New Urbanism propose to solve the problems of urban sprawl.

| SPEAKING |

Independent Task — In your opinion, what would be the most important principles for a new community to have, and why? Support your opinion with specific examples.

| SKILL FOCUS |

Using Detailed Examples — Using detailed examples shows your ability to provide concrete examples and specific information to illustrate an idea or to support a general statement.

| TOEFL® iBT TARGET SKILLS |

- Identify and express main ideas
- Identify and express details
- Make inferences
- Listen for details and paraphrase them
- Summarize a listening and relate it to a text on the same topic
- Link concrete information to abstract ideas

 For extra practice of TOEFL iBT skills, go to pages 242–259.

1 Listening

PRE-LISTENING VOCABULARY

Read the sentences. Guess the meaning of the boldfaced words and phrases. Then match each word or phrase with a definition or synonym from the list below. Work with a partner and compare your answers.

_____ **1.** The professor can't meet with us now because he **is about to** leave for his next class.

_____ **2.** Don't **give up** if you've been searching awhile for a job; you'll find something soon.

_____ **3.** If you overload yourself with English, chemistry, calculus, and history in one semester, you may have too much work and **end up** getting poor grades.

_____ **4.** I'm well-prepared for my sociology exam; **as a matter of fact**, I don't even need to study at all.

_____ **5.** Look over the course offerings for next semester and consider all the **options** that you have. Then let me know which courses you've selected.

_____ **6.** New compact cars **go for** more than $10,000, so I decided it would be more economical to buy a used car while I'm in school.

_____ **7.** My computer programming professor said that $1,200 is a **reasonable** amount to pay for a laptop computer with ample memory and speed.

_____ **8.** If you decide to live **off campus,** you will have to find the best way to commute to and from school and your home.

_____ **9.** My math professor is **a real pain!** He takes points off on our exams if we forget to put the parentheses in an equation. And he gives an exam *every week*.

_____ **10.** That girl is too beautiful to ever go out with me. She's **out of my league.**

a. actually

b. admit defeat, quit

c. an annoying person or thing

d. choices

e. cost

f. finish by

g. is ready to do (something) very soon

h. outside the college buildings and land

i. sensible, fair

j. superior to someone or something else

> **Culture Note:** For many "undergrads" (students seeking a two- or four-year degree), attending college marks an initiation into independent living. In the United States, for example, the majority of undergraduates live off campus, often with one or more roommates. Usually, this is a student's first experience with the responsibilities and challenges related to living on his or her own.

FIRST LISTENING

Read the questions. Listen to the conversation between two students. Take notes as you listen. Share your notes with a partner. Then use your notes to answer the questions.

1. What problem are the students discussing?

_____

_____

2. Why is the choice difficult?

_____

_____

3. What idea is finally proposed?

_____

_____

SECOND LISTENING

Read the questions. Listen to the conversation again. Add details to your notes. Then use your notes to answer the questions. Work with a partner and compare your answers.

1. What is the conversation mainly about?
    (A) A student's problem with finding good housing
    (B) The problems with traveling from home to school and work
    (C) The safety of neighborhoods in the students' city
    (D) The students' search for a house where they both can live

2. How does the male student say he travels to school?
    (A) By car
    (B) By bus
    (C) By train
    (D) On foot

Listen again to part of the conversation. Then answer question 3.

3. What is the student's attitude when he says, "And you know how plentiful parking spaces are at 8:45 in the morning!"?
    (A) He considers it common knowledge that parking spaces are plentiful.
    (B) He is asking for information about the availability of parking on campus.
    (C) He and his classmate both know that on-campus parking is hard to find.
    (D) He thinks it is too early to park at 8:45 in the morning.

Listen again to part of the conversation. Then answer question 4.

4. What is the student's purpose in saying this?
    (A) He is expressing agreement that none of these ideas is acceptable.
    (B) He is suggesting that his classmate should have accepted one of his ideas.
    (C) He is objectively restating all of the ideas that they already discussed.
    (D) He is preparing to offer several other proposals to his classmate.

Listen again to part of the conversation. Then answer question 5.

5. Why does the male student ask, "So . . . where is this ideal house?"?
    (A) He is disappointed in the idea.
    (B) He is doubtful about the idea.
    (C) He is excited about the idea.
    (D) He is against the idea.

ACADEMIC LISTENING

FIRST LISTENING

Listen to an excerpt from a radio interview with Douglas Frantz, a journalist who wrote a book about his experience living in the town of Celebration, Florida. Take notes as you listen. Work with a partner to combine your notes. Then use your notes to answer the questions.

1. What is the topic of the interview?

_____

2. What examples of town features does Frantz include? Write as many as you hear.

_____

3. In general, does Frantz have a positive or a negative feeling about Celebration?

_____

SECOND LISTENING

Read the questions. Listen to the interview again. Add details to your notes. Then use your notes to answer the questions. Work with a partner and compare your answers.

1. What is the subject of this conversation?
   (A) Planners designed a model for big-city life.
   (B) Planners designed parks and common areas.
   (C) Planners wanted to create the perfect small town.
   (D) Planners designed houses with front porches.

2. In the interview, Frantz mainly speaks about
   (A) ways to improve suburbs in America
   (B) causes for building neighborhoods with parks
   (C) effects of interaction among neighbors in small towns
   (D) reasons behind the planned community's design

3. Which of these statements most accurately reflects Frantz's evaluation of Celebration, Florida?
   (A) Frantz thinks the town planners did not achieve their goals.
   (B) Frantz believes that Celebration was an ideal place to live.
   (C) Frantz does not express his opinion about the town.
   (D) Frantz thinks that most suburbs are better than Celebration.

4. Which of the following describes Celebration?
   (A) Houses built far apart from each other
   (B) Lots of parks and common areas
   (C) Plenty of private yard space
   (D) Residents relaxing on front porches

Listen again to part of the interview. Then answer question 5.

5. What does Frantz mean when he says, "There are a couple of things going on."?
(A) Here are two causes of the failure.
(B) Here are two solutions to the failure.
(C) Here are two effects of the failure.
(D) Here are two descriptions of the failure.

ANALYSIS

It is helpful to know the purpose of a test item. There are three types of questions in the listening section.

1. Basic Comprehension

- main ideas
- details
- the meaning of specific sentences

2. Organization

- the way information is structured
- the way ideas are linked

3. Inference

- ideas are not directly stated
- speaker's intention, purpose, or attitude not explicitly stated

Go back to the listening questions and label each question with 1, 2, or 3. Then work with a partner to see if you agree. Check the Answer Key for the correct answers. Which questions did you get right? Which did you get wrong? What skills do you need to practice?

2 Reading

MAKING ENDS MEET

PRE-READING

Poverty, or not having enough money to live, is a significant problem in most communities. You will read an excerpt from a review of a book by Barbara Ehrenreich entitled *Nickled and Dimed: On (Not) Getting by in America.* Ehrenreich worked at minimum-wage (low-paying) jobs to find out what it is like to live in poverty.

Read the question. Then work with a partner to brainstorm answers. Include examples with specific details—facts, descriptive words, and so on. Use the chart below to organize your ideas.

What do you think life is like for people in the United States who try to support themselves with minimum-wage (low-paying) jobs?

DESCRIPTION OF DAILY LIFE	EXAMPLE	DETAILS
often sick	my neighbor Sam	had back problems, chronic pain, no medical insurance, no time to stand in lines at free clinics

READING

Read the passage and answer the questions. Then work with a partner and compare your answers. When you disagree, go back to the text to find helpful information.

Making Ends Meet

From a *New York Times* book review written by Dorothy Gallagher

1   In Key West, Florida, Ehrenreich found a job as a waitress at an inexpensive family restaurant. Her shift ran from 2:00 P.M. to 10:00 P.M. Salary: $2.43 an hour plus tips. To find an affordable rent, she had to move 30 miles out of town, a 45-minute commute on a crowded two-lane highway. How did her co-workers manage housing? One waitress shared a room in a $250 a week flophouse; a cook shared a two-room apartment with three others; another worker lived in a van parked behind a shopping center.

2   "There are no secret economies that nourish the poor," Ehrenreich writes. "If you can't put up the two months' rent you need to get an apartment, you end up paying through the nose for a room by the

(continued on next page)

week. If you have only one room, with a hotplate at best, you can't save by cooking up huge stews that can be frozen for the week ahead. You eat hot dogs and the Styrofoam cups of soup that can be microwaved at a convenience store." Without health insurance from work, you risk a small cut becoming infected because you can afford neither a visit to the doctor nor antibiotics.

3   In the summer tourist slump, Ehrenreich found her salary with tips dropped from about $7 an hour to $5.15. At this rate, the only way to pay her rent was to get a second job. So, for a while she worked 8:00 A.M. to 2:00 P.M. and then rushed to her regular shift at the first restaurant—a 14-hour day of brutal physical labor, as anyone who has waitressed for a living knows. With such a schedule, she could not, of course, keep her decent housing so far from town. Ehrenreich's new home was an eight-foot-wide trailer parked among others "in a nest of crime," where "desolation rules

night and day. . . . There are not exactly people here, but what amounts to canned labor, being preserved between shifts from the heat."

4   Moving to Maine, Ehrenreich took two jobs to make ends meet—a weekend job in a nursing home and a full-time job in a house-cleaning service. At Merry Maids, the cleaning service, the economics were as follows: the customer pays the service $25 an hour per cleaning person; the service pays $6.65 an hour to each cleaner. "How poor are my co-workers?" Ehrenreich asks. Half-bags of corn chips for lunch; dizziness from malnutrition; a toothache requiring frantic calls to find a free dental clinic; worries about makeshift childcare arrangements because a licensed day-care center at $90 a week is beyond any cleaner's budget; no one sleeping in a car, but everyone crowded into housing with far too many others, strangers or family; "signs of real difficulty if not actual misery ."

1. In general, what information does this passage present?
   (A) An explanation of wages in different cities
   (B) Advice about finding jobs
   (C) Suggestions for saving money
   (D) A description of living on too little money

2. All of the following characterized Ehrenreich's job in Key West, Florida, EXCEPT
   (A) working as a waitress
   (B) making a minimal salary
   (C) needing 15 minutes to get to work
   (D) commuting on a crowded highway

3. The word *you* throughout paragraph 2 refers to
   (A) the reader
   (B) a poor worker
   (C) an unemployed person
   (D) the author

4. The word *misery* in paragraph 4 is closest in meaning to
(A) anger
(B) poverty
(C) suffering
(D) pessimism

5. In paragraph 2, the author's primary purpose is
(A) to compare and contrast housing options in the United States
(B) to urge people to search for higher-paying jobs
(C) to inform readers about practices regarding rental payment
(D) to explain the causes and effects of living poor

6. The word *desolation* in paragraph 3 is closest in meaning to
(A) sadness
(B) confusion
(C) destruction
(D) anger

7. Based on the information in paragraph 3, what can be inferred about poor people?
(A) They need their homes to protect them from the heat.
(B) They do little more than work long hours.
(C) They spend most of their time in their homes.
(D) They are negatively affected by weather changes.

8. In paragraph 4, how does the author characterize the lives of poor workers?
(A) extremely hard
(B) completely hopeless
(C) somewhat bright
(D) rarely demanding

9. Look at the four squares ☐ that indicate where the following sentence could be added to the passage. Where would the sentence best fit? Circle the letter that shows the point where you would insert this sentence.

That didn't leave much money for housing.

In Key West, Florida, Ehrenreich found a job as a waitress at an inexpensive family restaurant. Her shift ran from 2:00 P.M. to 10:00 P.M. Salary: $2.43 an hour plus tips. **[A]** To find an affordable rent, she had to move 30 miles out of town, a 45-minute commute on a crowded two-lane highway. **[B]** How did her co-workers manage housing? **[C]** One waitress shared a room in a $250 a week flophouse; a cook shared a two-room apartment with three others; another worker lived in a van parked behind a shopping center.

[D] "There are no secret economies that nourish the poor," Ehrenreich writes. "If you can't put up the two months' rent you need to get an apartment, you end up paying through the nose for a room by the week."

10. Which of the following best expresses the essential information in this sentence from the passage?

> Without health insurance from work, you risk a small cut becoming infected because you can afford neither a visit to the doctor nor antibiotics.

(A) People without health insurance can only afford to pay for doctor visits.
(B) People who injure themselves at work need antibiotics to ensure their health.
(C) Health risks can occur when poor people are not able to pay for medical treatment.
(D) Medical care is provided so that workers do not have further health problems.

11. An introductory sentence for a brief summary of the passage is provided below. Complete the summary by circling the THREE answer choices that express the most important ideas in the passage. Some sentences do not belong in the summary because they express ideas that are not presented in the passage or are minor ideas in the passage.

> Poor Americans have difficulties making enough money to cover their living expenses.

(A) As a waitress, Ehrenreich earned $2.43 plus tips.
(B) Some people have to live in distant or unsafe housing.
(C) People must sometimes work two jobs to make ends meet.
(D) Freezing and microwaving food is an expensive way to eat.
(E) People can't afford medicine, and they have health problems.
(F) Trailer parks are practical housing options for the poor.

3 Writing

INTEGRATED TASK: READ, LISTEN, WRITE

In this section, you will read a short passage and listen to an excerpt on a related topic. Then you will write about the relationship between the two.

READING

Read the passage on the next page. As you read, fill in the following summary chart.

TOWN GOALS	EXAMPLES FOR MEETING GOALS	DETAILS ABOUT EXAMPLES
1. Social and civic interaction	a. Central Market Street district	• reduces traffic • • • •
	b.	• • • •
2.	a.	• 4,900 acres, with 4,700 acre greenbelt •
	b. High-rise office, apartment buildings	• •

The Celebration Experiment

1 In the 1960s, Walt Disney envisioned a futuristic utopian city with underground roads and a climate-controlled dome. The *real* community of Celebration, Florida, built in 1999, applies the social and environmental goals of both Disney and the New Urbanism movement.

2 Disney and the New Urbanists have envisioned communities that facilitate social and civic interaction. Celebration has a centralized Market Street district to reduce traffic and encourage social contacts. The idea is that if the downtown area is compact, people will walk and meet their

(continued on next page)

neighbors. Downtown events like art festivals also bring residents together. Narrow, tree-lined streets are "traffic calm"—with slower speed limits—to encourage bicycling and walking.

3   Moreover, housing in Celebration includes both single- and multi-family residences that encourage socialization. Apartment buildings are located close to downtown, and houses are built close together with small yards. They feature lobbies and porches to encourage residents to socialize.

4   "Many aspects of that kind of design are really aimed at maximizing social interaction between residents, not just on the streets but also in community institutions that are very much a part of public life there," says Andrew Ross, a New York University professor who lived in Celebration for one year.

5   Utopian communities such as Celebration are also designed with environmental preservation in mind. The town itself is built on 4,900 acres surrounded by a 4,700 acre protected greenbelt. The greenbelt, parks, and common areas accommodate native wildlife and animals.

6   High-rise office and apartment buildings provide high-density office and residential space in a small geographic area in order to reduce urban sprawl, the spread of today's cities onto nature areas. Buildings also minimize environmental impact by using energy-efficient cooling and electric systems with insulated glass, cooling towers, and low-wattage lamps.

7   "The town more or less borrows very heavily from New Urbanist principles . . . to create environmentally friendly alternatives to sprawl and to create communities around people rather than automobiles," Ross said.

LISTENING

Listen to a lecture. Use the outline on the next page to take notes as you listen.

Main Idea: U.S. cities and towns have experienced urban sprawl, leading to the
rise of anti-sprawl movements such as New Urbanism.

Definitions of *urban sprawl*

General definition:

Description:

Effects of urban sprawl

Negative

- robbing us of nature

-

Positive

- new homes, businesses

-

- less noise, crime

Solutions to urban sprawl—New Urbanism principles

Regions

-

- environmental protections

Cities

-

Neighborhoods

-

- walk to stores, public transportation, parks

WRITING

Write on the following topic. Follow the steps below to prepare.

Explain how the principles of New Urbanism propose to solve the problems of
urban sprawl discussed in the lecture. Include examples from the town of
Celebration to support your explanation.

Step 1

- Work with a partner. Skim the reading and your notes from the reading and
  listening tasks (pages 28–31) to answer the questions on the next page.

1. What are the problems of urban sprawl?

2. What are the principles of New Urbanism and the related solutions to urban sprawl?

3. How does Celebration, as an example of New Urbanism, try to stop the problems of urban sprawl?

- With your partner, fill in the chart below to organize your ideas on the topic. Use your answers to the questions above to help you. If necessary, review your notes from the reading task (pages 28–30). In the first column, write the major problems of urban sprawl. In the second column, write New Urbanism's solutions to these problems. In the third column, add detailed examples of features from the town of Celebration that relate to these solutions. Be sure to include specific details about the examples.

URBAN SPRAWL PROBLEMS	NEW URBANISM SOLUTIONS	CELEBRATION'S FEATURES

Step 2

Write for 20 minutes. Leave the last 5 minutes to edit your work.

To evaluate a partner's writing, use the Writing Evaluation Form on page 203.

4 Speaking

INDEPENDENT TASK

Speak on the following topic. Follow the steps below to prepare.

Imagine that you are helping to establish a new utopian community. Which principles would you recommend that the community adopt, and why? What are the best ways to uphold those principles? Support your opinions with specific examples.

Step 1

- Work in a group to brainstorm possible principles for your utopian community.

- On your own, choose the two or three principles that you think are most important for the community to adopt. Write them in the first column of the chart below. In the second column, write the reasons why each principle is important. In the third column, write examples of the best actions to take in order to uphold each principle. Include specific details in the examples.

UTOPIAN PRINCIPLE	WHY IS THE PRINCIPLE IMPORTANT?	WHAT IS THE BEST WAY TO UPHOLD THE PRINCIPLE?
The community should actively work to reduce traffic.	• traffic = bad for the environment • traffic lessens the quality of life; limits exercise and interaction with others	• carpool to work with 3 other co-workers • walk or ride my bike to the library, stores

Step 2

With a partner, take turns practicing a one-minute oral response to the topic. Be sure to use the information in your chart to help you.

Step 3

Change partners. Take turns giving a one-minute response to the topic again.

To evaluate your partner's response, use the Speaking Evaluation Form on page 204.

5 Skill Focus

USING DETAILED EXAMPLES

EXAMINATION

Look at the following items from the unit. Work with a partner and answer the questions about each item.

Item 1 (Reading, p. 26)

All of the following characterized Ehrenreich's job in Key West, Florida, EXCEPT
(A) working as a waitress
(B) making a minimal salary
(C) needing 15 minutes to get to work
(D) commuting on a crowded highway

- How did you remember which details were mentioned in the example about Ehrenreich's job, and which detail was not mentioned? Did you think about the main idea of the passage to help you make your choice?

- How do the details that were included support the author's main idea about Ehrenreich's experience?

Item 2 (Academic Listening, p. 23)

If necessary, listen again to the interview.

1. What is the topic of the interview?

2. What examples of town features does Frantz include? Write as many as you hear.

3. In general, does Frantz have a positive or a negative feeling about Celebration?

- Did Frantz's examples help you to understand more about the topic—life in the town of Celebration? What aspects of Celebration did the examples explain?

- Which examples helped you to understand Frantz's feeling about Celebration?

Item 3 (Integrated Task, p. 31)

Explain how the principles of New Urbanism propose to solve the problems of urban sprawl discussed in the lecture. Include examples from the town of Celebration to support your explanation.

- Review your written response to the topic. Did you use examples about Celebration to illustrate the problems of and solutions to urban sprawl? If so, highlight them. Show them to your partner and discuss your choices.

- In your response, did you include specific details in your examples? If so, underline them. Why did you include these details? Show them to your partner and discuss your choices.

- In your response, did you include any words to signal examples? If so, circle them. Show them to your partner and discuss your choices.

Tips

To do well on the TOEFL, it is essential to learn how to identify and use detailed examples. Examples can help you to understand a speaker or writer's main ideas or point of view, and they can help you to support and illustrate your own statements.

Listening and Reading

- Look and listen for specific words, phrases, and punctuation or non-verbal clues (intonation, pauses) that signal examples.

    Words/phrases: *for example, for instance, such as, include/including, like, following/as follows,* or *case* (*a case in point, one case,* and so on)

    Punctuation marks: colon (:) or long dash (—)

To answer **Item 1**, you probably remembered that the author used the example of Ehrenreich's job in Key West to show that her experience was very difficult. Choice (C) is the only detail about the example that doesn't support this idea.

To answer **Item 2**, you could have mentioned Frantz's examples of planning elements. Frantz uses a pause (indicated in written text with a dash) and the phrase "in our case" to signal these examples:

(continued on next page)

They've tried to look backward at small-town America and take the best of those planning elements—houses are all very close together. *In our case,* we were just 10 feet apart from our neighbors …

Elsewhere in the interview, Frantz uses two other examples of life in Celebration—the fact that people don't use their porches, and the fact that it's hot—to support his general idea that the town of Celebration was unsuccessful in some ways.

Speaking and Writing

- Choose effective examples which "prove" that a general statement is true or explain more about a general topic.

- Include specific details in your examples. Details about time, place, people, and events enhance the example.

- Use specific words, phrases, and punctuation to signal examples.

In your response to **Item 3**, you should have used examples about the town of Celebration to prove or explain the ideas you presented about sprawl. Your examples should have included specific details, such as the following:

Office buildings in Celebration minimize environmental impact by using energy-efficient cooling and electric systems with *insulated glass, cooling towers,* and *low-wattage lamps.*

PRACTICE

1 *Read the passages. Use the tips from the previous section to help you answer the questions that follow. Work with a partner and compare your answers.*

Passage 1

How about looking in the Museum district? There are tons of reasons to live there: It's close to campus. You wouldn't even have to take a bus. I've seen a lot of for-rent signs. There's also so much to do there—museums nearby, and great shopping. And there's a twenty-four-hour supermarket and video store right in the center. And it's very safe. I always see people walking around late at night.

Passage 2

Many consider urban sprawl to be very harmful, including environmental groups like the Sierra Club, which calls sprawl "irresponsible," a "cancer," a "virus" on the land. Sprawl misuses land that should be preserved for wildlife, parks, farmland, and it's robbing us of our nature, they say.

Passage 3

Moving to Maine, Ehrenreich took two jobs to make ends meet—a weekend job in a nursing home and a full-time job in a house-cleaning service. At Merry Maids, the cleaning service, the economics were as follows: the customer pays the service $25 an hour per cleaning person; the service pays $6.65 an hour to each cleaner.

- What is the general topic of each passage?

- What examples are used to explain or support the topics? Highlight them.

- What details are used to strengthen the examples? Underline them.

- In the passages, what words, phrases, or punctuation marks, if any, signal the example(s)? Circle them.

2 *Work with a partner. Read your partner's written response from the Integrated Task (pages 28–31). Highlight one or two places where more examples and details could improve the writing. Then suggest additions.*

Personality

| LISTENING |

Campus Conversation
A student talks to her professor about dropping a course.

Academic Listening
Radio commentary: *The Pollyanna Syndrome*

| READING |

Book Excerpt
Keeping Your Confidence Up

| SPEAKING |

**Integrated Task:
Read, Listen, Speak**
Categorize two students according to definitions of types of shyness. Explain your reasons.

| WRITING |

Independent Task
Describe and explain the most significant challenges and most effective strategies related to academic success.

| SKILL FOCUS |

Making Inferences
Inferences are guesses, predictions, or conclusions about information that is not stated directly.

| TOEFL® iBT TARGET SKILLS |

- Identify and express main ideas
- Identify and express details
- Infer a speaker's attitude or intention
- Listen and categorize information in a chart
- Link concrete information to abstract ideas
- Support a written answer using knowledge and experience

 For extra practice of TOEFL iBT skills, go to pages 242–259.

1 Listening

CAMPUS CONVERSATION

PRE-LISTENING VOCABULARY

Read the sentences. Guess the meaning of the boldfaced words and phrases. Write your ideas on the lines. Then match each word or phrase with a definition or synonym from the list on the next page. Work with a partner and compare your answers.

_____ 1. My apartment is a mess, my laundry is piling up, and I have two major class projects due in two days. I'm feeling fairly **overwhelmed** by all my responsibilities.

_____

_____ 2. When you sign up for classes next term, be **flexible**. If a daytime chemistry class doesn't fit in your schedule, then be willing to take an evening or Saturday class.

_____

_____ 3. **Freshmen** often need guidance in adjusting to college life. Many of them quickly discover that their first year of college requires different work habits from those they had in high school.

_____

_____ 4. My classmate Christian has trouble with physics, so he made a **standing appointment** with a learning lab tutor every Friday. The tutor goes over the basic concepts in each week's lectures.

_____

_____ 5. Charlie has a **gift for** music. He plays the drums like a professional, and in only a few weeks taught himself to play the guitar. Now he plays so well that he is performing in the student coffeehouse this weekend.

_____

_____ 6. In our history class, we have to read an entire book on mass movements by next Monday. I'm afraid that if I **fall behind**, I'll run out of time to finish the book, and then I won't be prepared to answer the professor's questions.

_____

_____ 7. We've been working *so* hard in our classes. If we can just **stick it out** until spring break—two weeks from now—the rest of the semester will fly by!

_____

_____ **8.** Remember that if you decide to **drop** your economics class, you will lose the time and money that you have invested in it so far.

_____

_____ **9.** Sally is starring in the student drama production. She has spent a lot of time memorizing her part. She **goes over** her lines every night so that she knows them perfectly.

_____

_____ **10.** Let's meet at the soccer field at 9:00 A.M. on Saturday. If you **run into** any problems and can't be there on time, please let me know beforehand.

_____

a. able to change

b. be late or slow in doing something

c. continue doing something difficult

d. encounter

e. first-year students

f. quit taking

g. regular meeting time

h. reviews

i. talent in

j. weighed down

> **Culture Note:** Professors generally establish rules at the beginning of a semester about whether to allow students to make up examinations or turn in assignments late. Students are responsible for contacting their professors to explain absences and ask about making up work.

FIRST LISTENING

Read the questions on the next page. Listen to the conversation between a student and a professor. Take notes as you listen. Share your notes with a partner. Then use your notes to answer the questions.

1. Why has the student come to speak to the professor?

_____

2. What is the professor's reaction?

_____

3. What advice and help does the professor offer? Write as many ideas as you hear.

_____

SECOND LISTENING

Read the questions. Listen to the conversation again. Add details to your notes. Then use your notes to answer the questions. Work with a partner and compare your answers.

1. Why does the student go to see the professor?
   (A) To ask when she can make up a missed test
   (B) To complain about all the work she has in her classes
   (C) To tell the professor she wants to drop the course
   (D) To get suggestions about how to improve her grades

2. What does the professor say to encourage the student to change her mind?
   (A) The student has made good grades in Arabic class so far.
   (B) The student got a passing grade on the first exam in the class.
   (C) The student is doing well in her other courses.
   (D) The student has a talent for learning languages.

Listen again to part of the conversation. Then answer question 3.

3. Why does the student say, "I feel really bad about this"?
   (A) She has become ill because her class load is too heavy.
   (B) She would like to defend her decision to drop the class.
   (C) She regrets that she will lose money when she drops the class.
   (D) She thinks she may disappoint the professor by dropping the class.

Listen again to part of the conversation. Then answer question 4.

4. What can be inferred about the professor?
   (A) She is uncertain about whether the student can find the website.
   (B) She expects the student to look up the website on her own.
   (C) She is not sure that the student will find the website helpful.
   (D) She is going to show the student the website on her computer.

5. In the conversation, what does the professor offer to do for the student?
   (A) Drop the grade of the student's missed examination
   (B) Help the student with difficult material in the textbook
   (C) Contact the language tutor to set up an appointment
   (D) Help the student to build self-confidence as a language learner

ACADEMIC LISTENING

FIRST LISTENING

Listen to a radio commentary in which host Julie Danis describes how "Pollyannas," or extreme optimists, react to life's problems. Take notes using the chart below. Work with a partner and combine your notes.

PROBLEM	POLLYANNA REACTION
Visit to eye doctor	• •
	• perfect for listening to language tapes and doing relaxation exercises
Computer crashes, hold time on help line is hours	• •
	• catch up on movies

SECOND LISTENING

Read the questions. Listen to the commentary again. Add details to your notes. Then use your notes to answer the questions. Work with a partner and compare your answers.

1. What is the main idea of this commentary?
   (A) Many people view life in a negative way.
   (B) Some people always see the bright side of problems.
   (C) Everyone should have a more positive outlook.
   (D) Most people take either a positive or a negative view of life.

2. How does the speaker organize the information she presents?
   (A) By contrasting the ways different people react to problems
   (B) By giving reasons for why people react to problems as they do
   (C) By suggesting better ways to handle life's problems
   (D) By examining the effects of problems on people's lives

Listen again to part of the commentary. Then answer question 3.

3. What does the speaker mean when she says, "She had made lemonade out of lemons."?
   (A) The coworker had come to the wrong conclusion.
   (B) The coworker had focused on the negative side of the problem.
   (C) The coworker had tried to offer her advice again.
   (D) The coworker had found something good about a bad situation.

Listen again to part of the commentary. Then answer question 4.

4. What is the speaker's attitude toward the people she is describing?
   (A) She finds them annoying.
   (B) She finds their ideas appealing.
   (C) She is confused by their ideas.
   (D) She admires their commitment.

Listen again to part of the commentary. Then answer question 5.

5. What does the speaker mean when she says, "Then go suck on some lemons and feel better in your own way."?
   (A) Disagree with positive people, even though you will feel bad afterwards.
   (B) Disagree with positive people and feel good about your opinion.
   (C) Pretend to agree with positive people, even though you do not agree.
   (D) Think about the situation, and then change your mind about it.

2 Reading

KEEPING YOUR CONFIDENCE UP

PRE-READING

Before you read, work with a partner to brainstorm descriptions of successful people. Think of successful people you know. What can you infer, or guess, about how they became successful? What characteristics, habits, or other factors might have led to their accomplishments? Make a list of your ideas on a separate piece of paper.

READING

Read the passage on the next page and answer the questions. Then work with a partner and compare your answers. When you disagree, go back to the text to find helpful information.

KEEPING YOUR CONFIDENCE UP

BY DENNIS O'GRADY

(from *Taking the Fear Out of Changing*)

1   Success seeks to help you become more accepting of your genuine strengths. Self-approval unleashes your best traits to be expressed in your work and family life, and in the world. How can you learn to accept your successes without panicking? Here are some practical ways to learn to celebrate all of your SUCCESSES.

2   SELF-ESTEEM. Being a genuine achiever means you acknowledge your strengths, hunt for your secret talents, and give your best to the world without being a braggart.

Build Self-Confidence: Learn from your failures.

3   UNDERSTANDING. Achievement means you are an intense person who expresses who you really are while staying open to growing and changing each and every day.

Build Self-Confidence: Thrive on responsibility.

4   CHILD DRIVE. You pay attention to inner urges that speak to you about what work you love to do and what insights you have to give the world.

Build Self-Confidence: Make work fun.

5   CURIOSITY. You talk, talk, and talk some more to people to find out what makes them tick. You soak up information like a sunbather taking in sunshine.
   Build Self-Confidence: Take good advice.

6   ENERGY. You maximize your energy by eating, sleeping, exercising, and working in recognition of your own special rhythms. You do what makes you feel most alive.
   Build Self-Confidence: Keep your energy high.

7   SET GOALS. You dignify life with long-term goals and mark your progression toward them.
   Build Self-Confidence: Choose commitment.

8   STAY FOCUSED. You intensely focus single-mindedly on the most important tasks to accomplish, and you say, "No way!" to nifty distractions.
   Build Self-Confidence: Accept self-discipline.

9   ERRORS. You make errors every day and know that if you aren't failing at least once a day then you aren't succeeding. You try again to hit the mark after you've missed it.
   Build Self-Confidence: Never accept failure as a permanent state.

10   SATISFACTION. You endorse yourself for your wins, follow a consistent set of values, and take humble pride in all of your accomplishments.
   Build Self-Confidence: Feel gratified.

11   Permit yourself to be a genuine achiever instead of an impostor. Real people aren't impostors— we are the genuine article. Take the risk, and be the real McCoy!

1. What is the text mainly about?
   (A) Learning from failures
   (B) Setting goals for success
   (C) Success through risk-taking
   (D) How to be successful

2. The word *thrive* in paragraph 3 is closest in meaning to
   (A) survive
   (B) grow
   (C) build
   (D) depend

3. In paragraph 4, the author suggests that
   (A) we should try not to act like children
   (B) we must only respond to our inner urges
   (C) we should follow our youthful impulses
   (D) we can only teach others when we are older

4. According to paragraph 5, if you ask questions
   (A) you will become curious
   (B) people will talk a lot
   (C) you will learn more
   (D) people will listen to you

5. Which of the following statements about failure can be inferred from paragraph 9?
   (A) Failure can be avoided.
   (B) Failure prevents you from succeeding.
   (C) It is difficult to try again after failing.
   (D) You learn when you fail.

6. The word *endorse* in paragraph 10 is closest in meaning to
   (A) thank
   (B) approve of
   (C) focus on
   (D) analyze

7. The word *we* in paragraph 11 refers to
   (A) achievers
   (B) impostors
   (C) articles
   (D) real people

8. Which of the following best expresses the essential information in this sentence from the passage?

   > Achievement means you are an intense person who expresses who you really are while staying open to growing and changing each and every day.

   (A) Constantly changing who you are will make you successful.
   (B) Believe in yourself, and you will accomplish what you want.
   (C) Passionate people get what they want by stating their views.
   (D) Be true to yourself, but try to improve, and you will succeed.

9. All of the following are recommendations for success EXCEPT
   (A) Celebrate your success.
   (B) Acknowledge your strengths.
   (C) Hunt for your secret talents.
   (D) Do not make mistakes.

10. Which of the following best describes the author's presentation of information in the passage?
    (A) The author describes problems related to success.
    (B) The author explains ways to be successful.
    (C) The author discusses the effects of success.
    (D) The author compares various methods for success.

ANALYSIS

It is helpful to know the purpose of a test item. There are four types of questions in the reading section.

1. Basic Comprehension

- main ideas
- details
- the meaning of specific sentences

2. Organization

- the way information is structured in the text
- the way ideas are linked between sentences or between paragraphs

3. Inference

- ideas are not directly stated in the text
- author's intention, purpose, or attitude not explicitly stated in the text

4. Vocabulary and Reference

- the meaning of words
- the meaning of reference words such as *his, them, this,* or *none*

Go back to the reading questions and label each question with 1, 2, 3, or 4. Then work with a partner to see if you agree. Check the Answer Key for the correct answers. Which questions did you get right? Which did you get wrong? What skills do you need to practice?

3 Speaking

INTEGRATED TASK: READ, LISTEN, SPEAK

In this section, you will read a short passage and listen to an excerpt on the same topic. Then you will speak about the relationship between the two.

READING

Read the passage on the next page. As you read, fill in the following summary chart with examples and descriptors for each category.

SITUATIONAL SHYNESS	CHRONIC SHYNESS
• shy, awkward if object of attention at social gathering • • • •	• can mark lives • • • • • • • • • • • •

Types of Shyness

1   How do you feel when you're the object of attention at a social gathering? If you sometimes feel shy or awkward, then you may be interested in knowing that many other people feel the same way. Actually, this type of *situational shyness* is a common, temporary feeling caused by a particular situation, according to Dr. Philip Zimbardo, a psychology professor at Stanford University who has researched shyness in adults.

2   Situational shyness is a momentary feeling of awkwardness that you might get on a blind date, or when asked to perform in public. Zimbardo points out that people experience temporary shyness because they are not prepared for the situation. As a result, arousal, negative thoughts, and physical tension occur. To counter such feelings, he gives this advice: "Say to yourself, 'Well, that's not me; that's that external situation which I have to avoid.'"

3   Zimbardo is more concerned with *chronic,* or *dispositional, shyness,* a type of shyness that he says can mark people's lives. When shyness becomes chronic and dispositional, it is something people carry around with them. Even if others don't notice it, it's there, ready to emerge.

4   Chronic shyness carries a range of negative effects. According to Zimbardo, chronically shy people are less popular, have fewer friends, and, thus, less social support and lower self-esteem. They make less money and have fewer leadership skills. In general, they have a more boring life and are more likely to be depressed. Later in life, they're also more inclined to be lonely.

LISTENING

Listen to a conversation. Use the chart to take notes as you listen. Write down any details that demonstrate the personalities of the two students in the conversation.

Main Idea: The personalities of two classmates are revealed as they prepare a class assignment.

MALE STUDENT—CHRIS	FEMALE STUDENT— MELISSA
• everybody knows him	• has always been shy
•	•
•	•
• outgoing: gives Melissa advice; invites her to lunch, computer lab	• school play:
	•

SPEAKING

Speak on the following topic. Follow the steps below to prepare.

Categorize the two students according to Zimbardo's definitions of types of shyness. Explain your reasons.

Step 1

- Work with a partner. Skim the reading and your notes from the reading and listening tasks (pages 49–50) to answer the following questions.

    1. In the reading, how does Zimbardo define situational shyness?

    2. How does he define chronic, or dispositional, shyness?

    3. Which student is situationally shy: Melissa or Chris? What information from the conversation helped you to decide?

    4. Which student is chronically shy? What information from the conversation helped you to decide?

- With your partner, fill in the chart on the next page to organize your ideas about the topic. First, define the two types of shyness. Then choose which student fits in each category. Write notes to answer the questions about the students' characteristics. Use your answers to the questions above to help you.

	SITUATIONAL SHYNESS	CHRONIC SHYNESS
Zimbardo's definition		
Which student fits in this category?		
How does the student in this category relate to others?		
How does the student in this category act in class?		
What kinds of situations make the student in this category feel shy?		
How does the student in this category deal with the other student?		

Step 2

With your partner, take turns practicing a one-minute oral response to the topic. Be sure to use the information in your chart to help you.

Step 3

Change partners. Take turns giving a one-minute response to the topic again.

> To evaluate your partner's response, use the Speaking Evaluation Form on page 204.

4 Writing

INDEPENDENT TASK

Write on the following topic. Follow the steps below to prepare.

Describe and explain the most significant challenges and most effective strategies related to academic success. Include examples from your own and your classmates' experiences to support your explanation.

Step 1

- Think of your own successful academic experiences. Answer the following questions.

  1. What were some classes, projects, or other times when you were successful?

  2. What challenges did you overcome?

  3. What did you do to succeed?

- Work in a group. Take turns sharing your experiences with academic success. Take notes on what you hear.

- On your own, evaluate what you have heard. What were the most significant challenges to academic success mentioned in your group? Which strategies for being academically successful worked the best? Which ideas could you use in your own writing?

- Prepare for your writing by making a list of the challenges and strategies that you will write about. For each one, take notes about the examples you will include. Refer to your list as you write.

Step 2

Write for 20 minutes. Leave the last 5 minutes to edit your work.

> To evaluate a partner's writing, use the Writing Evaluation Form on page 203.

5 Skill Focus

MAKING INFERENCES

EXAMINATION

Look at the following items from the unit. Work with a partner and answer the questions about each item.

Item 1 (Integrated Task, p. 50)

If necessary, listen again to the conversation.

Which student is situationally shy: Melissa or Chris? What information from the conversation helped you to decide?

Which student is chronically shy? What information from the conversation helped you to decide?

- Were you able to use the context, or surrounding information, to interpret the students' personalities?

- Did any specific words help you to interpret the students' personalities?

- Did the way the students said the words help you to interpret their personalities?

Item 2 (Academic Listening, p. 43)

If necessary, listen again to this part of the commentary.

> We all know people like this. They find the silver lining inside the darkest cloud … all the time … without fail … driving others to distraction with their "find the bright side" philosophy.
> "Oh well," they say, "a stop-and-go commute is perfect …"

What is the speaker's attitude toward the people she is describing?
(**A**) She finds them annoying.
(**B**) She finds their ideas appealing.
(**C**) She is confused by their ideas.
(**D**) She admires their commitment.

- Were you able to use the context to interpret the speaker's meaning or attitude?

- Did any specific words help you to interpret the speaker's meaning or attitude?

- Did the way the speaker said the words help you to interpret her meaning or attitude?

Item 3 (Reading, p. 47)

Which of the following statements about failure can be inferred from paragraph 9?
(A) Failure can be avoided.
(B) Failure prevents you from succeeding.
(C) It is difficult to try again after failing.
(D) You learn when you fail.

- Were you able to use the context to interpret the writer's meaning or attitude?

- Did any specific words or punctuation in the reading help you to interpret the writer's meaning or attitude? Go back to the reading and underline the parts that helped you. Show them to your partner and discuss your selections.

Tips

To do well on the TOEFL, it is essential to learn how to make inferences. Inferences are guesses, predictions, or conclusions about information that is not stated directly. Inference questions often ask about a speaker or writer's meaning, purpose, or attitude.

To answer inference questions:

- Use the context to help you interpret the speaker or writer's meaning. In other words, put together the information that you have.

To answer **Item 1**, you probably determined the students' personalities by connecting key ideas about the types of shyness explained in the reading with comments made in the conversation (Chris = "situations make me shy;" Melissa = "I've always been shy").

- Pay attention to word choices that can lead you to logical conclusions.

In **Item 2**, the phrases "all the time," "without fail," and "driving others to distraction" probably helped you to infer the speaker's attitude or feeling. In **Item 3**, the statements "If you aren't failing . . . then you aren't succeeding" and "Never accept failure as a permanent state" probably helped you to eliminate incorrect choices and select the right answer.

- Pay attention to non-verbal clues. Writers use italics, boldfaced type, and punctuation to show their attitude or feeling about a subject. Speakers change their stress, pitch, or intonation to show their attitude or feeling.

In the examples on the next page, intonation is used to show attitude.

Listen to the examples. Pay attention to the way the same phrase is spoken with different meanings.

> **Example 1:** Yes, I can.
> **Example 2:** Yes, I can.

In the first example, the speaker's stress and intonation indicate that she feels firm about the subject. In the second example, her stress and intonation reveal her irritable, defiant attitude. It's as if she were saying, "I don't care what you say! I'm going to do what I want anyway!"

PRACTICE

1 *Listen to each statement as it is spoken two times with different stress, pitch, and intonation. Write* A *or* B *next to the sentence that best expresses the speaker's attitude or emotion in versions A and B.*

1. _____ The speaker is surprised.

   _____ The speaker is critical.

2. _____ The speaker is optimistic.

   _____ The speaker is pessimistic.

3. _____ The speaker accepts the situation.

   _____ The speaker regrets the situation.

2 *Read an excerpt from a radio interview with Dr. Philip Zimbardo. Use the tips from the previous section to help you complete the activities that follow.*

1 **Alex Chadwick, Host:** Do you find these days that it's more difficult meeting people? In social situations with strangers do you wind up asking yourself, "Am I dressed wrong today or something?" Friends, take heart. A new study says it's not you at all. The problem is Americans are, generally speaking, more shy than many people would expect, and getting shyer all the time.

2   Philip Zimbardo is a professor of psychology at Stanford University who runs a shyness clinic in Palo Alto. He's the author of numerous studies on shyness. Good morning, Professor Zimbardo.

3 **Philip Zimbardo:** Good morning.

4 **AC:** Your earlier study showed shyness is already widespread, but what about the newest figures?

5 **PZ:** Our research, which we've been conducting since 1972, focused on adults who were shy. Before our research started, of course, the interest was always in shy children and, to our amazement, we discovered that about 40 percent of all Americans label themselves as currently shy, and over the past ten years that figure has increased to about 48 percent. What that means is two out of every five people you meet think of themselves as shy, and now that figure is moving toward one out of two, which is a surprise, especially to foreigners . . .

3 *Read the pairs of sentences below. Choose the sentence that best states the idea that the speaker intended to express. Then mark the words, ideas, or context clues in the passage that helped you choose your answer. Work with a partner and compare your answers.*

1. Paragraph 1   (A) People generally believe that shyness is a negative quality.

   (B) People generally believe that shyness is a positive quality.

2. Paragraph 1   (A) In this passage, the speaker wants to make people feel better about being shy.

   (B) In this passage, the speaker wants to help people overcome shyness.

3. Paragraph 5   (A) Before the 1970s, people were more concerned about shyness in adults than in children.

   (B) Before the 1970s, people were more concerned about shyness in children than in adults.

| LISTENING |

Campus Conversation A student asks a professor about buying a used car on eBay.

Academic Listening Radio interview: *Tipping Points in Fighting Crime*

| READING |

Essay *The Story of* Silent Spring

| WRITING |

Integrated Task: Read, Listen, Write Use concepts described in *The Tipping Point* to explain the success of Paul Revere.

| SPEAKING |

Independent Task Express your opinion about the reasons behind the popularity of a modern technological device, such as the cell phone.

| SKILL FOCUS |

Identifying and Using Main Ideas and Details Identifying and using main ideas and details of listening passages and reading excerpts show that you understand a writer's or speaker's most important point about a topic.

| TOEFL® iBT TARGET SKILLS |

- Identify and express main ideas
- Identify and express details
- Make inferences
- Listen and take notes in an outline
- Write definitions using main ideas and details
- Link concrete information to an abstract concept

 For extra practice of TOEFL iBT skills, go to pages 242–259.

1 Listening

CAMPUS CONVERSATION

PRE-LISTENING VOCABULARY

Read the sentences. Guess the meaning of the boldfaced words and phrases. Then match each word or phrase with a definition or synonym from the list below. Work with a partner and compare your answers.

_____ 1. The university library is holding an **auction** at noon today to sell some old bookcases and desks.

_____ 2. I didn't **come across** your biology book while I was cleaning up the house. Did you look for it in your car?

_____ 3. My friend Ali's car is **a lemon**! He has spent $500 to repair it, and it still runs badly.

_____ 4. If you like science fiction, read this novel. It's **all about** the adventures of a time traveler.

_____ 5. That new pizza café near campus has really **caught on**. Now, they have long lines at lunch and dinner.

_____ 6. This spaghetti sauce has a lot of ingredients, but when you **get right down to it**, it's actually easy to make.

_____ 7. The best way to learn about new music is through **word of mouth**. Ask your friends and classmates to share their opinions about their favorite bands.

_____ 8. One of my personal **principles** is to try to treat people respectfully.

_____ 9. Those ancient maps in the art museum are **phenomenal**! It's hard to believe that geographers could draw them so accurately with so little technology.

a. amazing

b. become popular

c. find

d. person-to-person communication

e. public sale where people offer money for items

f. really think about or do something

g. rules

h. something that does not work properly, usually a car

i. to be on or dealing with a subject

Culture Note: Many college and university students own cars because they study far away from home. In fact, at many schools in the United States, the *majority* of students are from another city, state, or country. Many of these students use cars as a form of transportation while at school and for traveling home.

FIRST LISTENING

Read the questions. Listen to the conversation between a student and a professor. Take notes as you listen. Share your notes with a partner. Then use your notes to answer the questions.

1. What does the student ask the professor about?

_____

_____

2. What are the student's main concerns about online shopping?

_____

_____

3. What reasons does the professor give for eBay's success?

_____

_____

SECOND LISTENING

Read the questions. Listen to the conversation again. Add details to your notes. Then use your notes to answer the questions. Work with a partner and compare your answers.

1. What is the conversation mainly about?
   (A) The principles of marketing
   (B) Getting advice about buying a car
   (C) The student's difficulties in marketing class
   (D) How to buy and sell things on eBay

Listen again to part of the conversation. Then answer question 2.

2. Why does the student ask, "But weren't you worried about buying a car online?"?
   (A) He wants the professor to give more information.
   (B) He expects the professor to agree with him.
   (C) He admires the professor for taking a risk.
   (D) He thinks the professor was not being careful.

3. What concern does the student raise about buying a car online?
   (A) He has no expertise about cars.
   (B) He does not know how to use eBay.
   (C) He is unsure about buying a car he hasn't seen.
   (D) He is opposed to buying anything online.

Listen again to part of the conversation. Then answer question 4.

4. What can be inferred about the marketing principles?
   (A) The professor did not talk about them much in the class.
   (B) The student did not understand them.
   (C) The student enjoyed learning about them.
   (D) The professor discussed them many times in the class.

5. What does the student decide to do in the end?
   (A) To buy a car from the eBay website
   (B) To look at the cars eBay has on sale
   (C) To use word-of-mouth sources to find a car
   (D) To ask for the professor's help again

ACADEMIC LISTENING

FIRST LISTENING

Listen to an excerpt from a radio interview with Malcolm Gladwell, author of a book that examines "tipping points," or events that trigger important societal changes. Take notes as you listen. Work with a partner to combine your notes. Then use your notes to answer the questions on the next page.

1. In what way did the level of crime in New York City change?

_____

2. What example does Gladwell use to explain the change?

_____

3. What causes criminals to commit crimes, according to Kelling?

_____

SECOND LISTENING

Read the questions. Listen to the interview again. Add details to your notes. Then use your notes to answer the questions. Work with a partner and compare your answers.

1. What is the interview mainly about?
 (A) Why crimes are committed
 (B) The types of crime in New York
 (C) How crime levels change
 (D) The psychology of criminals

Listen again to part of the interview. Then answer question 2.

2. What does Gladwell mean when he says this?
 (A) Influential people were certain to behave the way they did.
 (B) Influential people caused others to change their behavior.
 (C) Influential people's behavior was influenced by a sea of change.
 (D) Influential people stopped crime by hitting criminals hard.

3. Why does Gladwell mention the broken window theory?
 (A) To explain how crime occurs in cities
 (B) To describe how automobile thefts occur in cities
 (C) To persuade us to believe George Kelling's theory
 (D) To illustrate how environment affects crime levels

Listen again to part of the interview. Then answer question 4.

4. Why does Gladwell say "right?" at the end of this passage?
 (A) To indicate that he shares the conservative position
 (B) To disagree with the conservative point of view
 (C) To check that the listener agrees with him
 (D) To check the listener's understanding of the situation

5. What conclusion does Gladwell draw from the broken window example?
 (A) Criminal behavior is the result of a lack of moral values.
 (B) Criminals are insensitive to environments where they commit crimes.
 (C) Criminal behavior can be prevented by changing the environment.
 (D) Criminals are different from the average person.

ANALYSIS

It is helpful to know the purpose of a test item. There are three types of questions in the listening section.

1. Basic Comprehension

- main ideas
- details
- the meaning of specific sentences

2. Organization

- the way information is structured
- the way ideas are linked

3. Inference

- ideas are not directly stated
- speaker's intention, purpose, or attitude not explicitly stated

Go back to the listening questions and label each question with 1, 2, or 3. Then work with a partner to see if you agree. Check the Answer Key for the correct answers. Which questions did you get right? Which did you get wrong? What skills do you need to practice?

2 Reading

THE STORY OF SILENT SPRING

PRE-READING

Read the list of mass movements—united actions by groups of people who share the same beliefs and work together to achieve a particular aim. Work in a group to think about possible "triggers," or causes, for the movements listed. Write your ideas in the chart. Then add your own examples of mass movements and the triggers that caused them. Share your ideas with the class.

MASS MOVEMENT	POSSIBLE TRIGGERS
Nazism—a movement led by Adolf Hitler in Germany in the 1930s–40s	• global economic depression • unemployment • belief in racial superiority
English as an international language—the current movement to have English function as the common "world" language	
Anti-gun movement—current movement to ban or restrict the sale and use of guns in the United States	

READING

Read the passage and answer the questions. Then work with a partner and compare your answers. When you disagree, go back to the text to find helpful information.

THE STORY OF SILENT SPRING

(Adapted from A Natural Resources Defense Council Publication)

1   Developed in 1939, DDT was the most powerful pesticide the world had ever known. It was used throughout the 1940s and 1950s to clear regions of mosquitoes carrying malaria. Its inventor was awarded the Nobel Prize. When DDT became available for purely commercial

(continued on next page)

use and was sprayed over crops, only a few people, like Rachel Carson, felt that there was some danger. When she finally published her book, *Silent Spring,* her fears were heard loud and clear. The impact of *Silent Spring* was great; with this book, Rachel Carson laid the foundation for the modern environmental protection movement.

2   Carson did not originally intend to write a book about the harmful effects of DDT. Her interest in the subject was sparked by a letter from old friends telling about the damage that aerial spraying had done to the ecological system on their land. Although Rachel Carson was a best-selling author, no magazine would agree to her idea for an article investigating the negative effects of DDT. She decided to go ahead and deal with the issue in a book, *Silent Spring,* which took her four years to complete. It described how DDT entered the food chain and accumulated in the fatty tissues of animals, including human beings, and caused cancer and genetic damage. The book's most famous chapter, "A Fable for Tomorrow," depicted a nameless American town where all life—from fish to birds to apple blossoms to children—had been "silenced" by the insidious effects of DDT.

3   First serialized in *The New Yorker* magazine in June 1962, the book alarmed readers across the country and, not surprisingly, brought howls of anger from the chemical industry. "If man were to faithfully follow the teachings of Miss Carson," complained an executive of the American Cyanamid Company, "we would return to the Dark Ages, and the insects and diseases would once again inherit the earth." Some of the attacks were more personal, questioning Carson's integrity and even her sanity.

4   Her careful preparation, however, had paid off. Foreseeing the reaction of the chemical industry, she had written *Silent Spring* like a lawyer's brief, with no fewer than 55 pages of notes and a list of experts who had read and approved the manuscript. Many well-known and respected scientists rose to her defense, and when President John F. Kennedy ordered the President's Science Advisory Committee to examine the issues the book raised, its report supported both *Silent Spring* and its author. As a result, DDT came under much closer government supervision and was eventually banned.

5   Conservation had never attracted much public interest before Rachel Carson's book, but the dangers she analyzed were too frightening to ignore. For the first time, the need to regulate industry in order to protect the environment became widely accepted and environmentalism was born. Carson was well aware of the implications of her book. Appearing on a CBS documentary about her work shortly before her death from breast cancer in 1964, she remarked:

The public must decide whether it wishes to continue on the present road, and it can only do so when in full possession of the facts. We still talk in terms of conquest. We haven't become mature enough to think of ourselves as only a tiny part of a vast and incredible universe. Man's attitude toward nature is today critically important simply because we have now acquired a fateful power to alter and destroy nature. But man is part of nature, and his war against nature is inevitably a war against himself.

6   One of the landmark books of the 20th century, *Silent Spring* still speaks to us today, many years after its publication. Equally inspiring is the example of Rachel Carson herself. Against overwhelming difficulties and hardship, despite her own shyness and reserve, and motivated only by her love of nature, she rose like a gladiator in its defense.

1. What is the reading mainly about?
   (A) The background and impact of *Silent Spring*
   (B) The negative effects of DDT on agriculture
   (C) The story of Rachel Carson's life and her work
   (D) The modern environmental protection movement

2. According to paragraph 1, which of the following was true about DDT before 1960?
   (A) It was used solely to stop the spread of disease.
   (B) It was globally condemned after its invention.
   (C) Most people thought it was a powerful product.
   (D) Many people were concerned about its effects.

3. The word *foundation* in paragraph 1 is closest in meaning to
   (A) basis
   (B) organization
   (C) definition
   (D) cause

4. According to paragraph 2, what started Carson's investigation into DDT?
   (A) Carson asked a magazine to publish an article on DDT.
   (B) Carson wanted to write a best-selling book on the effects of DDT.
   (C) Carson saw the damage caused by spraying DDT on farmland.
   (D) Carson heard about the negative effects of DDT from friends.

5. What can be inferred from paragraph 4 about John F. Kennedy?
   (A) He was among the experts who approved Carson's book.
   (B) He was a member of the Science Advisory Committee.
   (C) He had either read Carson's book or knew of its contents.
   (D) He defended the chemical industry's reaction to the book.

6. In paragraph 4, what does the word *its* refer to in the clause beginning "its report supported . . ."?
   (A) The committee
   (B) The book
   (C) The report
   (D) DDT

7. The word **banned** in paragraph 4 is closest in meaning to
   (A) criticized
   (B) denied
   (C) forbidden
   (D) examined

8. All of the following are mentioned in paragraph 5 about Carson EXCEPT
   (A) She was interviewed on television about her book.
   (B) She died of cancer after the book was published.
   (C) She did not expect her book to have a major impact.
   (D) Her book triggered an interest in environmental issues.

9. In the quotation in paragraph 5, Carson states that
   (A) Humans want to triumph over the environment.
   (B) Humans think of themselves as one small part of nature.
   (C) Humans have little authority over the environment.
   (D) Humans live in harmony with the environment.

10. Look at the four squares ☐ that indicate where the following sentence could be added to the passage. Where would the sentence best fit? Circle the letter that shows the point where you would insert this sentence.

    > This was surely due to the fact that, at that time, most Americans believed science worked for the good of society.

    Carson did not originally intend to write a book about the harmful effects of DDT. Her interest in the subject was sparked by a letter from old friends telling about the damage that aerial spraying had done to the ecological system on their land. [A] Although Rachel Carson was a best-selling author, no magazine would agree to her idea for an article investigating the negative effects of DDT. [B] She decided to go ahead and deal with the issue in a book, *Silent Spring,* which took her four years to complete. [C] It described how DDT entered the food chain and accumulated in the fatty tissues of animals, including human beings, and caused cancer and genetic damage. [D] The book's most famous chapter, "A Fable for Tomorrow," depicted a nameless American town where all life—from fish to birds to apple blossoms to children—had been "silenced" by the insidious effects of DDT.

11. Which of the following best expresses the essential information in this sentence from the passage?

> Foreseeing the reaction of the chemical industry, she had written *Silent Spring* like a lawyer's brief, with no fewer than 55 pages of notes and a list of experts who had read and approved the manuscript.

(A) Carson supported the claims in her book with only 55 pages of notes.
(B) Carson gained legal approval for her manuscript from experts.
(C) Carson included strong evidence for her claims because she expected opposition.
(D) Carson wrote her book in the same way that a lawyer would prepare a case.

12. An introductory sentence for a brief summary of the passage is provided below. Complete the summary by circling the THREE answer choices that express the most important ideas in the passage. Some sentences do not belong in the summary because they express ideas that are not presented in the passage or are minor ideas in the passage.

> Rachel Carson's book *Silent Spring* laid the groundwork for the environmental movement.

(A) The book first appeared in *The New Yorker* magazine in 1962.
(B) The book described the negative impact of DDT on humans and the environment.
(C) Chemical industry leaders accused Carson of being insane.
(D) Carson died before realizing the impact that her book would have.
(E) Before the book was published, there was little interest in environmentalism.
(F) After the book appeared, a government study was ordered, and DDT was later banned.

3 Writing

INTEGRATED TASK: READ, LISTEN, WRITE

In this section, you will read a short passage and listen to an excerpt on a related topic. Then you will write about the relationship between the two.

READING

Read the passage on the next page. As you read, fill in the following summary chart with definitions and details for each category.

CATEGORY	DEFINITION	DETAILS
Mavens		•
Connectors		• •
Salesmen		•

The Forces behind Trends

1   Why did the New York City crime rate drop so dramatically in the 1990s? Why did fax machines become popular so quickly in the United States? Author Malcolm Gladwell has explored the forces behind the sudden, swift transmission of ideas that change society, and he has found that new ideas and trends originate with three types of exceptional people: mavens, connectors, and salesmen.

2   In his book, *The Tipping Point: How Little Things Can Make a Big Difference,* Gladwell profiles the three groups to explain how word-of-mouth epidemics take hold in society.

3   Gladwell says mavens, the type of people who have specialized knowledge, are the first group of exceptional people responsible for trends. If you examine why you make certain decisions, such as where to shop or dine or what movie to see, he says, you find that you are relying on the same person—a maven—over and over again for recommendations.

4   Connectors are the kind of people who know everybody, the handful of individuals in any social group who have extraordinary social ties. Gladwell explains that connectors are incredibly powerful in generating word-of-mouth epidemics because if they like something, they can spread information about it five or six times, much farther than the average person.

5   Once a new idea has spread, Gladwell attributes the ability to persuade people to adopt it to the third group, the salesmen. Salesmen have an extraordinary natural ability to win people over, to get hold of an idea and make it go a long way, he says.

LISTENING

Listen to a lecture. Use the outline to take notes as you listen.

Main Idea: Paul Revere was a "connector" who succeeded in spreading news of an American Revolutionary War battle.

Paul Revere's ride

- rode from Boston to Lexington to warn of British attack
- learned of attack from several sources
-

Revere's social connections

- was a "connector": knew everybody, the type you go to for news
-
-

    - businesses:
    - clubs and organizations:
    - grand juror

-
-

WRITING

Write on the following topic. Follow the steps below to prepare.

Use concepts described in *The Tipping Point* to explain the success of Paul Revere. Include details from Revere's life to support your explanation.

Step 1

- Work with a partner. Skim the reading and your notes from the reading and listening tasks (pages 67–69) to answer the following questions. Then share your answers in a group. Take notes on what you hear.

  1. How does Gladwell define a connector?

  2. What characteristics or behaviors make a person a connector, according to Gladwell?

  3. What specific aspects of Revere's life and personality made him a connector?

- On your own, evaluate what you have heard. Which characteristics or behaviors of Revere best define him as a connector? Which details could you use in your own writing?

- Fill in the chart below to organize your ideas about the topic. In the first column, write the characteristics of a connector. In the second column, add notes about the related activities and characteristics that made Revere a connector. Use your answers to the questions above to help you.

A CONNECTOR...	REVERE'S ACTIVITIES / CHARACTERISTICS
...knows everybody	

Step 2

Write for 20 minutes. Leave the last 5 minutes to edit your work.

To evaluate a partner's writing, use the Writing Evaluation Form on page 203.

4 Speaking

INDEPENDENT TASK

Speak on the following topic. Follow the steps below to prepare.

> **Express your opinion about the reasons behind the popularity of a modern technological device, such as the cell phone. What factors caused the development of this device? Why has it become so widely used?**

Step 1

- Work in a group. Brainstorm a list of technological devices that are popular today. Take turns describing one device, its origin, and the reasons for its popularity.

- On your own, evaluate what you have heard. Which technological device do you consider the most popular? Which one do you have the most knowledge about? Choose a device to speak about.

- After you have chosen a topic, organize your ideas by filling in the outline below.

Introduction—Main Idea Sentence: _____

_____
(State the device, and briefly state the reasons that you think it has gained popularity.)

Main Point (Reason 1): _____
(Introduce the first reason for your opinion.)

Details: _____
(Use details to support this reason.)

Main Point (Reason 2): _____
(Introduce the second reason for your opinion.)

Details: _____
(Use details to support this reason.)

Conclusion: _____

_____
(Restate your main idea.)

Step 2

With a partner, take turns practicing a one-minute oral response to the topic. Be sure to use the information in your outline to help you.

Step 3

Change partners. Take turns giving a one-minute response to the topic again.

> To evaluate your partner's response, use the Speaking Evaluation Form on page 204.

5 Skill Focus

IDENTIFYING AND USING MAIN IDEAS AND DETAILS

EXAMINATION

1 *Look at the following items from the unit. Write* MI *next to the items that ask about the main idea. Write* D *next to those that ask about supporting details. (Some items may deal with both types.) Work with a partner to discuss your choices and answer the questions about the items.*

- For the items you labeled *MI*, how did you identify the correct main idea or choose which main ideas were incorrect?

- For the items you labeled *D*, how did you identify the details that support the main idea?

- In Item 3, how did you distinguish between details that belong in the summary and those that do not belong?

Item 1 (Campus Conversation, p. 60) _____

What is the conversation mainly about?
(A) The principles of marketing
(B) Getting advice about buying a car
(C) The student's difficulties in marketing class
(D) How to buy and sell things on eBay

Item 2 (Reading, p. 66) _____

All of the following are mentioned in paragraph 5 about Carson EXCEPT
(A) She was interviewed on television about her book.
(B) She died of cancer after the book was published.
(C) She did not expect her book to have a major impact on people.
(D) Her book triggered an interest in environmental issues.

Item 3 (Reading, p. 67) _____

An introductory sentence for a brief summary of the passage is provided below. Complete the summary by selecting the THREE answer choices that express the most important ideas in the passage. Some sentences to do not belong in the summary because they express ideas that are not presented in the passage or are minor ideas in the passage.

> Rachel Carson's book *Silent Spring* laid the groundwork for the environmental movement.

(A) The book first appeared in *The New Yorker* magazine in 1962.
(B) The book described the negative impact of DDT on humans and the environment.
(C) Chemical industry leaders accused Carson of being insane.
(D) Carson died before realizing the impact that her book would have.
(E) Before the book was published, there was little interest in environmentalism.
(F) After the book appeared, a government study was ordered, and DDT was later banned.

2 *Look at the following task from the unit. Work with a partner and answer the questions about the task.*

Item 4 (Independent Task, p. 71)

Express your opinion about the reasons behind the popularity of a modern technological device, such as the cell phone. What factors caused the development of this device? Why has it become so widely used?

• Review the outline you created to prepare for your oral response to the topic. What was your main idea—what were the reasons that the device you chose became popular?

• Did you include details to support your main idea? If so, which details did you include and why did you choose them?

• How did you organize the points and details that support your main idea?

Tips

To do well on the TOEFL, it is essential to learn how to identify a speaker or writer's most important points and to make your own ideas clear when you speak and write. Paying attention to important supporting details can help you understand and communicate main ideas.

Listening and Reading

- Identify main ideas, or the general ideas about the topic that are supported by the other information in the text.

- Identify details that support and explain the main ideas. These may include facts, reasons, examples, steps, or other kinds of evidence. To identify details, look for specific information about the main ideas. Then focus on the details that present the information that is most important in supporting the main idea.

In **Item 1**, you probably identified the topic of the conversation as *buying a car*. The conversation involved a student getting advice from a counselor about buying a car, so those two ideas together—getting advice about buying a car—form the main idea.

In **Item 2**, you should have identified choice (C) as the detail that is not mentioned in the paragraph. The text expresses the opposite idea: "Carson was well aware of the implications of her book." In **Item 3**, you probably read over the details and the introductory (main idea) sentence in order to decide which details would fit and which would not.

Speaking and Writing

- State the topic and your main points about the topic in a main idea sentence. In writing, the main idea sentence is called a *thesis statement,* and the main point sentences for each paragraph are called *topic sentences.*

- Include important details that will best support your main idea.

Your outline related to **Item 4** should have clearly stated your main ideas and included effective details, as in the following example:

Main Idea: The <u>cell phone</u> has gained sudden popularity because
of its <u>convenience and safety benefits</u>.

> **Main Point 1:** The cell phone is a convenient, portable device.
> **Detail 1:** You can use it almost anywhere—at home, at work, on a bus, or at a shopping mall.
> **Detail 2:** It's so small that it can fit on your belt, in your pocket, or in your backpack.
> **Main Point 2:** The cell phone also makes people safer. . . .

PRACTICE

1 *Read the passage. Use the tips from the previous section to help you complete the activity that follows. Work with a partner and compare your answers.*

Ideaviruses

1   Have you ever wondered why people believe what they believe, wear what they wear, and do what they do? In his book *Unleashing the Ideavirus*, Seth Godin argues that an idea can spread as rapidly as a bad cold. This occurs when people use person-to-person communication to produce significant changes in attitude, preference, or habits.

2   According to Godin, if a company wants to transmit an idea, it needs to create an "ideavirus." To persuade people, he explains, companies need a "virusworthy" idea, something everyone wants to talk about. "And if the right people get a hold of the idea, it will spread incredibly fast." A good example is the e-mail system Hotmail. Since every piece of Hotmail has the Hotmail name on it, no one is immune to the Hotmail ideavirus.

3   Godin calls the people who spread ideaviruses "sneezers." Oprah Winfrey, the well-known actress and talk show host, is one. He says when Winfrey began recommending books on her show, those books would suddenly become hot best-sellers. Each viewer would tell his or her friend or neighbor. The friend or neighbor would tell another friend and then another. "The group of readers just got bigger and bigger, like a stone thrown in a pond. The recommendations created a ripple effect," Godin says.

2 *Read the sentences. Copy them onto the appropriate lines of the outline that follows to show the main ideas and supporting details of the passage above.*

- Everyone knows Hotmail because the name appears on its e-mail messages.

- Oprah Winfrey is an example of someone who spreads ideas.

- New ideas spread like viruses through person-to-person communication.

- Companies can transmit ideas in the same way that viruses spread.

- Viewers follow Winfrey's recommendations about books.

- The people who disseminate information can be called "sneezers."

- Hotmail illustrates a "virusworthy" idea.

Introduction—Thesis Statement (main idea of passage): _____

_____

Topic Sentence (main idea of paragraph): _____

_____

    Detail 1: _____

    Detail 2: _____

Topic Sentence (main idea of paragraph): _____

_____

    Detail 1: _____

    Detail 2: _____

3 *Work with a partner. Read your partner's written response from the Integrated Task (pages 67–71). Highlight one or two places where more (or better) details could improve the writing. Then suggest additions.*

Cross-Cultural Insights

| LISTENING |

Campus Conversation
A student talks with a counselor about his feeling of helplessness during a family crisis, when he's far from his family.

Academic Listening
Radio interview: *Feng Shui in the Newsroom*

| READING |

Newspaper Article
In One School, Many Sagas

| SPEAKING |

**Integrated Task:
Read, Listen, Speak**
Debate options for redesigning a college visitor center. Which model should be followed: Victorian design or the philosophy of feng shui?

| WRITING |

Independent Task
Which country or culture has made the most significant contributions throughout history?

| SKILL FOCUS |

Using Context Clues
Using context clues means using surrounding information to understand meaning and details, and make inferences.

| TOEFL® iBT TARGET SKILLS |

- Identify and express main ideas
- Identify and express details
- Make inferences
- Recognize a speaker's attitude
- Understand vocabulary in context
- Scan for information and organize it
- Use details to support an opinion

 For extra practice of TOEFL iBT skills, go to pages 242–259.

1 Listening

CAMPUS CONVERSATION

PRE-LISTENING VOCABULARY

Read the sentences. Guess the meaning of the boldfaced words and phrases. Then match each word or phrase with a definition or synonym from the list below. Work with a partner and compare your answers.

_____ 1. Your assignment is to research your cultural **heritage**, to interview family members, and to prepare a family history.

_____ 2. The concert tickets go on sale next week, but I don't know how much they'll cost. I'll **be in touch with** you as soon as I find out the details.

_____ 3. A lot is **at stake** if I don't do well on this job interview. I need the experience on my résumé, and I really need the extra money.

_____ 4. I have two term papers due Monday, a big test next week, and a bad cold. I'm **a wreck!**

_____ 5. Don't be angry at yourself for one low test score. You can bring your grade up later in the semester, so **give yourself a break**.

_____ 6. Since Amy struggles so much in her biology class, she should **face the fact** that nursing is not the right major for her.

_____ 7. John is looking for a good used car. **First and foremost**, he wants one that's reliable.

_____ 8. If you don't want to **flunk out**, you had better start doing your homework! Remember that the advisor said you may not be allowed to return to school next semester if you don't pass all your courses.

a. fail in school

b. in danger of being lost

c. mentally stressed

d. most importantly

e. realize

f. talk to

g. traditions

h. stop criticizing yourself

Culture Note: Most colleges and universities have counseling centers where students can talk to professional counselors about problems or stresses in their personal and academic lives. The counseling is confidential and usually free of charge. These centers also provide helpful information about healthy living and stress management.

FIRST LISTENING

Read the questions. Listen to a conversation between a student and a counselor. Take notes as you listen. Share your notes with a partner. Then use your notes to answer the questions.

1. What are the student and the counselor discussing?

   _____

   _____

2. Why is the student upset?

   _____

   _____

3. What does the counselor suggest the student do?

   _____

   _____

SECOND LISTENING

Read the questions. Listen to the conversation again. Add details to your notes. Then use your notes to answer the questions. Work with a partner and compare your answers.

1. Why does the student go to see the counselor?
   (A) To discuss his concerns about his family's current crisis
   (B) To request another appointment to discuss his situation
   (C) To explain the differences between Haitian and American families
   (D) To talk about the role of oldest sons in Haitian culture

2. How does the student feel about his situation?
   (A) He is angry.
   (B) He is optimistic.
   (C) He is worried.
   (D) He is confident.

Listen again to part of the conversation. Then answer question 3.

3. Why does the counselor say, "Luc, give yourself a break!"?
   (A) He wants the student to think clearly about his actions.
   (B) He wants the student to criticize himself less.
   (C) He wants the student to learn from his mistakes.
   (D) He wants the student to stop thinking about his actions.

4. What solution does the student reach in the end?
   (A) He will return to Haiti and help his family.
   (B) He will call his family and ask what he can do.
   (C) He will ask his aunt to help his family.
   (D) He will call his friends and ask them to help.

5. Why does the counselor suggest the student make another appointment?
   (A) He enjoyed talking to Luc and wants to get to know him better.
   (B) He thinks Luc has deeper problems that may continue to bother him.
   (C) He always suggests that students make another appointment.
   (D) He wants to keep track of how Luc's family is doing.

ACADEMIC LISTENING

FIRST LISTENING

Listen to an excerpt from a radio interview with Kirsten Lagatree, author of a book about feng shui. Take notes as you listen. Work with a partner and combine your notes. Then use your notes to answer the questions.

1. What does the radio host ask Lagatree to do?

   _____

   _____

2. What is Lagatree's overall reaction to the newsroom?

   _____

   _____

3. What comments does Lagatree make relating to directions (north, south, east, etc.) in the room? Write as many ideas as you hear.

   _____

   _____

SECOND LISTENING

 Read the questions. Listen to the interview again. Add details to your notes. Then use your notes to answer the questions. Work with a partner and compare your answers.

    1. What is the interview mainly about?
      (A) How to become a better writer
      (B) How to enhance an area with feng shui
      (C) The importance of helping people in their careers
      (D) The way to pay attention to emotions in a room

    2. How does Lagatree explain the concepts of feng shui?
      (A) By describing the features of the newsroom
      (B) By contrasting the newsroom with other spaces
      (C) By describing the work of people in the newsroom
      (D) By defining the main principles of feng shui

 Listen again to part of the interview. Then answer question 3.

    3. Why does the host say, "Am I blocked up a little bit?"?
      (A) He wants to know if he should clean off his desk.
      (B) He is concerned that there is not enough space around him.
      (C) He is asking if his desk should face in a different direction.
      (D) He is worried that the color red might be a negative force.

 Listen again to part of the interview. Then answer question 4.

    4. Why does Lagatree say, "Well, one thing at a time."?
      (A) To go back to her previous point
      (B) To think about what to say about the fish tank
      (C) To begin to talk about the fish tank at this moment
      (D) To disagree with the other speaker

    5. What point does Lagatree make about fountains or fish tanks in feng shui design?
      (A) Water creates energy.
      (B) Water equals cash flow.
      (C) Water brings good health.
      (D) Water indicates happiness.

    6. What does Lagatree recommend that the radio host do in the end?
      (A) Move his desk to face northeast in order to become a better writer
      (B) Add items to his southeast wall so that he can become rich
      (C) Enhance the southwest wall to promote his personal relationships
      (D) Determine his goals, and then change the space accordingly

2 Reading

IN ONE SCHOOL, MANY SAGAS

PRE-READING

Read this excerpt from the passage that follows and answer the questions. Do not use a dictionary. Work with a partner and compare your answers. Share your answers with the rest of your class.

In One School, Many Sagas

1   Mrs. Contrepois realize[d] that she knew nothing of the background of the young people of different races whom she faced every day. Clearly, some students' parents came to France simply to find work. Others came fleeing wars and dictatorships. Yet Mrs. Contrepois, who comes from an immigrant
5   family herself, also wondered whether the teenagers themselves knew why they were in France. Did they know their own family history?

1. What does the word *sagas* in the title probably mean? Write your guess. Explain your answer.

_____

_____

2. What does the word *fleeing* in line 3 probably mean? Write your guess. Explain your answer.

_____

_____

READING

Read the passage on the next page and answer the questions. Then work with a partner and compare your answers. When you disagree, go back to the text to find helpful information.

In One School, Many Sagas

By Alan Riding (from the *New York Times*)

1   Sabine Contrepois well remembers the day two years ago when she explained to her high school class how the Vietnam War eventually spilled into Cambodia. Suddenly, Meak, an Asian girl in the front row, burst into tears. "I asked her what was wrong," Mrs. Contrepois recalled. "She said her father was shot the day the Khmer Rouge took power in Cambodia in 1975. She and her mother spent years in concentration camps before they escaped through Thailand. There was absolute silence in the classroom."

2   The incident set the teacher thinking. A traditional role of French schools is to prepare children of immigrants to become French citizens. Yet Meak's reaction made Mrs. Contrepois realize that she knew nothing of the background of the young people of different races whom she faced every day. Clearly, some students' parents came to France simply to find work. Others came fleeing wars and dictatorships. Yet Mrs. Contrepois, who comes from an immigrant family herself, also wondered whether the teenagers themselves knew why they were in France. Did they know their own family history?

3   A year ago, seeking answers, she gave the 120 students in her six classes a research project titled: "In what way has your family been touched by history?" If they did not know, she told them, they should ask their parents and grandparents. The result is "History, My History," a document in which 41 students, mostly in their late teens, describe the tumultuous paths—wars in Armenia, Spain, Algeria, Vietnam, and the former Yugoslavia; repression in Poland, Portugal, and Cameroon—that brought their families here.

4   Mrs. Contrepois sees the problem through the prism of her students at Frederic Mistral High School in this town south of Paris. Her job is to teach youths who are considered by the school system to be slow learners. Many are immigrant children who have trouble finding jobs after school.

5   To Mrs. Contrepois, the youths' main liability is not a lack of ability, but confusion about their identity. "It's easier for them to accept being French if they can also come to terms with their roots," she said. "This project tried to do that. It made them communicate with their parents. In many cases, they discovered things that made them proud. And I think it taught them tolerance toward each other."

6   Yassine, a 19-year-old born in France of Algerian parents, said he discovered that his grandfather had been tortured and killed by French troops during Algeria's war of independence. "I didn't know anything about this," he said. "We never spoke about Algeria at home. I had never dared ask before."

7   Stephanie, also 19, said she learned that her grandfather was shot by invading German troops in Poland in 1939. "My father came here illegally in 1946, but this topic was taboo at home," she said. "He died two years ago and my mother told me the story. When she saw the final project, she cried. She was very proud."

1. What is the passage mainly about?
   (A) The difficulties of immigrants
   (B) A class project on family histories
   (C) The after-effects of war on families
   (D) A teacher's effort to know her students

2. In paragraph 1, the author's primary purpose is
   (A) To provide an example of a student's family history
   (B) To illustrate one of the nationalities of students in the school
   (C) To describe the incident that led to the teacher's assignment
   (D) To emphasize the dramatic content of the students' stories

3. Based on the information in paragraph 1, what can be inferred about the classmates' reaction to the student's story?
   (A) They did not pay attention.
   (B) They were shocked.
   (C) They were bored.
   (D) They had heard it before.

4. Which of the following statements about immigrants can be inferred from paragraph 2?
   (A) They know their family histories.
   (B) They have been in France for many years.
   (C) The teacher lacks any background knowledge of them.
   (D) French schools do not have a strong role in educating them.

5. According to paragraph 3, which of the following is true about the student research project?
   (A) The teacher compiled some of the papers into one document.
   (B) The teacher produced a document consisting of all her students' writing.
   (C) The students had to rely solely on their own knowledge to write their papers.
   (D) The papers focused on families' experiences after they immigrated.

6. The word *liability* in paragraph 5 is closest in meaning to
   (A) disadvantage
   (B) asset
   (C) circumstance
   (D) reason

7. All of the following are mentioned in paragraph 5 as benefits of the research project EXCEPT
   (A) The project gave students pride in themselves.
   (B) The project taught students about their family histories.
   (C) The project encouraged students to talk to their parents.
   (D) The project helped students learn about French history.

8. The word *this* in paragraph 6 refers to
   (A) Algeria
   (B) the grandfather
   (C) Algeria's war of independence
   (D) the grandfather's torture and death

9. The word *taboo* in paragraph 7 is closest in meaning to
   (A) forbidden
   (B) popular
   (C) unauthorized
   (D) uncommon

10. Which of the following information is NOT true of the family histories mentioned in paragraphs 6 and 7?
    (A) Both stories explained the death of a grandparent.
    (B) Both stories occurred during war-time periods.
    (C) Both stories were openly discussed in the students' homes.
    (D) Both stories told about violence in the students' homes.

11. Look at the four squares ☐ that indicate where the following sentence could be added to the passage. Where would the sentence best fit? Circle the letter that shows the point where you would insert this sentence.

    > She thought they might be as uninformed about their family roots as she was at that age.

    The incident set the teacher thinking. A traditional role of French schools is to prepare children of immigrants to become French citizens. **A** Yet Meak's reaction made Mrs. Contrepois realize that she knew nothing of the background of the young people of different races whom she faced every day. **B** Clearly, some students' parents came to France simply to find work. Others came fleeing wars and dictatorships. **C** Yet Mrs. Contrepois, who comes from an immigrant family herself, also wondered whether the teenagers themselves knew why they were in France. Did they know their own family history? **D**

    A year ago, seeking answers, she gave the 120 students in her six classes a research project titled: "In what way has your family been touched by history?"

12. An introductory sentence for a brief summary of the passage is provided below. Complete the summary by circling the THREE answer choices that express the most important ideas in the passage. Some sentences do not belong in the summary because they express ideas that are not presented in the passage or are minor ideas in the passage.

    > Students in a French school researched their immigrant families' histories for a class project.

    (A) The collection of stories was called "History, My History."
    (B) The project required the students to write a paper on the effects of history on their families.

(continued on next page)

(C) The teacher hoped the project would help her students improve their language skills.

(D) Their stories told of the difficult experiences that led their families to immigrate.

(E) The project helped the students accept both their lives in France and their origins.

(F) The project required students to conduct their research on the Internet.

ANALYSIS

It is helpful to know the purpose of a test item. There are four types of questions in the reading section.

1. Basic Comprehension

- main ideas

- details

- the meaning of specific sentences

2. Organization

- the way information is structured in the text

- the way ideas are linked between sentences or between paragraphs

3. Inference

- ideas are not directly stated in the text

- author's intention, purpose, or attitude not explicitly stated in the text

4. Vocabulary and Reference

- the meaning of words

- the meaning of reference words such as *his*, *them*, *this*, or *none*

Go back to the reading questions and label each question with 1, 2, 3, or 4. Then work with a partner to see if you agree. Check the Answer Key for the correct answers. Which questions did you get right? Which did you get wrong? What skills do you need to practice?

3 Speaking

INTEGRATED TASK: READ, LISTEN, SPEAK

In this section, you will read a short passage and listen to an excerpt on a related topic. Then you will speak about the relationship between the two.

READING

Read the passage on the next page. As you read, fill in the following summary chart.

FEATURES OF VICTORIAN DESIGN	DETAILS AND EXAMPLES
Filled spaces	• • Peninsula Hotel: • • •
	• cloth is a primary material in Victorian rooms • • • Peninsula Hotel: •
Decoration of walls	Peninsula Hotel: • • • results: rooms that overflow with decorative, elegant elements

The Victorian Style of Design

The Peninsula Hotel, Hong Kong

1   One of the most enduring styles of interior design is the Victorian style, named for Queen Victoria of England. The style emerged in the late 1800s, at the height of the prosperous Industrial Revolution, when middle-class Britons wanted to display their affluence, status, and cultural interests. What better way to do so than to decorate their homes with ornate interiors? Thus, Victorian design gained immediate fame. Even today, the style remains popular across the globe, especially in Asia, where designers look to the past to create opulent, decorated spaces that convey wealth and status.

2   One of the key features of Victorian design is the notion that bareness in a room shows poor taste. Victorian designers fill interior spaces with as many objects as possible. The renowned Peninsula Hotel in Hong Kong exemplifies this principle with its ornate wood furniture, and tabletops and walls adorned with decorative objects and art. The Peninsula's lobby may seem cluttered to some, yet the size and number of its ornamental elements give it an impressive, elegant atmosphere.

3   A second important part of Victorian design is the use of rich, brightly colored fabrics. Cloth is a primary material in Victorian rooms. Windows are rarely left uncovered, but rather are wrapped in

thick draperies, as in the Peninsula Hotel. The richness of drapery fabrics—velvet, silk, and satin—compensates for the loss of natural light flowing into Victorian spaces. Furniture is also covered in fabric, often in colors to coordinate with draperies and walls. The woven fabric element is carried out in plush carpets and rugs, often with complex patterns.

4   The decoration of walls is yet another aspect of Victorian style. As in the Peninsula Hotel, walls and ceilings are embellished with molding, colorful wallpapers, and paint. The wall moldings add texture and depth to the already complicated interiors. The results are rooms that overflow with elegant, decorative elements—exactly what the first Victorian designers had in mind.

LISTENING

Listen to a lecture. Use the chart on the next page to take notes as you listen.

Fallingwater home in Mill Run, Pennsylvania, by Frank Lloyd Wright

Main Idea: Feng shui influenced the architecture of Frank Lloyd Wright and has become increasingly popular in the West.

FENG SHUI CONCEPTS AND WRIGHT	
Balance	**Energy Flow**
• Chinese believe in yin, yang: balance in everything	• Wright's open, bright spaces encouraged energy flow
•	•
• yang—low ceilings	• no clutter, tight spaces
•	•
• balanced use of 5 Chinese elements: fire, water, earth, wood, metal	• waterfall = negative energy

SPEAKING

Speak on the following topic. Follow the steps below to prepare.

Debate options for redesigning a college visitor center. Which model should be followed: Victorian design or the philosophy of feng shui?

Step 1

• Work with a partner. Skim the reading and your notes from the reading and listening tasks (pages 87–90) to answer the following questions.

  1. What is Victorian style in interior design? How could it be applied to the redesign of a college visitor center where visitors and potential students come to find out about a college?

  2. How could the feng shui philosophy be applied to the redesign of a college visitor center?

• With your partner, brainstorm ideas for redesigning a college visitor center according to each of the models: Victorian and feng shui. Take notes on your ideas.

Step 2

With your partner, practice debating the ideas for redesigning the visitor center. Take turns advocating one model and refuting the other. Then switch roles and debate again. Be sure to use the information in your notes to help you.

Step 3

Change partners. Debate the issue for two minutes. One student will act as a Victorian design advocate, and one as a feng shui supporter. Then switch roles and debate again.

To evaluate your partner's response, use the Speaking Evaluation Form on page 204.

4 Writing

INDEPENDENT TASK

Write on the following topic. Follow the steps below to prepare.

Which country or culture has made the most significant contributions throughout history? Include examples to support your opinion.

Step 1

- As a class, brainstorm important contributions or discoveries that various countries or cultures have made throughout history. Think about aspects of everyday life that are present around the world: food, clothing, housing, furniture, technology, and so on. Write your ideas on the board.

- On your own, evaluate what you have heard. Which country or culture do you think has made the most significant contributions? What are the most important contributions that it has made? What makes them so important? How widely are they used today?

- Prepare for your writing by making a list. Title the list with the name of the country or culture. First list the reasons that you consider the country or culture to have made the most significant contributions. Then list several contributions that you will write about. For each contribution, take notes about detailed examples that you will include. Refer to your list as you write.

Step 2

Write for 20 minutes. Leave the last 5 minutes to edit your work.

> To evaluate a partner's writing, use the Writing Evaluation Form on page 203.

5 Skill Focus

USING CONTEXT CLUES

EXAMINATION

1 *Look at the following items from the unit. Work with a partner and answer this question about the items.*

- Did any surrounding words or ideas help you choose the correct answers? Go back to the reading passage and mark the parts that helped you.

Item 1 (Reading, p. 84)

The word *liability* in paragraph 5 is closest in meaning to
(A) disadvantage
(B) asset
(C) circumstance
(D) reason

Item 2 (Reading, p. 85)

The word *this* in paragraph 6 refers to
(A) Algeria
(B) the grandfather
(C) Algeria's war of independence
(D) the grandfather's torture and death

Item 3 (Reading, p. 85)

Which of the following information is NOT true of the family histories
mentioned in paragraphs 6 and 7?
(A) Both stories explained the death of a grandparent.
(B) Both stories occurred during war-time periods.
(C) Both stories were openly discussed in the students' homes.
(D) Both stories told about violence in the students' homes.

2 *Look at the following item from the unit. Work with a partner and answer these
questions about the item.*

- Did any surrounding words or ideas help you choose the correct answer?

- Did you include these words or ideas in your notes? Go back to your notes
  and mark the parts that helped you. If necessary, listen again to the
  conversation and take notes on the parts that helped you.

Item 4 (Campus Conversation, p. 80)

Why does the counselor suggest the student make another appointment?
(A) He enjoyed talking to Luc and wants to get to know him better.
(B) He thinks Luc has deeper problems that may continue to bother him.
(C) He always suggests that students make another appointment.
(D) He wants to keep track of how Luc's family is doing.

Tips

To do well on the TOEFL, it is essential to learn how to use context clues,
or surrounding information, to understand meaning. The TOEFL evaluates
your ability to interpret context clues in three categories of test items:
vocabulary/reference, detail, and inference items.

Vocabulary/Reference

The TOEFL contains two types of vocabulary test items:

1. Synonym items, in which you choose the word with the same or similar meaning as the target word.

2. Referent items, in which you identify the noun or idea to which a pronoun such as *he* or *this* refers.

• Reread the sentence in which the target word appears, as well as a few sentences before and after the target word. This will help you to "frame" the word in its larger context.

• Choose the answer that best fits the sentence in which the target word appears. Go back to the reading and substitute each answer choice to see which one fits. Pay attention to number (singularity and plurality) in making your choice.

To answer **Item 1**, you likely guessed that the word *liability* must have a negative meaning, based on the context, which tells about the students' problems. The word *disadvantage*—choice (A)—is the answer that most logically fits when substituted for *liability* in the original sentence.

For **Item 2**, you probably used the context to figure out that *this* had to mean "the grandfather's torture and death"—choice (D). Of the choices, this fact is most likely the one that the student might *not* have heard about.

Details

On the TOEFL, test items about details have these characteristics:

1. Questions focus on important details in texts.

2. Answer choices may include details not presented in the text.

• Look for important details as you read or listen, and write them down in your notes. These are the details that you are most likely to be tested on.

• Keep in mind the larger context of a detail as you listen or read. If you put the ideas together, you can better comprehend each detail because you will see how it fits into the speaker or writer's main idea(s).

To answer **Item 3**, you probably put together the important details about each story related in paragraphs 6 and 7. The details in both paragraphs that indicate the students did *not* previously know the stories probably helped you make the correct choice, (C).

Inference

Context clues include key ideas, words, or nonverbal clues—such as punctuation in writing or intonation in speaking—that convey meaning or attitude.

- Put together important ideas and think about their implications. This will help you reach logical conclusions based on the information at hand.

- Pay attention to words and structures that fit together to indicate the writer or speaker's meaning.

To answer **Item 4**, you probably paid attention to the questions that the counselor asked in the course of the conversation. Put together, the questions imply that the counselor is concerned about Luc's deeper feelings about living away from his family—choice (B).

PRACTICE

1 *Read the passage. Use the tips from the previous section to help you answer the items that follow. Work with a partner and compare your answers.*

The Meaning and Origin of Feng Shui

1   Feng shui, meaning "wind" and "water" in Chinese, is an ancient form of geomancy, or the art of arranging the physical surroundings to create harmony and good luck. An art and a science, feng shui is concerned with creating both physical and psychological comfort. Practitioners believe that the arrangement of the elements in our environment can affect many aspects of our lives, such as health, happiness, and fortune.

2   Feng shui grew out of the practical experience of farmers in southern China over 3,000 years ago. Those who built their huts facing north were battered by the wind and dust from the Gobi Desert in Mongolia. In contrast, those who built their huts facing south enjoyed the warmth of the sun and protection from the wind. As a result, south became the favored direction. Over the years, it came to be associated with fame, fortune, summer, the color red, and the number nine.

1. All of the following are mentioned in paragraph 1 as characteristics of feng shui EXCEPT
   (A) Feng shui is a very old practice.
   (B) Feng shui can affect our minds and our bodies.
   (C) Feng shui involves ideas, not objects.
   (D) Feng shui relates to making us comfortable.

2. The word *huts* in paragraph 2 probably means _____.
   (Write an appropriate synonym or synonymous phrase.)

3. The pronoun *it* in paragraph 2 refers to _____.
   (Write the noun or noun phrase that the pronoun replaces.)

4. Based on the information in paragraph 2, what can be inferred about life in this area of China at the time?
   (A) There were few challenges.
   (B) Living there was comfortable.
   (C) Life there was very difficult.
   (D) It was impossible to live there.

5. According to the passage, the practice of feng shui
   (A) became instantly popular
   (B) developed over time
   (C) originated with scientists
   (D) was taught to Chinese farmers

2 *Listen to a passage from the book* Lost in Translation, *the story of a Polish girl who immigrated to Canada with her family. Use the chart below to take notes. Then use your notes and the tips from the previous section to help you answer the questions that follow. Work with a partner and compare your answers.*

Main Idea: A girl learns about cultural differences as an immigrant in a new country.

CULTURAL DIFFERENCE	DETAILS
	Teacher says to sit on hands while describing frog digestive system
Cultural distances	
	Penny is offended, thinks gesture means aggression, not friendliness
Walking arm-in-arm	

Listen again to part of the passage. Then answer question 1.

1. What does the speaker's mother mean by "becoming English"?
   (A) She admires English behavior.
   (B) Her daughter is becoming cold like the English.
   (C) Becoming English is painful.
   (D) She does not like the cold English weather.

Listen again to part of the passage. Then answer question 2.

2. Why does the teacher tell the student to sit on her hands and then try talking?
   (A) To get her to speak more clearly
   (B) To get her to use fewer gestures
   (C) To get her to change her answer
   (D) To get her to look at other students

3. What point does the speaker make about cultural distance in Canada?
   (A) People stand closer together.
   (B) People do not tell her where to stand.
   (C) People do not like her to stand so close.
   (D) People stand about the same distance apart.

4. What does the speaker learn from her two friends?
   (A) To control the ways she shows her feelings
   (B) Not to be embarrassed by her actions
   (C) Not to pay attention to her own movements
   (D) To express intimacy and friendliness freely

Faith

| LISTENING |

Campus Conversation   A student consults his advisor about whether or not he should attend a summer spiritual retreat instead of taking courses.

Academic Listening   Radio interview: *Describing Monastic Life*

| READING |

Encyclopedia Entry   *Religion*

| WRITING |

Integrated Task: Read, Listen, Write   Explain fasting as a means to increase spirituality. Include details from Thomas Merton's life to support your explanation.

| SPEAKING |

Independent Task   Discuss the ways in which religious beliefs or practices have affected your life or the lives of others you know or have read about.

| SKILL FOCUS |

Summarizing   Summarizing means finding the essential information from a written or spoken text, and leaving out less important details, then using this information in writing or speaking.

| TOEFL® iBT TARGET SKILLS |

- Identify and express main ideas
- Identify and express details
- Make inferences
- Recognize a speaker's or writer's attitude
- Scan for important information
- Paraphrase information in notes

 For extra practice of TOEFL iBT skills, go to pages 242–259.

1 Listening

CAMPUS CONVERSATION

PRE-LISTENING VOCABULARY

Read the sentences. Guess the meaning of the boldfaced words and phrases. Write your ideas on the lines. Then match each word or phrase with a definition or synonym from the list on the next page. Work with a partner and compare your answers.

_____ 1. My roommate Diane **meditates** every afternoon. Sitting quietly and focusing her thoughts relaxes her and reduces her stress.

_____

_____ 2. Since Calvin is majoring in chemical engineering, he needs to take several **core classes** in chemistry.

_____

_____ 3. I've been working on my English assignment for two hours, so I need some fresh air. I need to take a walk before I can **get this out of the way.**

_____

_____ 4. I didn't make an appointment, so if I've **caught you** at a bad time, just let me know. I can come back later.

_____

_____ 5. After talking to a few chemists, Michelle **had second thoughts about** choosing chemistry as her line of work.

_____

_____ 6. With classes and study time, my weekdays are filled, but I still find time for the International Students' Club and other **extracurricular** activities on the weekends.

_____

_____ 7. Walking in the woods is a **spiritual** activity for Shawn. It makes him recognize that all living things are connected.

_____

_____ 8. Nadia was chosen to join the **honors program** because she made excellent grades in her first two semesters of college.

_____

_____ **9.** To be a better person, **strive** to be thoughtful to others and mindful of their needs.

_____

_____ **10.** Reading e-mail is a **time-consuming** task, so I usually do it late at night after I've finished my classes.

_____

a. apply effort

b. central courses

c. finish something

d. met someone who was not prepared

e. not relating to school work

f. program for exceptional students

g. reconsidered

h. reflects, thinks deeply

i. relating to god or the soul

j. taking a long time

> **Culture Note:** Most colleges and universities offer a wide variety of extracurricular clubs and activities, including volunteer projects, political and social organizations, campus journalism, and sports activities. Students are strongly encouraged to participate in these activities as a way to make friends and build a support system that will help them cope with the challenges of academic life.

FIRST LISTENING

Read the questions on the next page. Listen to a conversation between a student and an advisor. Take notes as you listen. Share your notes with a partner. Then use your notes to answer the questions.

1. What is the student's dilemma (choice)?

_____

_____

2. Why does the student want to attend the retreat?

_____

_____

3. What does the advisor say in the end?

_____

_____

SECOND LISTENING

Read the questions. Listen to the conversation again. Add details to your notes. Then use your notes to answer the questions. Work with a partner and compare your answers.

1. What is the conversation mainly about?
(A) A student's concern about his progress in biology
(B) A student's practice of the Buddhist religion
(C) A student's plans for taking psychology in the summer
(D) A student's decision about whether to attend a spiritual retreat

2. How does the student feel about his own meditation?
(A) He thinks he should start meditating later in the day.
(B) He thinks he can no longer meditate in the proper way.
(C) He thinks it is difficult to find time to meditate.
(D) He thinks there is no value in meditation anymore.

Listen again to part of the conversation. Then answer question 3.

3. Why does the advisor mention the student's extracurricular activities?
(A) He thinks the student may be doing too many activities.
(B) He is impressed by the student's participation in so many activities.
(C) He wants the student to tell him more about his school newspaper job.
(D) He thinks the student should take fewer courses and do more activities.

4. Why is the student hesitating about whether to attend the retreat?
(A) He feels distracted from his religion.
(B) He worries about keeping up with his studies.
(C) He thinks that he cannot afford the trip.
(D) He was dissatisfied with his experiences there.

Listen again to part of the conversation. Then answer question 5.

5. What can be inferred from the advisor's response?
   (A) He thinks the student should go on the retreat.
   (B) He thinks the student should focus only on his studies.
   (C) He thinks the student should meditate at home.
   (D) He thinks the student should use his own judgment.

6. What solution does the student reach in the end?
   (A) He will attend summer school classes.
   (B) He will go to the Buddhist retreat.
   (C) He will think about the problem more.
   (D) He will make a new degree plan.

ACADEMIC LISTENING

FIRST LISTENING

 Listen to a radio interview about author William Claassen's visits to and book on monastic communities. Take notes as you listen. Work with a partner to combine your notes. Then use your notes to answer the questions.

1. What specific types of work do the monks at Wat Tham Krabok do? Write as many ideas as you hear.

   _____

2. How does this work make Wat Tham Krabok different from other monasteries?

   _____

3. What are "day trippers," or "two-legged wolves"?

   _____

SECOND LISTENING

 Read the questions. Listen to the interview again. Add details to your notes. Then use your notes to answer the questions. Work with a partner and compare your answers.

1. What does Claassen mainly focus on in his report on monastic life?
   (A) The increase in public interest in monasteries
   (B) The solitude of the monastic life
   (C) The activities that occur at monasteries
   (D) Traditions in forest monastic communities

2. What is one important reason Claassen visits the monasteries?
   (A) To escape from Western life
   (B) To work with AIDS patients
   (C) To join a religious community
   (D) To tell about monastic life

Listen again to part of the interview. Then answer question 3.

3. What does Claassen suggest about the work of the Wat Tham Krabok monks?
   (A) They spend most of their time chanting in solitude.
   (B) They spend less time chanting than monks usually do.
   (C) They work outside their communities, like most monks do.
   (D) They have a regular daily schedule, like most monks do.

Listen again to part of the interview. Then answer question 4.

4. Why does the interviewer say, "Isn't that fair to say?"?
   (A) To indicate that he disapproves of the listener's actions.
   (B) To show that he agrees with the listener's actions.
   (C) To defend his right to ask the question.
   (D) To invite the listener to explain the subject.

5. What point does Claassen make about why "two-legged wolves" visit the monastic community?
   (A) They are considering living there permanently.
   (B) They wish to write about their experiences.
   (C) They want to observe the special way of life.
   (D) They enjoy visiting the beaches of Thailand.

6. What does Claassen imply about the lives of monks in both communities?
   (A) Their lives are improved by outsiders.
   (B) Their lives are disturbed by outsiders.
   (C) Outsiders have little effect on the monks' lives.
   (D) The monks want to live more like outsiders.

ANALYSIS

It is helpful to know the purpose of a test item. There are three types of questions in the listening section.

1. Basic Comprehension

- main ideas
- details
- the meaning of specific sentences

2. Organization

- the way information is structured
- the way ideas are linked

3. Inference

- ideas are not directly stated
- speaker's intention, purpose, or attitude not explicitly stated

Go back to the listening questions and label each question with 1, 2, or 3. Then work with a partner to see if you agree. Check the Answer Key for the correct answers. Which questions did you get right? Which did you get wrong? What skills do you need to practice?

2 Reading

RELIGION

PRE-READING

Skim the topic sentences, or first sentences, of each paragraph of the passage on the next page. Work with a partner to predict what each paragraph will say about religion. Take notes about your predictions. An example for the first paragraph is provided. Work in a group to share your ideas.

Paragraph 1 predictions: Maybe this paragraph will talk about how thoughts of death helped to start religions. It may also discuss how religions treat the subject of death and people's fears about it.

READING

Read the passage on the next page and answer the questions. Then work with a partner and compare your answers. When you disagree, go back to the text to find helpful information.

RELIGION

FROM *COMPTON'S INTERACTIVE ENCYCLOPEDIA*

1   It has been said that thoughts of death lead necessarily to the development of religion. It is difficult to imagine what need there would be for religion in a world in which no one ever died or became ill. The literatures of all religions attempt to give answers to basic questions: From where did the world come? What is the meaning of human life? Why do people die and what happens afterward? Why is there evil? How should people behave? In the distant past, these questions were answered in terms of mythology. In literature, they are dealt with in poetry. Modern sciences try to investigate them.

2   As a word religion is difficult to define, but as a human experience it seems to be universal. The twentieth century German-born American theologian Paul Tillich gave a simple and basic definition of the word. "Religion is ultimate concern." This means that religion encompasses that to which people are most devoted or that from which they expect to get the most fundamental satisfaction in life. Consequently, religion provides adequate answers to the most basic questions posed above.

3   Four centuries earlier the German social reformer Martin Luther spoke in similar terms about God. He stated that to have a god was to "have something in which the heart trusts completely." Putting Tillich's and Luther's definitions together, it is possible to see that religion does not necessarily have to be involved with shrines, temples, churches, or synagogues. It does not need complex doctrines or clergy.[1] It can be anything to which people devote themselves that fills their lives with meaning.

4   In Western civilization, religion has traditionally been defined as belief in and worship of one god. This is true for Judaism, Christianity, and Islam. The statements by Tillich and Luther make it clear, however, that such a definition may be too narrow. In original Buddhism in India and Confucianism in China, there was no recognition of a supreme being. Both of these philosophies were basically concerned with patterns of human behavior.

5   Regardless of definition, all religions (as the word is normally used) have certain elements in common: rituals to perform, prayers to recite, places to frequent or avoid, holy days to keep, means by which to predict the future, a body of literature to read and study, truths to affirm, charismatic leaders to follow, and ordinances to obey. Many have buildings set aside for worship, and there are activities such as prayer, sacrifice, contemplation, and perhaps magic.

---

[1] *clergy*: a group of men and women who are religious leaders

6   Closely associated with these elements is personal conduct. Although it is possible to separate ritual observances from moral conduct, worship has normally implied a type of relationship with a god from which certain behavior patterns are expected to follow. A notable exception in history is the official state religion of ancient Rome, which was kept separate from personal commitment and morality.

1. The passage focuses on which of the following aspects of religion?
   (A) The patterns of human behavior
   (B) The rituals in different religions
   (C) The differences among religions
   (D) The meaning and elements of religion

2. According to paragraph 1, which of the following is NOT a present-day attempt to answer questions about life, death, and human existence?
   (A) Science
   (B) Literature
   (C) Mythology
   (D) Religion

3. The word *them* in paragraph 1 refers to
   (A) religions
   (B) sciences
   (C) thoughts of death
   (D) the questions

4. Why does the author ask the questions in paragraph 1?
   (A) To persuade readers to find the answers
   (B) To explain why religion exists
   (C) To contrast religion with other things
   (D) To introduce answers to the questions

5. In paragraph 2, the word *encompasses* is closest in meaning to
   (A) includes
   (B) permits
   (C) supports
   (D) causes

6. In paragraphs 2 and 3, the author defines the concept of religion by
   (A) supporting one of two definitions
   (B) combining two definitions
   (C) contrasting two definitions
   (D) describing two religious leaders

7. According to paragraph 3, which of the following is a necessary element of religion?
(A) Complex beliefs
(B) Faithful believers
(C) Religious thinkers
(D) Places of worship

8. Which of the following statements about the East and the West can be inferred from paragraph 4?
(A) The West and East describe religion in similar ways.
(B) In the East and the West, religions relate to the belief in gods.
(C) The definition of religion is biased toward Western religions.
(D) Eastern religions probably influenced Western religions.

9. Which of the following statements can be inferred from the passage?
(A) Most people believe in one god.
(B) People usually agree about what religion is.
(C) People tolerate many types of religion.
(D) Religion means many things to many people.

10. Look at the four squares ☐ that indicate where the following sentence could be added to the passage. Where would the sentence best fit? Circle the letter that shows the point where you would insert this sentence.

> One might also say that religion exists because people need to understand the meaning of birth and life.

It has been said that thoughts of death lead necessarily to the development of religion. It is difficult to imagine what need there would be for religion in a world in which no one ever died or became ill. **[A]** The literatures of all religions attempt to give answers to basic questions: From where did the world come? What is the meaning of human life? Why do people die and what happens afterward? Why is there evil? How should people behave? **[B]** In the distant past, these questions were answered in terms of mythology. **[C]** In literature, they are dealt with in poetry. Modern sciences try to investigate them. **[D]**

As a word religion is difficult to define, but as a human experience it seems to be universal. The twentieth century German-born American theologian Paul Tillich gave a simple and basic definition of the word. "Religion is ultimate concern."

11. Which of the following best expresses the essential information in this sentence in the passage?

> Although it is possible to separate ritual observances from moral conduct, worship has normally implied a type of relationship with a god from which certain behavior patterns are expected to follow.

(A) Religious ceremonies must be kept apart from personal behavior.
(B) Religion does not specify the way you must live your life.
(C) Religious belief usually influences both personal behavior and ceremonies.
(D) Religious belief means a person must engage in rituals.

12. An introductory sentence for a brief summary of the passage is provided below. Complete the summary by circling the THREE answer choices that express the most important ideas in the passage. Some sentences do not belong in the summary because they express ideas that are not presented in the passage or are minor ideas in the passage.

> There are many different kinds of religions, yet certain commonalities exist among them.

(A) Religion answers basic questions about death, life, and human existence.
(B) Religion can be anything that gives meaning to people's lives.
(C) Martin Luther started the Lutheran Church.
(D) In ancient Rome, personal behavior was separated from devotion.
(E) All religions share elements such as ceremonies and rules of conduct.
(F) To most people, religion means belief in one god.

3 Writing

INTEGRATED TASK: READ, LISTEN, WRITE

In this section, you will read a short passage and listen to an excerpt on a related topic. Then you will write about the relationship between the two.

READING

Read the passage on the next page. As you read, fill in the following summary chart. Then write a short summary of the reading using the information in your chart.

Main Idea: Fasting exists in different forms in many religions.

IMPORTANT POINTS ABOUT FASTING	DETAILS
	• Judaism, Christianity, Islam: roots = ancient prophets • Eastern religions: roots – ancient yogic, ascetic traditions
General purpose of fasting	• •
Benefits of fasting	Eck: • • Ahmed: • vital to spiritual well-being • replenishment of the soul • without it, people become spiritually exhausted •

The Religious Tradition of Fasting

Duncan Moon: Fasting is an ancient tradition. The three Abrahamic religions, Judaism, Christianity and Islam, all trace it back to the prophets of the Old Testament. For example, many people believe the prophet Mohammed's first fast was probably Yom Kippur. Many Eastern religions trace their roots of fasting to ancient yogic and ascetic traditions. But while there are differences in approach and style, those who fast are most often hoping to increase spirituality and come closer to the divine. Dr. Diana Eck, professor of comparative religion at Harvard Divinity School, says fasting accomplishes this in part by breaking an attachment to material things.

Dr. Diana Eck: And of course the most repetitive attachment to earthly things is that that we enact every day by our desire for food. So there is a way in which breaking that, even in a symbolic way, speaks against the consumption, the materialism that is so pervasive in our world.

Moon: In Islam during the holy month of Ramadan, Muslims fast from sunrise to sunset, refraining from food, water, smoking, and sex. Dr. Ahbar Ahmed, a professor of Islamic studies at American University, says in this time of rapid change and fear, fasting is vital to spiritual well-being.

Dr. Ahbar Ahmed: Because if you do not withdraw during the day, then the replenishment of the soul is not being affected, and when that does not happen, then over time the individual begins to become exhausted, spiritually exhausted.

Moon: Dr. Ahmed says the rhythm of life has become so hectic, so fast moving, that finding time to pull back from our daily lives, even temporarily, has become more difficult than ever. But he says that only means the need for it has never been greater, and that the ancient tradition of fasting is still necessary, even in the twenty-first century.

LISTENING

Listen to a lecture. Use the outline to take notes as you listen.

Main Idea: Thomas Merton struggled to follow ascetic practices, but he eventually was able to live a rich life as a monk.

Merton's struggle to follow ascetic practices

- felt drawn to God, committed himself to Catholic faith
-
-
- suffered through loneliness, rigors of monastic life
- had to give up smoking, drinking, talking
-

Merton's rich life as a monk

- made him somber
- developed a gift for writing
- for 20 years, "talked" by writing about life, faith, human issues
-
-
-
-

(continued on next page)

●

  ● met Dalai Lama, brought deeper understanding between Buddhists and Christians

●

WRITING

Write on the following topic. Follow the steps below to prepare.

Explain fasting as a means to increase spirituality. Include details from Thomas Merton's life to support your explanation. How did he use fasting and other ascetic practices to increase spirituality, and what results did he experience?

Step 1

● Work with a partner. Skim the reading and your notes from the reading and listening tasks (pages 107–110) to answer the following questions. Then share your answer in a group. Take notes on what you hear.

  1. What are the main goals of fasting, according to the reading and Merton?

  2. What benefits does fasting provide?

  3. What ascetic practices did Merton follow?

  4. What impact did Merton make on himself and others by living an ascetic life?

● On your own, evaluate what you have heard. What is the connection between fasting and spirituality? Which details from Merton's life best illustrate this connection? Which details could you include in your own writing?

● Fill in the outline below to organize your ideas on the topic.

Introduction—Thesis Statement (fasting and spirituality): _____

_____

Topic Sentence (Merton's ascetic practices): _____

_____

  Details: _____

Topic Sentence (impact of Merton's ascetic practices): _____

_____

  Details: _____

Conclusion: _____

_____

Step 2

Write for 20 minutes. Leave the last 5 minutes to edit your work.

To evaluate a partner's writing, use the Writing Evaluation Form on page 203.

4 Speaking

INDEPENDENT TASK

Speak on the following topic. Follow the steps below to prepare.

How important is religion in a person's life? Discuss the ways in which religious beliefs or practices have affected your life or the lives of others you know or have read about.

Step 1

- Work in a group to brainstorm a list of religions and their beliefs or practices. Take turns discussing these beliefs or practices and their impact on people's lives. Use the chart to take notes on ideas that you might use in your speaking.

BELIEF OR PRACTICE	IMPACT ON YOUR LIFE OR OTHER PEOPLE'S LIVES
daily meditation	makes me feel calm, centered, happier

- On your own, evaluate what you have heard. Which beliefs or practices are the most important or interesting? Are their effects positive or negative? Which ones can you speak about best?

- After you have chosen which beliefs or practices you will discuss, take more notes about them. Then, summarize your ideas in preparation for your oral presentation.

Step 2

With a partner, take turns practicing a one-minute oral response to the topic. Be sure to use the information in your summary to help you.

Step 3

Change partners. Take turns giving a one-minute response to the topic again.

> To evaluate your partner's response, use the Speaking Evaluation Form on page 204.

5 Skill Focus

SUMMARIZING

EXAMINATION

1 *Look at the following items from the unit. Work with a partner and answer the questions about each item.*

Item 1 (Campus Conversation, p. 100)

What is the conversation mainly about?
(A) A student's concern about his progress in biology
(B) A student's practice of the Buddhist religion
(C) A student's plans for taking psychology in the summer
(D) A student's decision about whether to attend a spiritual retreat

- How did you identify the main idea?

- Did you listen for key ideas and words that appeared throughout the conversation?

- Did you include these ideas and words in your notes? Go back to your notes and mark the parts that helped you. If necessary, listen again to the conversation and take notes on the parts that helped you.

Item 2 (Reading, p. 107)

An introductory sentence for a brief summary of the passage is provided below. Complete the summary by circling the THREE answer choices that express the most important ideas in the passage. Some sentences to do not belong in the summary because they express ideas that are not presented in the passage or are minor ideas in the passage.

> There are many different kinds of religions, yet certain commonalities exist among them.

(**A**) Religion answers basic questions about death, life, and human existence.
(**B**) Religion can be anything that gives meaning to people's lives.
(**C**) Martin Luther started the Lutheran Church.
(**D**) In ancient Rome, personal behavior was separated from devotion.
(**E**) All religions share elements such as ceremonies and rules of conduct.
(**F**) To most people, religion means belief in one god.

- How did you identify the important points?

- Did you reread parts of the reading passage? Go back to the passage and mark the parts that express the points that you included in the summary.

2 *Look at the following task from the unit. Work with a partner and answer the questions about the task.*

Item 3 (Integrated Task, p. 107)

Read the passage. As you read, fill in the summary chart. Then write a short summary of the reading using information in the chart.

- Review the summary you wrote for this task. How did you identify the important points to include in your summary?

- Did you reread parts of the passage in order to complete the task? Go back to the text and mark the parts that express the points that you included in your chart and summary.

Tips

To do well on the TOEFL, it is essential to learn how to summarize. When you summarize, you present the essential information from a written or spoken text, leaving out unimportant details.

Listening and Reading

- Look for the statement in the answer choices that summarizes the main idea.

- Pay attention to the main idea sentence. It will express the idea that is supported throughout the text.

- Look for the statements that express the most important points that support the main idea sentence.

To answer **Item 1**, you probably identified the topic of the conversation as *the student's decision*. The main point about his dilemma was whether he should attend a spiritual retreat or summer school. Together, these form the main idea that is expressed in answer choice (D).

To answer **Item 2**, you probably read over the details and the main idea sentence in order to decide which points belonged in the summary and which did not.

Speaking and Writing

- Begin your summary with a main idea sentence.

- Include only the most essential points. Omit unimportant details. Your summary should be short, about 25 percent of the original text or less.

- Use your own words, when possible, and identify the sources of important ideas by using quotation marks or indirect speech.

- Avoid including your own opinions.

- Use transition words to show relationships among ideas.

  Transition words: *moreover, in fact, for instance, in contrast, as a result, finally,* and so on

To answer **Item 3**, you probably reread the text and your summary chart notes to identify the most important points to include in the summary. Then, you should have started the summary with a main idea sentence, used your own words, and cited sources.

PRACTICE

1 *Read the passage from an interview with the Dalai Lama, the religious leader of the Tibetan Buddhist community. Use the tips from the previous section to help you answer the question and complete the activity that follows. Work with a partner and compare your answers.*

PEACE PREVAILS, Part One

By Claudia Dreifus (from the *New York Times Magazine*)

1   **Interviewer:** Three years ago, you predicted that the next hundred years would be a century of peace, hope, and justice. Since then, there have been massacres in Rwanda and Burundi, the Northern Irish peace discussions have been blown apart, and the Chinese have kidnapped the young boy you designated to be the Panchen Lama. Are you still optimistic about the future?

2   **Dalai Lama:** Oh, yes. Of course. A handful of shortsighted people have always existed. But overall, their day is over because the public's attitude towards war and violence has become much healthier than at any time in history. People used to be much more jingoistic and nationalistic compared with the way they are now.

3   Recently I was talking with the English Queen Mother[1]. I asked her, "What changes have you seen in your lifetime?" She answered, "When I was young, we had not much concern about the outside world. Now people have a great concern about what is happening all over the world." This is a very positive change.

4   So I believe that due to [the revolution in] information, generally speaking, any leader, if he tried to mobilize the whole nation for war, would find it impossible. In previous times, it was quite possible. Well, small-scale wars, perhaps they can still do. But large-scale wars, I think, are not likely. I do believe that in the next century we have to seriously think about putting a complete stop to the arms trade.

[1] The Queen Mother died on March 29, 2002, at the age of 101.

1. An introductory sentence for a brief summary of the passage is provided below. Complete the summary by circling the THREE answer choices that express the most important ideas in the passage. Some sentences do not belong in the summary because they express ideas that are not presented in the passage or are minor ideas in the passage.

> There are thoughtless people in the world, but most people want wars and violence to end, according to the Dalai Lama.

(A) The Chinese kidnapped the young boy that the Dalai Lama named to be the Panchen Lama.

(B) The religious leader believes that people today are not so focused on a single nation's interest as in the past.

(continued on next page)

(C) The English Queen Mother died in 2002 at the age of 101.

(D) The Dalai Lama says people today pay more attention to the world around them.

(E) The Dalai Lama thinks that because of the information revolution, there is no longer a possibility for large, national wars.

(F) The Dalai Lama doubts that countries will be able to wage smaller, nationwide wars in the future.

2. Write a summary paragraph of the passage, using the sentences you selected above. Add appropriate transition words to show the relationships among ideas. Where necessary, you may replace subjects with subject pronouns.

2 *Listen to a continuation of the interview with the Dalai Lama. As you listen, take notes on the main points. Then use your notes and the tips from the previous section to help you prepare a one-minute summary of the Dalai Lama's answer to the question. Work with a partner. Take turns giving your summaries.*

The Workplace

| LISTENING |

Campus Conversation
A student interviews for a work-study position in the university library.

Academic Listening
Call-in radio program: *Comments on Workplace Privacy*

| READING |

Textbook Passage
Coca-Cola Thinks International

| SPEAKING |

Integrated Task: Read, Listen, Speak
Imagine that your employer has asked you to help develop its employee monitoring program.

| WRITING |

Independent Task
Describe your ideal job. Discuss the work you would do, where you would work, your colleagues, and the salary and benefits you would receive.

| SKILL FOCUS |

Skimming and Scanning
Skimming is reading a passage quickly to understand the general meaning, the gist. Scanning is reading a passage quickly to find specific information, such as names and dates.

| TOEFL® iBT TARGET SKILLS |

- Identify and express main ideas
- Identify and express details
- Make inferences
- Take notes on speakers' main points
- Scan a passage for specific information
- Skim a paragraph for the main idea
- Relate abstract ideas to concrete information for problem solving

 For extra practice of TOEFL iBT skills, go to pages 242–259.

1 Listening

CAMPUS CONVERSATION

PRE-LISTENING VOCABULARY

Read the sentences. Guess the meaning of the boldfaced words and phrases. Then match each word or phrase with a definition or synonym from the list below. Work with a partner and compare your answers.

_____ 1. The reference librarian gave me a list of five **criteria** for evaluating websites, which has helped me select the best sites for my research.

_____ 2. Kevin is majoring in English education, so he wanted to get teaching experience while earning extra money. Luckily, he found a **work-study** job as a reading tutor in the learning lab.

_____ 3. Many U.S. college students apply for **financial aid** online. They provide information about their family's income, and the federal government sends the data to the students' college or university.

_____ 4. My sister enjoys being an office manager because it requires **multitasking**. She would be bored with a job where she always did one single task.

_____ 5. Whether at work or school, we all have to deal with people that we **can't stand** to be around. Sometimes avoiding them is the best solution.

_____ 6. Since you can't meet on Saturday to research our speech project, we could do it on Sunday instead. Would that **work for** you?

_____ 7. In astronomy class, we have learned that there is **a myriad of** stars. I'm amazed by the number and sizes of stars that exist.

_____ 8. People work more closely with **colleagues** than they do with supervisors. That's why many disagree more often with their peers than with bosses.

_____ 9. My brother Martin has a **promising** career in pharmacy research. He has just developed a new drug that his company thinks will become very widely used.

_____ 10. Jennifer is not very athletic. She can't even throw a ball, **let alone** play baseball!

a. a large number of

b. and certainly can't

c. be convenient for

d. coworkers

e. dislike very much

f. doing many things at one time

g. employment program for students

h. likely to be successful

i. money given or loaned to students

j. requirements

> **Culture Note:** As tuition and living expenses rise, many students are required to "work their way through school." Consequently, more students seek on-campus employment, called work-study jobs, to help pay for their education. Examples of work-study jobs include working in campus libraries, cafeterias, admissions offices, or IT (information technology) departments.

FIRST LISTENING

Read the questions. Listen to the conversation between a student and a supervisor. Take notes as you listen. Share your notes with a partner. Then use your notes to answer the questions.

1. What are the student and the supervisor discussing?

   _____

   _____

2. What kinds of work does the job involve? Write as many ideas as you hear.

   _____

   _____

3. What does the supervisor decide about the job in the end?

   _____

   _____

SECOND LISTENING

Read the questions. Listen to the conversation again. Add details to your notes. Then use your notes to answer the questions. Work with a partner and compare your answers.

1. Why does the student go to see the library supervisor?
   (**A**) To study the workings of the library
   (**B**) To interview for a job in the library
   (**C**) To share her interest in libraries
   (**D**) To ask for information on financial aid

Listen again to part of the conversation. Then answer question 2.

2. Which sentence best expresses how the supervisor probably feels?
   (A) She is pleasantly surprised.
   (B) She is deeply suspicious.
   (C) She is very amused.
   (D) She is somewhat concerned.

3. What does the supervisor say is a general feature of the job?
   (A) Working directly with students
   (B) Doing one task repeatedly
   (C) Answering reference questions
   (D) Performing a variety of tasks

 Listen again to part of the conversation. Then answer question 4.

4. What does the supervisor mean when she says, "I do have to consult with my colleagues before I can make the final decision"?
   (A) She is not yet prepared to offer the student the work-study position.
   (B) She prefers to wait until later to tell the student she will not get the job.
   (C) She does not want the student to return to ask about the decision.
   (D) She does not care whether the student is chosen for the position.

5. What does the supervisor tell the student in the end about the job?
   (A) She promises that the student will get the job.
   (B) She tells the student to come back later for the decision.
   (C) She asks the student to meet with the supervisor's colleagues.
   (D) She says that the student can start working that day.

ACADEMIC LISTENING

FIRST LISTENING

 Listen to a call-in radio program about workplace privacy. Take notes about each caller as you listen. Work with a partner to combine your notes. Then use your notes to answer the questions.

Caller 1—Bob

1. What is the caller's position? (Circle one.)   **Employer   Employee**

2. What is the caller's main point about

   workplace privacy? _____

   _____

Caller 2—Mary

1. What is the caller's position? (Circle one.)   **Employer**   **Employee**

2. What is the caller's main point about

   workplace privacy? _____

   _____

Caller 3—Louis

1. What is the caller's position? (Circle one.)   **Employer**   **Employee**

2. What is the caller's main point about

   workplace privacy? _____

   _____

Caller 4—Susan

1. What is the caller's position? (Circle one.)   **Employer**   **Employee**

2. What is the caller's main point about

   workplace privacy? _____

   _____

SECOND LISTENING

Read the questions. Listen to the radio program again. Add details to your notes. Then use your notes to answer the questions. Work with a partner and compare your answers.

1. What is the program mainly about?
   (A) Employers' rights in workplace communication
   (B) Companies' reasons for using workplace monitoring
   (C) Ways to monitor employees in the workplace
   (D) Differing opinions about workplace monitoring

2. How does Bob (Caller 1) describe the employee monitoring at his workplace?
   (A) His employer does not monitor workers.
   (B) The employer observes employees with cameras.
   (C) The employer monitors workers' e-mails.
   (D) The workers know when they are being observed.

3. What is similar about Bob's (Caller 1's) and Mary's (Caller 2's) experiences?
   (A) Both have been monitored in the workplace.
   (B) Both are observed at work by video cameras.
   (C) Both left their jobs after being monitored at work.
   (D) Both are unaware of when they are monitored.

Listen again to part of the program. Then answer question 4.

4. What can be inferred about Mary (Caller 2)?
   (A) She did not work independently.
   (B) She was suspicious of her employers.
   (C) She wanted to feel good about her work.
   (D) She felt her boss appreciated her work.

Listen again to part of the program. Then answer question 5.

5. What is Bob's (Caller 1's) attitude toward the radio host's comment about monitoring?
   (A) He disagrees strongly with the radio host's comment.
   (B) He thinks the host has not experienced monitoring.
   (C) He wants to explain the technology behind monitoring.
   (D) He thinks that the host's comments are interesting.

6. Select the sentence that best expresses Louis's (Caller 3's) opinion about employee monitoring.
   (A) Employee privacy should be protected.
   (B) Employers can monitor workers if they give warnings.
   (C) Employees are watched for good reasons.
   (D) Employers have a right to monitor workers' phone calls.

Listen again to part of the program. Then answer question 7.

7. Why does Louis (Caller 3) say, "I mean, you'd have to agree our privacy deserves some protections."?
   (A) To invite the radio host to state her opinions
   (B) To draw a conclusion from his previous points
   (C) To discourage the radio host from stating her opinions
   (D) To introduce a new recommendation

8. Select the sentence that best expresses Susan's (Caller 4's) employee monitoring practices.
   (A) She uses computer chips to monitor employees.
   (B) She believes that monitoring harms employees.
   (C) She checks workers' e-mails to prevent theft.
   (D) She monitors workers' language in e-mails.

2 Reading

COCA-COLA THINKS INTERNATIONAL

PRE-READING

1 *Read the questions. Then quickly read the passage that follows to answer the questions. Write on the lines the number of the paragraph in which you found each answer. Work with a partner to compare your answers.*

_____ **1.** In how many countries does Coca-Cola operate?

_____ **2.** How many employees did Coca-Cola transfer in its leadership development program?

_____ **3.** Who is the president of Coca-Cola, and where was he born?

_____ **4.** Where does Coca-Cola earn the greater portion of its profits?

2 *Quickly read paragraph 1 of the passage. What is the general idea of the paragraph? Work with a partner to compare your answers.*

READING

Read the passage and answer the questions. Then work with a partner and compare your answers. When you disagree, go back to the text to find helpful information.

COCA-COLA THINKS INTERNATIONAL

1   Coca-Cola has been operating internationally for most of its 100-year history. Today the company has operations in 160 countries and employs over 400,000 people. The firm's human resource management (HRM) strategy helps to explain a great deal of its success. In one recent year Coca-Cola transferred more than 300 professional and managerial staff from one country to another under its leadership development program, and the number of international transferees is increasing annually. One senior-level HRM manager explained the company strategy by noting:

From *International Business: A Strategic Management Approach*, by Alan M. Rugman and Richard M. Hodgetts, McGraw-Hill, 1995, p. 323. Reproduced with permission of the McGraw-Hill Companies.

We recently concluded that our talent base has to be multilingual and multicultural. . . . To use a sports analogy, you want to be sure that you have a lot of capable and competent bench strength,[1] ready to assume broader responsibilities as they present themselves.

2   In preparing for the future, Coca-Cola includes a human resources recruitment forecast in its annual and long-term business strategies. The firm also has selection standards on which management can focus when recruiting and hiring. For example, the company likes applicants who are fluent in more than one language because they can be transferred to other geographic areas where their fluency will help them be part of Coca-Cola's operation. This multilingual, multicultural emphasis starts at the top with the president, Roberto Goizueta, a Cuban-born American who has been chairman for over a decade, and with the 21 members of the board, of whom only four are American.

3   The firm also has a recruitment program that helps it to identify candidates at the college level. Rather than just seeking students abroad, Coca-Cola looks for foreign students who are studying in the United States at domestic universities. The students are recruited stateside and then provided with a year's training before they go back to their home country. Coca-Cola also has an internship program for foreign students who are interested in working for the company during school break, either in the United States or back home. These interns are put into groups and assigned a project that requires them to make a presentation to the operations personnel on their project. This presentation must include a discussion of what worked and what did not work. Each individual intern is then evaluated, and management decides the person's future potential with the company.

4   Coca-Cola believes that these approaches are extremely useful in helping the firm to find talent on a global basis. Not only is the company able to develop internal sources, but the intern program provides a large number of additional individuals who would otherwise end up with other companies. Coca-Cola earns a greater portion of its income and profit overseas than it does in the United States. The company's human resource management strategy helps to explain how Coke is able to achieve this feat.

---

[1] *bench strength:* players sitting on the sidelines, ready to play if needed

1. What is the passage mainly about?
  (A) The history of the Coca-Cola company
  (B) Coca-Cola's employee development strategies
  (C) The future of Coca-Cola's international profits
  (D) Coca-Cola's college recruitment program

2. In paragraph 1, the authors' primary purpose is
  (A) to illustrate the size of the company
  (B) to compare Coca-Cola and sports
  (C) to describe Coca-Cola's college interns
  (D) to explain the firm's international success

3. In the quotation in paragraph 1, why does the Coca-Cola manager use a sports analogy?
  (A) To explain the company's strategy
  (B) To increase the reader's interest in management
  (C) To suggest the global nature of sports
  (D) To emphasize the need for a strong team in sports

4. In paragraph 2, why do the authors mention Coca-Cola's president and its board?
  (A) To illustrate the company's international emphasis
  (B) To show that Americans serve in high positions in the firm
  (C) To encourage foreigners to work for the company
  (D) To prove that the company has long-time workers

5. The word *recruitment* in paragraph 3 is closest in meaning to
  (A) management
  (B) hiring
  (C) unity
  (D) planning

6. The word *internship* in paragraph 3 is closest in meaning to
  (A) management
  (B) supervision
  (C) presentation
  (D) training

7. What can be inferred about student interns in paragraph 3?
  (A) The company would rather hire American-born college students.
  (B) The company ignores students' schedules when planning internships.
  (C) Interns are encouraged to work independently to show their potential.
  (D) Interns may get permanent jobs in the company after their internships.

8. Select the appropriate phrases from the answer choices below and match them to the group they characterize. TWO of the answer choices will NOT be used.

HRM Strategies

- _____

- _____

- _____

Recruitment Strategies

- _____

- _____

(A) Employee transfers
(B) Greater overseas income
(C) Internship program
(D) Multicultural emphasis
(E) Identifying college candidates
(F) Language fluency standards
(G) 100-year history in 160 countries

9. All of the following are mentioned in paragraph 4 about the intern program EXCEPT
(A) The program helps the company identify skilled international workers.
(B) Some people might go to work for other firms if the program did not exist.
(C) The company believes the program contributes to its international success.
(D) Coca-Cola hopes the program will increase its profits in the United States.

10. Which of the following best expresses the essential information in this sentence from the passage?

> Not only is the company able to develop internal sources, but the intern program provides a large number of additional individuals who would otherwise end up with other companies.

(A) The intern program provides the company with internal sources as well as additional people who might have gone to work with other firms.
(B) Hiring interns enables the company to develop internal sources.
(C) A large number of individuals might have found jobs with other companies.
(D) The company has developed internal sources by providing individuals with work in other firms.

11. Look at the four squares ☐ that indicate where the following sentence could be added to the passage. Where would the sentence best fit? Circle the letter that shows the point where you would insert this sentence.

> The company believes that these foreign-born employees can better represent its interests in their own countries than employees from the United States can.

The firm also has a recruitment program that helps it to identify candidates at the college level. ☐A☐ Rather than just seeking students abroad, Coca-Cola looks for foreign students who are studying in the United States at domestic universities. The students are recruited stateside and then provided with a year's training before they go back to their home country. [B] Coca-Cola also has an internship program for foreign students who are interested in working for the company during school break, either in the United States or back home. These interns are put into groups and assigned a project that requires them to make a presentation to the operations personnel on their project. [C] This presentation must include a discussion of what worked and what did not work. [D] Each individual intern is then evaluated, and management decides the person's future potential with the company.

12. An introductory sentence for a brief summary of the passage is provided below. Complete the summary by circling the THREE answer choices that express the most important ideas in the passage. Some sentences do not belong in the summary because they express ideas that are not presented in the passage or are minor ideas in the passage.

> Coca-Cola succeeds internationally because it develops a multicultural work force.

(A) The company has operations in 160 countries and employs over 400,000 people.
(B) One Coca-Cola manager compared the company's strategy to a sports team.
(C) To expand its multilingual, multicultural work force, Coca-Cola transfers employees from country to country.
(D) The firm's internship program identifies skilled foreign workers who may be hired to work for the company in their home countries.
(E) Coca-Cola believes these approaches help the firm identify and utilize global talent.
(F) Coca-Cola earns more of its profits in the United States than in other countries.

ANALYSIS

It is helpful to know the purpose of a test item. There are four types of questions in the reading section.

1. Basic Comprehension

- main ideas
- details
- the meaning of specific sentences

2. Organization

- the way information is structured in the text
- the way ideas are linked between sentences or between paragraphs

3. Inference

- ideas are not directly stated in the text
- author's intention, purpose, or attitude not explicitly stated in the text

4. Vocabulary and Reference

- the meaning of words
- the meaning of reference words such as *his, them, this,* or *none*

Go back to the reading questions and label each question with 1, 2, 3, or 4. Then work with a partner to see if you agree. Check the Answer Key for the correct answers. Which questions did you get right? Which did you get wrong? What skills do you need to practice?

3 Speaking

INTEGRATED TASK: READ, LISTEN, SPEAK

In this section, you will read a short passage and listen to an excerpt on a related topic. Then you will speak about the relationship between the two.

READING

Read the passage. As you read, fill in the following summary chart.

WORKPLACE SURVEILLANCE	
Tools for workplace surveillance	• video cameras • •
Things that companies monitor	• e-mail • • •
Reasons that companies monitor	• to protect themselves and employees legally; to detect legal violations • •

Workplace Surveillance on the Rise

1   More and more U.S. companies today are monitoring their employees at work—through video cameras, audio recorders, and computer software. This practice is being hotly debated, with companies arguing that it is legitimate and necessary.

2   Nearly 80 percent of all U.S. companies record and review employee communication on the job, through e-mail, Internet connections, phone communication, and computer files, according to the American Management Association (AMA). More than 900 major U.S. companies told the AMA that they engage in these practices to protect themselves and their workers legally, to measure productivity, and to deter theft.

3   AMA surveys indicate that many companies monitor employees in part to detect legal violations. Recently, Xerox Corporation fired 40 employees for spending a majority of their workdays viewing pornographic websites.

4   Other companies keep an eye on employees to measure productivity. Monitoring software and phone taps reveal when employees are wasting time in Internet and phone-based communication. A smaller percentage of employers view employees by video cameras to measure productivity and deter theft.

5   Eric Greenberg, director of management studies at the AMA, defends such practices. He says employers have a legitimate interest in a worker's performance, so they have a right to review workplace activities.

LISTENING

Listen to an excerpt from a radio interview. Use the outline to take notes as you listen.

Main Idea: Employers should have legitimate reasons for monitoring workers.

Problems with workplace surveillance

- often demeans workers
- overmonitoring (counting key strokes)
-
-

Recommendations about workplace surveillance

- protect workers' dignity
-
-
-

SPEAKING

Speak on the following topic. Follow the steps below to prepare.

Imagine that your employer has asked you to help develop its employee monitoring program. How could you design a program that addresses both the company's security needs and its employees' concerns about privacy?

Step 1

- Work with a partner. Skim the reading and your notes from the reading and listening tasks (pages 128–129) to answer the following questions.

  1. How are employees monitored at work?

  2. Why do companies monitor employees?

  3. What are employees' concerns about monitoring?

  4. How could a monitoring program meet employers' needs while protecting employees' privacy?

- With your partner, discuss what employers/managers and employees want in a monitoring program. Discuss how each "side" can accommodate the other side's needs and concerns. In the box below, make a list of practices that might satisfy both groups. Use your answers to the questions above to help you.

Monitoring Practices to Satisfy Both Sides

Step 2

With your partner, practice a two-minute role play, acting as a manager and an employee who are working together to establish a company's monitoring program. Take turns stating and responding to key points. Discuss ways to satisfy both sides' needs and concerns. Then switch roles and repeat the role play. Be sure to use the information in your list to help you.

Step 3

Change partners. Take turns doing the two-minute role play again. Then switch roles and repeat the role play.

> To evaluate your partner's response, use the Speaking Evaluation Form on page 204.

4 Writing

INDEPENDENT TASK

Write on the following topic. Follow the steps below to prepare.

Describe your ideal job. Discuss the work you would do, where you would work, your colleagues, and the salary and benefits you would receive.

Step 1

- Work in a group. Brainstorm ideas about appealing or interesting jobs. Share ideas about the following aspects of the jobs: duties, workplace and schedule, coworkers and managers, salary and benefits. Take notes on what you hear.

- On your own, evaluate what you have heard. What are the most appealing or interesting jobs that were mentioned? What are the characteristics of those jobs? Which ideas could you use in your own writing?

- Choose the job that you would most like to have. Organize your ideas by filling in the chart below with information about the job.

MY IDEAL JOB	
Description of job job title, type of work, duties	
Workplace inside/outside, atmosphere, hours, colleagues/managers	
Compensation salary, benefits	

Step 2

Write for 20 minutes. Leave the last 5 minutes to edit your work.

> To evaluate a partner's writing, use the Writing Evaluation Form on page 203.

5 Skill Focus

SKIMMING AND SCANNING

EXAMINATION

Look at the following items from the unit. Work with a partner and answer these questions about the items.

- Did you reread the text to answer the questions? If so, did you reread it quickly or slowly?

- Exactly how much of the text did you reread? Go back to the text and mark any parts that helped you. Discuss your selections with your partner.

Item 1 (Reading, p. 127)

An introductory sentence for a brief summary of the passage is provided below. Complete the summary by circling the THREE answer choices that express the most important ideas in the passage. Some sentences do not belong in the summary because they express ideas that are not presented in the passage or are minor ideas in the passage.

> Coca-Cola succeeds internationally because it develops a multicultural work force.

(A) The company has operations in 160 countries and employs over 400,000 people.
(B) One Coca-Cola manager compared the company's strategy to a sports team.
(C) To expand its multilingual, multicultural work force, Coca-Cola transfers employees from country to country.
(D) The firm's internship program identifies skilled foreign workers who may be hired to work for the company in their home countries.
(E) Coca-Cola believes these approaches help the firm identify and utilize global talent.
(F) Coca-Cola earns more of its profits in the United States than in other countries.

Item 2 (Reading, p. 125)

The word *internship* in paragraph 3 is closest in meaning to
(A) management
(B) supervision
(C) presentation
(D) training

Item 3 (Reading, p. 126)

All of the following are mentioned in paragraph 4 about the intern program
EXCEPT
(A) The program helps the company identify skilled international workers.
(B) Some people might go to work for other firms if the program did not exist.
(C) The company believes the program contributes to its international success.
(D) Coca-Cola hopes the program will increase its profits in the United States.

Tips

To do well on the TOEFL, it is essential to learn how to skim and scan. When you skim, you read text quickly to find general ideas. When you scan, you read text quickly to find specific information and facts, such as dates, numbers, and terms.

Skimming Tips

- Go back to the text and reread it quickly.

- Read the first and last sentences of paragraphs.

Scanning Tips

- Do not read each word.

- Look at text quickly to find key word(s).

To answer **Item 1**, you probably skimmed the whole text to find the main ideas to include in the summary. In contrast, for **Items 2** and **3**, you probably scanned the paragraph mentioned to find and mark the specific information or answer you were looking for.

PRACTICE

Read the passage on the next page about the founder of the Dell Computer Corporation. Use the tips from the previous section to help you answer the items that follow. Work with a partner and compare your answers.

A YOUNG GENIUS NAMED DELL

1   The success of Michael Dell, founder of the Dell Computer Corporation, illustrates that entrepreneurial skills are not limited to experienced businesspeople; they are often found in young men and women. As a college student, he started the Dell Computer empire, now one of the world's most profitable companies.

2   Dell was interested in business at an early age, launching his first business venture at age twelve selling stamps to collectors. He targeted customers who used auction houses and sent them a twelve-page catalogue. When orders came in, he went out to find the stamps people wanted. He may not have amassed very much money at first, but the direct sales, just-in-time inventory model for Dell Computer was born. At age fifteen, Dell became a full-fledged salesman selling subscriptions to *The Houston Post* and earning $18,000 in commissions in the first twelve months. Thus, years before he headed for college, Dell knew he had a talent for business.

3   Today, Dell is chairman of the board of a major corporation, but he started his career by selling computers from his dorm room at the University of Texas at Austin. When he finished his freshman year in college in 1984, he told his parents he wanted to leave school to start his own computer company. They were upset and reluctant to approve his decision. He did it anyway.

4   Dell acquired old computers and upgraded them, selling them directly to the customer without a store dealer as the middleman. There was no ambiguity about the results: He was getting a great many orders because people wanted custom-made computers to fit their needs.

5   Michael Dell's way of tackling the problem of cost was to build the computers only when the orders came in. This reduced inventory and allowed him to use upgraded and cheaper components as soon as they were available. Unlike his peers in the computer business, Dell was able to integrate new products without having to get rid of old models. Dell has left a legacy that many young entrepreneurs admire: In fifteen years, he has built a vast business empire.

1. Skim each paragraph. Then, write the general idea of each paragraph below.

Paragraph 1: _____

Paragraph 2: _____

Paragraph 3: _____

Paragraph 4: _____

Paragraph 5: _____

2. Where and when did Dell start his computer business? Underline the sections of the text that provide this information.

3. How did Dell handle his inventory? Underline the sections of the passage that provide this information.

4. Scan the passage to find the phrase "his decision." Then scan the surrounding sentences to determine what the phrase refers to. Write the answer here.

_____

5. Scan the passage to find the word *tackling*. Then scan the surrounding sentences to see how the word is used in the passage. Write a word or phrase that is close in meaning to the word *tackling* as it is used here.

_____

Perspectives on War

| LISTENING |

Campus Conversation   A student talks to an Army ROTC recruiter about joining the military.

Academic Listening   Radio interview: *Michael Ignatieff's Views on War*

| READING |

Newspaper Article   *Asmara Journal: In Peace, Women Warriors Rank Low*

| WRITING |

Integrated Task: Read, Listen, Write   Contrast the positions of the ICRC and Doctors without Borders using points presented in a reading and a listening.

| SPEAKING |

Independent Task   State your views about the legitimacy of war. Do you think war is sometimes necessary to solve conflicts between groups? Do you think war is never legitimate? Or do you have other views about war? Explain.

| SKILL FOCUS |

Paraphrasing   Paraphrasing is the ability to restate ideas from other sources in your own words without changing the meaning.

| TOEFL® iBT TARGET SKILLS |

- Identify and express main ideas
- Identify and express details
- Complete an outline of important ideas and details
- Paraphrase important points in a reading
- Contrast opinions from two sources

 For extra practice of TOEFL iBT skills, go to pages 242–259.

1 Listening

CAMPUS CONVERSATION

PRE-LISTENING VOCABULARY

Read the sentences. Guess the meaning of the boldfaced words and phrases. Write your ideas on the lines. Then match each word or phrase with a definition or synonym from the list on the next page. Work with a partner and compare your answers.

_____ 1. My history professor decided to **embark on** a new career. He wants to become a journalist.

_____

_____ 2. Many out-of-town journalists came to Miami to report on the storm. The mayor allowed the press **corps** to use a large room in the city hall as their headquarters.

_____

_____ 3. My bank has a large central office downtown with several small **branches** across the city. The branches offer fewer services but greater convenience than the main location.

_____

_____ 4. Don't worry if you don't have any money. I'll **take care of** lunch, and then you can pay me back tomorrow.

_____

_____ 5. My interview went so well today that that the employer offered me the job immediately. I'm **on the road** to success!

_____

_____ 6. At the new student **orientation,** a group of returning students showed us around the campus and gave us advice about college life.

_____

_____ 7. Annette recently became a member of Phi Beta Kappa, the academic honor society. To qualify for membership, she maintained a very high **GPA** in her courses.

_____

_____ 8. A bachelor of arts (B.A.) degree signifies that graduates have taken a balanced **curriculum** of English, arts, sciences, mathematics, and social sciences courses.

_____

a. begin

b. course of study

c. grade point average
(the average of all of a student's grades)

d. group of people

e. introductory session

f. on the way

g. parts of a larger organization

h. pay for

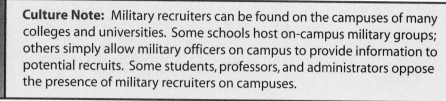

Culture Note: Military recruiters can be found on the campuses of many colleges and universities. Some schools host on-campus military groups; others simply allow military officers on campus to provide information to potential recruits. Some students, professors, and administrators oppose the presence of military recruiters on campuses.

FIRST LISTENING

Listen to a conversation between a student and a military recruiter. Take notes as you listen. Share your notes with a partner. Then use your notes to answer the questions.

1. What are the student and the recruiter discussing?

_____

_____

2. What information does the recruiter give the student? Write as many ideas as you hear.

_____

_____

3. What are the student's main questions about the ROTC?

_____

_____

SECOND LISTENING

 Read the questions. Listen to the conversation again. Add details to your notes. Then use your notes to answer the questions. Work with a partner and compare your answers.

1. What is the conversation mainly about?
   (A) The role of nurses in the U.S. military
   (B) The requirements and advantages of the ROTC
   (C) The reasons for quitting school and joining the military
   (D) The training and duties of U.S. Army officers

 Listen again to part of the conversation. Then answer question 2.

2. Why does the recruiter say, "It's important to know"?
   (A) He wants the student to know that it is important to graduate.
   (B) He is telling the student that it is important to have free tuition.
   (C) He is emphasizing one of the benefits of the ROTC.
   (D) He is indirectly pointing out a duty of ROTC members.

 Listen again to part of the conversation. Then answer question 3.

3. What is the student's attitude when the recruiter asks about the scholarship?
   (A) She is fairly unresponsive.
   (B) She is mildly interested.
   (C) She is somewhat nervous.
   (D) She is quite fascinated.

 Listen again to part of the conversation. Then answer question 4.

4. Why does the student ask, "But what about my nursing courses?"?
   (A) To request an explanation of the nursing curriculum requirements
   (B) To find out if she will use her nursing skills in the army
   (C) To find out if the ROTC will accept the courses she has taken
   (D) To emphasize that she already knows a lot about nursing

5. What would the student have to do after graduation if she joined the program?
   (A) Serve for three years in the army
   (B) Take required nursing courses
   (C) Attend a summer orientation session
   (D) Receive specialized job training

6. What does the student say she will do in the end?
   (A) Consider attending an orientation session
   (B) Call the recruiter for more information
   (C) Start the training the next summer
   (D) Sign up to join the ROTC

ACADEMIC LISTENING

FIRST LISTENING

Listen to a radio interview with author Michael Ignatieff. Take notes using the chart below. Work with a partner and combine your notes.

IMPORTANT POINTS	DETAILS
Toronto in the 1960s	•
	•
Ignatieff's views of war; Red Cross ethic	•
	•
	•
Red Cross rules of war	•
	•
	•
	•

SECOND LISTENING

Read the questions. Listen to the interview again. Add details to your notes. Then use your notes to answer the questions below. Work with a partner and compare your answers.

1. What is the interview mainly about?
   (A) The speaker's current antiwar views
   (B) The change in the speaker's views on war
   (C) The reasons people fight wars
   (D) The Red Cross views on war

2. How does Ignatieff introduce his explanation of the Red Cross ethic about war?
   (A) He explains how the ethic has changed over time.
   (B) He gives examples of work that the Red Cross does.
   (C) He contrasts the ethic with his original antiwar views.
   (D) He lists the rules that the Red Cross enforces.

Listen again to part of the interview. Then answer question 3.

3. Why does Ignatieff say, "dare I say it"?
   (A) To find out if the listeners support the idea of war
   (B) To emphasize that many people defend the idea of war
   (C) To admit that his opinion about war is controversial
   (D) To argue that war is sometimes unnecessary

Listen again to part of the interview. Then answer question 4.

4. What is Ignatieff's attitude toward the Red Cross ethic?
   (A) He disagrees with the ethic.
   (B) He thinks the ethic is too simple.
   (C) He does not express his opinion.
   (D) He approves of the ethic.

5. What is Ignatieff's conclusion about war?
   (A) We cannot stop war, but we should try to control behavior in war.
   (B) We must try to stop war and find other ways to solve human conflicts.
   (C) We cannot control the way humans act when they engage in war.
   (D) We must work to free oppressed groups around the world.

ANALYSIS

It is helpful to know the purpose of a test item. There are three types of questions in the listening section.

1. Basic Comprehension

- main ideas
- details
- the meaning of specific sentences

2. Organization

- the way information is structured
- the way ideas are linked

3. Inference

- ideas are not directly stated
- speaker's intention, purpose, or attitude not explicitly stated

Go back to the listening questions and label each question with 1, 2, or 3. Then work with a partner to see if you agree. Check the Answer Key for the correct answers. Which questions did you get right? Which did you get wrong? What skills do you need to practice?

2 Reading

ASMARA JOURNAL: IN PEACE, WOMEN WARRIORS RANK LOW

PRE-READING

Work with a partner. Read these excerpts from the passage that follows. Write paraphrases, or restatements of each excerpt in different words.

Excerpt 1

In Peace, Women Warriors Rank Low

_____

_____

Excerpt 2

Some days Nuria Mohammed Saleh says she actually finds herself missing the war—not the fear and horror, not even the adrenaline kick and camaraderie of soldiering. She misses being treated like a man.

_____

_____

_____

Excerpt 3

Like most women who are veterans here, she has found it hard to return to the deeply traditional and patriarchal society she left behind as a teenager.

_____

_____

_____

Excerpt 4

But if women who were guerrillas had hoped that fighting and dying in the war would change their status in Eritrean society, they have discovered instead that society's traditions die hard.

_____

_____

_____

READING

Read the passage and answer the questions. Then work with a partner and compare your answers. When you disagree, go back to the text to find helpful information.

Asmara Journal: In Peace, Women Warriors Rank Low

By James C. McKinley (from the *New York Times*)

1 Some days Nuria Mohammed Saleh says she actually finds herself missing the war—not the fear and horror, not even the adrenaline kick and camaraderie of soldiering. She misses being treated like a man. Like thousands of other Eritrean women, Mrs. Saleh fought side by side with the men in the rebel army that freed this rocky land from Ethiopian rule in 1991. Like most women who are veterans here, she has found it hard to return to the deeply traditional and patriarchal society she left behind as a teenager.

2 A few years ago, she recalled, she was hammering the enemy with mortar fire. Now she sweeps floors for a dollar a day in an office building near the capital she helped liberate. The only hints of her past are the shrapnel scars around her lips. Mrs. Saleh is one of about 20,000 women who have been discharged from the Eritrean Army in the last two years as part of a larger demobilization of nearly 52,000 troops. Though about 3,000 remain in the army, the vast majority of women were sent home. Some had spent their entire adult lives in the Eritrean People's Liberation Front. Most have little education, having quit school to join the guerrillas.

3 The front changed their lives, they said. The rebel commanders were Marxists by training and treated women as equals. The front's soldiers were taught to ignore sexual, tribal, and religious differences.

Women were trained to drive tanks, fight, and handle big guns. Though not many women had the education to become officers, a handful rose to command rebel battalions. Many married fighters from other religions and tribes.

4 Even outside the army in rebel-controlled regions, because the Liberation Front required most men to be in combat, women broke out of traditional molds, working as dentists, medical technicians, administrators, factory workers, mechanics, and teachers, a United Nations report said.

5 But if women who were guerrillas had hoped that fighting and dying in the war would change their status in Eritrean society, they have discovered instead that society's traditions die hard. Several said their

families had rejected their mixed marriages and employers had been reluctant to hire them for skilled jobs. Even more galling for some women is that, once they put on civilian clothes, men started expecting them to play subservient roles again.

6   Aster Haile was 12 when she joined the rebels. While she fought and worked for the front as a teacher, her sister spent the war in Saudi Arabia. After liberation, Ms. Haile said, she could not find work teaching, so she borrowed from her sister and opened a dress shop on Victory Avenue. Despite her military service, she said many men she meets still resist treating her like a businesswoman.

7   Other women who were veterans have banded together in cooperatives, pooling their savings and severance pay to start textile and honey-making businesses. Along with male veterans, they have been undergoing retraining at government expense to work as truck drivers and carpenters.

8   Here in Asmara, the capital, one group of women who were fighters have opened a fish market, the Gejeret Fish Retail Shop, built with the help of grants from the United States and the United Nations. Nine women work there, having traded in their AK-47s for fillet knives. They share the profits with other female veterans who are partners. Each woman takes home about $72 a month. Ghenet Berhe, a 30-year-old mother, said she did not mind filleting fish, since the whole country is struggling to get back on its feet economically. But when she was asked if she missed her life in the rebel army, she smiled and said, "Of course." "We had equality," she said. "We had common goals and common ends."

1. What is the passage mainly about?
   (A) The experiences of women soldiers during the war
   (B) The financial struggles of women in Eritrea
   (C) The struggles of women soldiers after the war
   (D) The role of women in the Eritrean revolution

2. According to paragraph 1, which of the following does NOT represent the experiences of Mrs. Saleh after the war?
   (A) She finds it difficult to return to the traditional society of her youth.
   (B) She misses being treated as an equal with men.
   (C) She has had more difficulties than most former female soldiers have had.
   (D) She does not miss the friendships with soldiers in the war.

3. In paragraph 1, why does the author begin the article with a description of Mrs. Saleh's experiences?
   (A) To illustrate the typical experiences of women veterans in her country
   (B) To demonstrate the negative experiences of wars in general
   (C) To show that Mrs. Saleh's experiences in Eritrea were extraordinary
   (D) To describe what happened during the Eritrean revolutionary war

4. In paragraph 2, why does the author mention Mrs. Saleh's scars?
   (A) To emphasize that Mrs. Saleh is no longer attractive
   (B) To point out that she was wounded during the war
   (C) To explain why she cannot get a well paying job
   (D) To show that she no longer serves in the army

5. The word *Some* in paragraph 2 refers to
   (A) the 52,000 troops in the Eritrean army
   (B) women who remained in the army
   (C) men and women who were sent home from the army
   (D) women who were discharged from the army

6. All of the following are mentioned in paragraphs 3 and 4 as roles that women held during the war EXCEPT
   (A) battalion commanders
   (B) religious leaders
   (C) tank drivers
   (D) dentists

7. The word *galling* in paragraph 5 is closest in meaning to
   (A) irritating
   (B) exciting
   (C) embarrassing
   (D) comforting

8. What can be inferred from paragraph 5 about what women veterans expected would happen after the war?
   (A) They thought their contributions in the war would change their status.
   (B) They expected their families to reject their mixed marriages.
   (C) They expected to be offered skilled jobs after they left the army.
   (D) They thought that women would return to their traditional roles.

9. In paragraphs 6 to 8, the author's primary purpose is
   (A) to illustrate the typical work of Eritrean women
   (B) to contrast the work of urban and rural women
   (C) to describe ways women have succeeded in the workplace
   (D) to emphasize the range of retail products sold in Eritrea

10. The phrase *broke out of* in paragraph 4 is closest in meaning to
    (A) reduced
    (B) lost
    (C) faced
    (D) escaped

11. The phrase *die hard* in paragraph 5 is closest in meaning to
    (A) suffer
    (B) grow strong
    (C) don't change
    (D) disappear

12. Look at the four squares ☐ that indicate where the following sentence could be added to the passage. Where would the sentence best fit? Circle the letter that shows the point where you would insert this sentence.

> Just like male soldiers, they met the enemy and were wounded and killed in battle.

> The front changed their lives, they said. **[A]** The rebel commanders were Marxists by training and treated women as equals. **[B]** The front's soldiers were taught to ignore sexual, tribal, and religious differences. Women were trained to drive tanks, fight, and handle big guns. **[C]** Though not many women had the education to become officers, a handful rose to command rebel battalions. Many married fighters from other religions and tribes. **[D]**

13. Which of the following best expresses the essential information in this sentence from the passage?

> Even outside the army in rebel-controlled regions, because the Liberation Front required most men to be in combat, women broke out of traditional molds, working as dentists, medical technicians, administrators, factory workers, mechanics, and teachers, a United Nations report said.

(A) Outside the army, women worked as mechanics, dentists, and teachers.
(B) Most men served in the army or held traditional jobs such as dentistry.
(C) Traditional gender roles determined the types of work that women did in the army.
(D) In society, women did traditionally male jobs because men were serving in the army.

14. An introductory sentence for a brief summary of the passage is provided below. Complete the summary by circling the THREE answer choices that express the most important ideas in the passage. Some sentences do not belong in the summary because they express ideas that are not presented in the passage or are minor ideas in the passage.

> Women veterans of the Eritrean war have found it difficult to return to their traditional places in society.

(A) Many women veterans miss being treated as equals to men.
(B) After the war, Eritrea gained its independence from Ethiopia in 1991.
(C) Nearly 20,000 women were killed in the Eritrean revolutionary war.
(D) Being in the war changed women's lives by allowing them to escape traditional gender roles.
(E) Women have made their own opportunities in society, becoming entrepreneurs.
(F) Aster Haile was 12 when she joined the rebels, serving as a soldier and teacher.

3 Writing

INTEGRATED TASK: READ, LISTEN, WRITE

In this section, you will read a short excerpt and listen to an excerpt on a related topic. Then you will write about the relationship between the two.

READING

Read the passage. As you read, fill in the following summary chart.

Main Idea: Dr. Sandra Martino, a Red Cross physician, supports the ICRC's principles of neutrality and the warrior's honor during wartime.

IMPORTANT POINTS	DETAILS
	• • studied the ICRC and Geneva Conventions; fascinated by neutrality ethic
Barriers to joining the ICRC	• wondered if she could do job: see misery, have no comforts, stay neutral • •
ICRC's principles and work	• we all share moral tradition: warrior's honor • warriors must tame, control aggression • •

Dear Editor:

1   For years, I had been drawn to the idea of doing relief work. So, last year, after receiving my medical degree, I joined the International Committee of the Red Cross.

2   As I had grown up in a wealthy San Francisco suburb, I wondered whether I could do the job. Could I truly relate to and identify with the devastating misery of victims in war-torn regions? I questioned my ability to do without the comforts of home and family that I took for granted. But more important, could I truly live by the principles of the ICRC, especially the principles of neutrality?

3   My parents were firmly opposed to my decision to join the ICRC. My father had been a draft evader and had participated in

many antiwar demonstrations in Berkeley, California, during the 1960s. Raised as a pacifist, my mother has always equated war with barbarism and believes that war has no legitimacy whatsoever.

4   My parents had advised me to join the group Doctors without Borders, a human rights group which provides medical relief to populations in volatile war zones. Unlike the ICRC, Doctors without Borders takes a firm position against those that unleash aggression and hostility against innocents. Doctors without Borders does not claim to remain neutral at all times.

5   However, I had studied the ICRC and the Geneva Conventions in college and was fascinated by the alternative ethic of neutrality. What I'd like to get at here is that the Red Cross is trying to remind people that we all share one moral tradition: the warrior's honor. In other words, "warriors" in all human societies must be trained to tame and discipline their aggression. The codes of the ICRC, the Geneva Conventions, are really simply common-sense rules that remind people to follow the tradition of the warrior's honor.

6   In the ICRC, my role is not only to provide medical services, but also to disseminate information in a clear, meaningful way. It's important that people all over the world be aware of the valuable work of the ICRC.

Sandra Martino, M.D.

LISTENING

Listen to a radio interview. Use the outline to take notes as you listen.

Main Idea: Dr. David Chan, a Doctors without Borders physician, believes that the principles of the warrior's honor and neutrality are unrealistic.

Chan's views of war and the warrior's honor

- soldiers must try to follow rules of war
- does not equate war with barbarism, savagery
-
-

Chan's views of neutrality

- not realistic for observers to be neutral
-
-
-
-

WRITING

Write on the following topic. Follow the steps below to prepare.

> **Contrast the positions of the ICRC and Doctors without Borders using points presented in both the reading and the listening.**

Step 1

- Work with a partner. Skim the reading and your notes from the reading and listening tasks (pages 148–149) to answer the following questions.

    1. What are the ICRC's views on the warrior's honor?

    2. What is the ICRC's ethic of neutrality?

    3. What is the Doctors without Borders' position on the warrior's honor?

    4. What does the Doctors without Borders organization say about neutrality? What positions do they take on wartime events that they observe?

- With your partner, take notes to fill in the outline below. Use your answers to the questions above to help you. Share your answers in a group.

Introduction—Thesis Statement: _____

_____

The warrior's honor

ICRC: _____

_____

Doctors without Borders: _____

_____

Neutrality

ICRC: _____

_____

Doctors without Borders: _____

_____

Conclusion: _____

_____

- On your own, evaluate what you have heard. What are the contrasting views that each side holds on the warrior's honor? On neutrality? What details should you include about each of these points? Add any new ideas to your outline. Refer to your outline as you write.

Step 2

Write for 20 minutes. Leave the last 5 minutes to edit your work.

To evaluate a partner's writing, use the Writing Evaluation Form on page 203.

4 Speaking

INDEPENDENT TASK

Speak on the following topic. Follow the steps below to prepare.

State your views about the legitimacy of war. Do you think war is sometimes necessary to solve conflicts between groups? Do you think war is never legitimate? Or do you have other views about war? Explain.

Step 1

- Work in a group. Take turns discussing the questions in the topic above. State your views about the legitimacy of war. Give reasons and examples to support your opinions. Take notes on ideas from your discussion.

VIEWS	REASONS AND EXAMPLES
War may be necessary sometimes.	It may be necessary to fight for independence, democratic rights, or against oppression. Example: Eritrean revolutionary war

- On your own, evaluate what you have heard. Did any of your classmates share your opinions about war? Did you hear any interesting reasons or examples that you could use in your writing?

- Organize your ideas by revising your notes on the views, reasons, and examples that you will speak about.

Step 2

With a partner, take turns practicing a one-minute oral response to the topic. Be sure to use the information in your notes to help you.

Step 3

Change partners. Take turns giving a one-minute response to the topic again.

To evaluate your partner's response, use the Speaking Evaluation Form on page 204.

5 Skill Focus

PARAPHRASING

EXAMINATION

1 *Look at the following items from the unit. Work with a partner and answer the questions about the items.*

- How did you identify the correct answers? Did you pay attention to the use of key ideas or words when making your choices?

- For Item 1, did you include key ideas and words in your notes? Go back and mark the parts of your notes that helped you. If necessary, listen again to the interview and take notes on the parts that helped you.

- For Item 2, mark the essential ideas in the sentence from the passage that are included in the paraphrased statement you selected.

- For Item 3, go back to the passage and mark the key ideas and words that are paraphrased in the summary sentences you selected.

Item 1 (Academic Listening, p. 142)

What is Ignatieff's conclusion about war?
(A) We cannot stop war, but we should try to control behavior in war.
(B) We must try to stop war and find other ways to solve human conflicts.
(C) We cannot control the way humans act when they engage in war.
(D) We must work to free oppressed groups around the world.

Item 2 (Reading, p. 147)

Which of the following best expresses the essential information in this sentence from the passage?

> Even outside the army in rebel-controlled regions, because the Liberation Front required most men to be in combat, women broke out of traditional molds, working as dentists, medical technicians, administrators, factory workers, mechanics, and teachers, a United Nations report said.

(**A**) Outside the army, women worked as mechanics, dentists, and teachers.
(**B**) Most men served in the army or held traditional jobs such as dentistry.
(**C**) Traditional gender roles determined the types of work that women did in the army.
(**D**) In society, women did traditionally male jobs because men were serving in the army.

Item 3 (Reading, p. 147)

An introductory sentence for a brief summary of the passage is provided below. Complete the summary by circling the THREE answer choices that express the most important ideas in the passage. Some sentences do not belong in the summary because they express ideas that are not presented in the passage or are minor ideas in the passage.

> Women veterans of the Eritrean war have found it difficult to return to their traditional places in society.

(**A**) Many women veterans miss being treated as equals to men.
(**B**) After the war, Eritrea gained its independence from Ethiopia in 1991.
(**C**) Nearly 20,000 women were killed in the Eritrean revolutionary war.
(**D**) Being in the war changed women's lives by allowing them to escape traditional gender roles.
(**E**) Women have made their own opportunities in society, becoming entrepreneurs.
(**F**) Aster Haile was 12 when she joined the rebels, serving as a soldier and teacher.

2 *Look at the following task from the unit. Work with a partner and answer the questions on the next page.*

Item 4 (Integrated Task, p. 150)

Contrast the positions of the ICRC and Doctors without Borders using points presented in both the reading and the listening.

- Review your written response to the topic. How did you paraphrase the points from the reading and listening passages? Did you simplify the grammar or language in your response?

- Did you include key words from the passages? Did you use synonyms? Mark these words or phrases in your response. Show them to your partner and discuss your choices.

Tips

To do well on the TOEFL, it is essential to learn how to paraphrase information. When you paraphrase, you restate ideas or information in your own words without changing the speaker's or writer's original meaning.

Effective Paraphrases

- Restate key information.

- Omit unimportant information.

- Include key words from the original source, as well as synonyms of original words.

- Use simpler grammar and language.

To answer **Item 1**, you probably looked for the statement—(A)—that restated the speaker's main point in the conclusion of the conversation.

In **Item 2**, you probably identified the statement—(D)—that included all the main points in the original sentence.

For **Item 3**, you should have selected the statements that paraphrased entire paragraphs or important ideas while omitting unimportant or incorrect ideas.

In your written response to **Item 4**, you should have identified the main points in the sources and then restated this information in a simplified form, using key words from the original sources and some different words of your own.

PRACTICE

1 *Read the passage on the next page. Use the tips from the previous section to help you answer the questions that follow. Work with a partner and compare your answers.*

THE FIRST GENEVA CONVENTION

1   In 1864, the wealthy Swiss businessman Jean-Henri Dunant wanted to create an international volunteer organization to care for the wounded on both sides of a battle. He wanted an international agreement that would give protection and legitimacy to these tireless volunteers. Dunant had been inspired by the devastating scene of thousands of dead Austrian and French soldiers in a volatile regional conflict of the time. He witnessed firsthand the horrific battlefield: bloody corpses, severed body parts, and wounded and dead horses. Shocked by the barbarism and savagery he had witnessed, Dunant wrote a book in which he explained his ideals.

2   With his influence, Dunant persuaded the Swiss government to organize an international meeting to discuss his proposals. In 1864, representatives of 12 governments met and ratified an agreement. It was the first version of the Geneva Conventions, or the "rules of war." As the first attempt to institutionalize guidelines for wartime behavior, it was the beginning of the modern humanitarian law movement.

3   Dunant's ideas were controversial then, just as they are today. Some people thought his beliefs were illogical, going against a natural way of thinking. Critics did not believe that codes could help restrain soldiers during conflicts, yet Dunant argued that these laws were fundamental human universals, with origins in every culture.

4   The original 1864 Conventions prevailed until 1949, when four more were added. One of these requires the sparing of civilian lives during wartime. Now more than 180 countries subscribe to the Geneva Conventions. The Red Cross devotes a great deal of effort to disseminating information about the conventions.

1. An introductory sentence for a brief summary of the passage is provided below. Complete the summary by circling the THREE answer choices that express the most important ideas in the passage.

> Swiss businessman Jean-Henri Dunant organized the Geneva Conventions, or "rules of war," which are still used today.

(A) In 1864, Dunant wanted to create an international agreement to establish rules of wartime behavior.

(B) He wrote a book about his ideals after he witnessed thousands of dead soldiers in a European battlefield.

(C) He saw thousands of dead Austrian and French soldiers, severed body parts, and wounded and dead horses.

(D) Dunant convinced the Swiss government to organize an international meeting and discuss his ideas.

(E) In 1864, representatives met and ratified the first version of the Geneva Conventions, or "rules of war."

(F) Now more than 180 countries support and follow the Geneva Conventions.

2. Which of the following best expresses the essential information in this sentence from the passage?

> Critics did not believe that codes could help restrain soldiers during conflicts, yet Dunant argued that these laws were fundamental human universals, with origins in every culture.

(A) Critics doubted that the codes of law could make soldiers control their behavior during war.

(B) Dunant believed that codes of law are basic, universal human laws that exist in any culture.

(C) Critics did not believe that conflicts would cause soldiers to use control, but Dunant thought the laws would be accepted in every culture.

(D) Critics did not think rules would make soldiers control themselves in war, but Dunant thought the codes were basic human traits in every culture.

2 *Listen to a conversation between a Red Cross volunteer and the prisoner of war (POW) he is visiting in a detention camp. As you listen, use the chart below to take notes related to the main points in the conversation. Then work with a partner and take turns paraphrasing the main points from the conversation. Use your notes to help you.*

MAIN POINTS	NOTES
General situation	
POW's question about photos	
Volunteer's warning about photos	

POW's question about a bag	
Volunteer's response and further questions	
POW's explanation about the bag	

The Arts

| LISTENING |

Campus Conversation A student discusses her choice for a future career with a career counselor.

Academic Listening Radio interview: *Music, Art, and the Brain*

| READING |

Novel Excerpt *The Soloist*

| SPEAKING |

Integrated Task: Read, Listen, Speak Debate the merits of arts education. What are its benefits? What are its disadvantages?

| WRITING |

Independent Task Explain the importance of music in your life.

| SKILL FOCUS |

Identifying and Using Cohesive Devices Cohesive devices are words and phrases that connect parts of text or speech and signal the type of organization used.

| TOEFL® iBT TARGET SKILLS |

- Identify and express main ideas
- Identify and express details
- Make inferences
- Complete a chart of important points and details
- Recognize words to introduce connections and transitions
- Use rhetorical devices to present contrasting opinions

 For extra practice of TOEFL iBT skills, go to pages 242–259.

1 Listening

CAMPUS CONVERSATION

PRE-LISTENING VOCABULARY

Read the sentences. Guess the meaning of the boldfaced words and phrases. Write your ideas on the lines. Then match each word or phrase with a definition or synonym from the list on the next page. Work with a partner and compare your answers.

_____ 1. Colleges collect many **statistics** to determine their students' graduation rate. They study the number and type of graduates to understand the reasons for the students' success.

_____

_____ 2. In the United States, the Census **Bureau** surveys the population every ten years. The bureau staff collects information and puts it together in a report.

_____

_____ 3. The novel we are reading in English class doesn't **paint a pretty picture** of life. The main character had a disturbing childhood and troubled teenage years.

_____

_____ 4. After Dave took one design course, he felt such a **keen** interest in the subject that he changed his major to architecture.

_____

_____ 5. Elizabeth constantly changes her hemline to match the latest **trends**; one month, her skirts are long, and the next, they're short.

_____

_____ 6. Officer Scott doesn't earn enough money from his full-time job as a police officer, so he **moonlights** as a security guard to increase his income.

_____

_____ 7. Mara is so busy that she rarely eats a decent lunch. She has to **supplement** her poor diet with vitamins.

_____

_____ 8. Jenny is interested in both art history and sociology, so she's doing a **double major** in both fields. That way, she will have twice the career options when she graduates.

_____

_____ 9. Carrie's major is French, but she enjoys studying languages so much that she's **minoring in** German as well.

_____

_____ 10. Will you at least think about going on a date with my brother? He's a very nice guy, and you never know what may **come of it**.

_____

_____ 11. There are many interesting topics for my psychology term paper, but **the bottom line** is I need to choose one and start my research today.

_____

_____ 12. Recent college graduates often have a hard time **making ends meet**, especially if they have to repay college loans *and* pay bills as they start off in their careers.

_____

a. add to

b. balancing income and expenses

c. concentrated study of two disciplines

d. current styles or movements

e. groups of numbers

f. happen as a result of something

g. main fact about a situation

h. office or organization

i. present a favorable description

j. studying a discipline for a secondary degree

k. very strong

l. works an extra job

> **Culture Note:** Double or even triple majoring has become an increasingly popular trend on college and university campuses. More and more students are pursuing bachelor's degrees in more than one discipline, primarily to make themselves more attractive to future employers. Students can complete a double major in roughly the same amount of time that a single major requires, although some double majors may require an extra year of study. Popular double majors include economics/finance, mathematics/computer science, geography/history, chemistry/chemical engineering, and physics/biochemistry.

FIRST LISTENING

 Read the questions. Listen to a conversation between a student and a career counselor. Take notes as you listen. Share your notes with a partner. Then use your notes to answer the questions.

1. What are the student and the counselor discussing?

_____

_____

2. What information does the counselor give the student about her career choice? Write as many ideas as you hear.

_____

_____

3. What does the counselor suggest that the student do in the end?

_____

_____

SECOND LISTENING

 Read the questions. Listen to the conversation again. Add details to your notes. Then use your notes to answer the questions. Work with a partner and compare your answers.

1. What is the conversation mainly about?
   (A) A student's choice of a future career
   (B) A counselor's research into career choices
   (C) The differences between music and education careers
   (D) The benefits of a choosing a career in the arts

2. What does the student wish she could become?
   (A) A music teacher
   (B) A school teacher
   (C) A full-time musician
   (D) A part-time pianist

Listen again to part of the conversation. Then answer question 3.

3. What is the counselor's attitude toward the student's career choice?
   (A) She is upset.
   (B) She is curious.
   (C) She is pessimistic.
   (D) She is unconcerned.

4. What does the counselor suggest that the student do?
   (A) Find a steady job and give up music
   (B) Find a job in a restaurant while taking classes
   (C) Do more research into careers in music
   (D) Study another discipline along with music

Listen again to part of the conversation. Then answer question 5.

5. Which sentence best expresses how the student probably feels?
   (A) She is completely optimistic about her future.
   (B) She has changed her opinion about her career.
   (C) She is very worried about her future success.
   (D) She is slightly less confident about her future.

Listen again to part of the conversation. Then answer question 6.

6. Why does the counselor ask, "What about teaching? Do you like children?"?
   (A) To start a discussion about the student's childhood
   (B) To introduce an idea about a possible career
   (C) To discourage the student from continuing her music
   (D) To remind the student about her interest in children

ACADEMIC LISTENING

FIRST LISTENING

Listen to a radio interview about music and the brain. Take notes using the chart on the next page. Work with a partner and combine your notes.

IMPORTANT POINTS	DETAILS

	• baby born with circuits that do crucial things:
	  • •
	  • •
	  • •

Music and math	• • • •
	• two- and three-year-olds got music lessons • • • • •

SECOND LISTENING

Read the questions. Listen to the interview again. Add details to your notes. Then use your notes to answer the questions. Work with a partner and compare your answers.

1. What is the interview mainly about?
   (A) The senses that babies are born with
   (B) The role of parents in a child's education
   (C) The role of school in music education
   (D) The effects of music on mental development

2. How does Begley explain the crucial brain functions that babies are born with?
   (A) By presenting examples of essential bodily activities
   (B) By contrasting the babies' abilities with those of adults
   (C) By explaining the connection between music and the brain
   (D) By describing the research of neuroscientists on babies

Listen again to part of the interview. Then answer question 3.

3. Why does the host say, "I had always assumed that musical talent and mathematics kind of went together because they had something to do with each other"?
   (A) To share his knowledge about the subject
   (B) To contrast his ideas with the guest's ideas
   (C) To elicit confirmation and explanation of his ideas
   (D) To invite description of various kinds of music

4. According to Begley, what did neuroscientists learn from their research with preschool children?
   (A) Music interferes with children's creativity.
   (B) Music increases certain thinking abilities.
   (C) Mathematics and music are left-brain activities.
   (D) Spatial and logical thinking affect musical abilities.

 Listen again to part of the interview. Then answer question 5.

5. What does the host mean when he says, "it's sort of scary"?
   (A) He is worried that he did not teach his children well in the past.
   (B) He is scared that he will not teach his children well in the future.
   (C) He is afraid that he did not give his children enough play time.
   (D) He is concerned that he did not have a role in raising his children.

2 Reading

THE SOLOIST

PRE-READING

You will read an excerpt from a novel about a famous concert cellist who loses his ability to perform due to the nervous pressure of playing concerts. In this excerpt, he finds a way to reconnect with his music.

Work with a partner. Read these excerpts from the passage that follows. Circle the words that indicate a connection to previous or later information in the passage. Then take notes about possible ideas or events that might come before or after each excerpt. Share your ideas with the class.

Excerpt 1

After improvising for a while, I started playing the D minor Bach suite, still in the darkness.

Before: _____

After: _____

Excerpt 2

For the first time I didn't think about how it would sound to anyone else, and slowly, joyfully, gratefully, I started to hear again.

Before: _____

After: _____

(continued on next page)

Excerpt 3

After an hour or so I looked up, and in the darkness saw the outline of the cat sitting on the floor in front of me, cleaning her paws and purring loudly. I had an audience again, humble as it was.

Before: _____

After: _____

READING

Read the passage and answer the questions. Then work with a partner and compare your answers. When you disagree, go back to the text to find helpful information.

THE SOLOIST

BY MARK SALZMAN

1   An idea came to me, and I turned off the lights in the studio. In the darkness, I put the cello's spike into a loose spot on the carpet, tightened the bow and drew it across the open strings. I took off my shirt and tried it again; it was the first time in my life I'd felt the instrument against my bare chest. I could feel the vibration of the strings travel through the body of the instrument to my own body. I'd never thought about that; music scholars always talk about the resonating[1] properties of various instruments, but surely the performer's own body must have some effect on the sound. As I dug into the notes I imagined that my own chest and lungs were extensions of the sound box; I seemed to be able to alter the sound by the way I sat, and by varying the muscular tension in my upper body.

2   After improvising for a while, I started playing the D minor Bach suite, still in the darkness. Strangely freed of the task of finding the right phrasing, the right intonation, the right bowing, I heard the music

[1] *resonating:* making a deep, rich sound that vibrates the material of the instrument or the body

through my skin. For the first time I didn't think about how it would sound to anyone else, and slowly, joyfully, gratefully, I started to hear again. The notes sang out, first like a trickle, then like a fountain of cool water bubbling up from a hole in the middle of a desert. After an hour or so I looked up, and in the darkness saw the outline of the cat sitting on the floor in front of me, cleaning her paws and purring loudly. I had an audience again, humble as it was.

3   So that's what I do now with my cello. At least once a day I find time to tune it, close my eyes, and listen. It's probably not going to lead to the kind of comeback I'd fantasized about for so long—years of playing badly have left scars on my technique, and, practically speaking, classical musicians returning from obscurity are almost impossible to promote—but I might eventually try giving a recital if I feel up to it. Or better yet, I may play for Dr. Polk if our date at the concert goes well. Occasionally I feel a stab of longing, and I wish I could give just one more concert on a great stage before my lights blink off, but that longing passes more quickly now. I take solace in the fact that, unlike the way I felt before, I can enjoy playing for myself now. I feel relaxed and expansive when I play, as if I could stretch out my arms and reach from one end of the apartment to the other. A feeling of completeness and dignity surrounds me and lifts me up.

1. What is the passage mainly about?
   (A) A musician's feelings when he plays the cello
   (B) A musician's desire to return to his former profession
   (C) A musician finding joy in playing music again
   (D) A musician playing the cello for his cat

2. According to paragraph 1, what relationship does the cellist experience between his body and his music?
   (A) His body affects the sound.
   (B) His body improves the sound.
   (C) His body becomes tense as he plays.
   (D) His body stops the vibrations as he plays.

3. Based on the information in paragraph 1, what can be inferred about the effect of a performer's body on musical sound?
   (A) The cellist had not read about it before.
   (B) The cellist thought scholars had talked about it.
   (C) The cellist had previously written about it.
   (D) The cellist had experienced it before.

4. In paragraph 1, what does the word *it* refer to in the sentence, "I took off my shirt and tried it again."?
   (A) Drawing the bow across the strings
   (B) Turning off the lights in the studio
   (C) Taking off the shirt
   (D) Tightening the bow

5. In paragraph 2, the author's primary purpose is
   (A) to explain the cellist's feelings of playing before an audience
   (B) to describe the sound when the cellist plays next to his skin
   (C) to identify specific pieces of music that the cellist plays
   (D) to describe the cellist's experience of playing next to his skin

6. All of the following are mentioned in paragraph 2 as part of the cellist's new way of playing EXCEPT
   (A) playing the instrument in the dark
   (B) thinking of how the music sounded to others
   (C) "hearing" music through his bare skin
   (D) not worrying about finding the right phrasing

7. What can be inferred from paragraph 3 about the cellist?
   (A) He had always enjoyed playing for himself.
   (B) He had continually performed over the years.
   (C) Previously, he had never played before an audience.
   (D) Previously, he only wanted to play for an audience.

8. Based on the information in paragraph 3, what can be inferred about the cellist's attitude toward playing?
   (A) He feels optimistic.
   (B) He is discouraged.
   (C) He feels nervous.
   (D) He is reluctant.

9. The word *solace* in paragraph 3 is closest in meaning to
   (A) relaxation
   (B) enjoyment
   (C) comfort
   (D) pride

10. Which of the following best expresses the essential information in this sentence from the passage?

    It's probably not going to lead to the kind of comeback I'd fantasized about for so long—years of playing badly have left scars on my technique, and, practically speaking, classical musicians returning from obscurity are almost impossible to promote—but I might eventually try giving a recital if I feel up to it.

    (A) The cellist may perform in public, but he will probably not be able to return to concert performance, since he has practiced badly for years and it is hard to make a comeback.

(B) The cellist, like most musicians, finds it difficult to make a comeback after not performing for some time, so he probably will not be able to do it.

(C) The cellist may try to give a public performance even though he has scars from playing the cello for so many years, but he cannot make a comeback.

(D) The cellist played badly for so many years that it affected his career as a classical musician, but he will try to make the comeback that he had dreamed about.

11. Look at the four squares ☐ that indicate where the following sentence could be added to the passage. Where would the sentence best fit? Circle the letter that shows the point where you would insert this sentence.

> My body does not actually extend to the edges of my living space, but the sounds of my music reverberate from wall to wall, filling the room.

So that's what I do now with my cello. At least once a day I find time to tune it, close my eyes, and listen. [A] It's probably not going to lead to the kind of comeback I'd fantasized about for so long—years of playing badly have left scars on my technique, and, practically speaking, classical musicians returning from obscurity are almost impossible to promote—but I might eventually try giving a recital if I feel up to it. [B] Or better yet, I may play for Dr. Polk if our date at the concert goes well. [C] Occasionally I feel a stab of longing, and I wish I could give just one more concert on a great stage before my lights blink off, but that longing passes more quickly now. I take solace in the fact that, unlike the way I felt before, I can enjoy playing for myself now. I feel relaxed and expansive when I play, as if I could stretch out my arms and reach from one end of the apartment to the other. [D] A feeling of completeness and dignity surrounds me and lifts me up.

12. An introductory sentence for a brief summary of the passage is provided below. Complete the summary by selecting the THREE answer choices that express the most important ideas in the passage. Some sentences do not belong in the summary because they express ideas that are not presented in the passage or are minor ideas in the passage.

> By experiencing the sounds and sensations of playing his cello next to his skin, a former cello soloist discovers the joy of playing for himself.

(A) He tightens his bow and draws it across the strings of the cello.

(B) His body becomes part of the musical instrument as he plays it next to his skin.

(C) He loses himself in the beauty and emotion of playing the cello.

(D) He has no audience except for his cat, who purrs as he plays the instrument.

(E) It is difficult for musicians to return to public performance after an absence.

(F) He regrets that he can no longer play in concert but enjoys playing in his home.

ANALYSIS

It is helpful to know the purpose of a test item. There are four types of questions in the reading section.

1. Basic Comprehension

- main ideas

- details

- the meaning of specific sentences

2. Organization

- the way information is structured in the text

- the way ideas are linked between sentences or between paragraphs

3. Inference

- ideas are not directly stated in the text

- author's intention, purpose, or attitude not explicitly stated in the text

4. Vocabulary and Reference

- the meaning of words

- the meaning of reference words such as *his, them, this,* or *none*

Go back to the reading questions and label each question with 1, 2, 3, or 4. Then work with a partner to see if you agree. Check the Answer Key for the correct answers. Which questions did you get right? Which did you get wrong? What skills do you need to practice?

3 Speaking

INTEGRATED TASK: READ, LISTEN, SPEAK

In this section, you will read a short passage and listen to an excerpt on a related topic. Then you will speak about the relationship between the two.

READING

Read the passage on the next page. As you read, fill in the following summary chart.

IMPORTANT POINTS	DETAILS
What the schools want	•
	•
Why they want it	•
	•
Editors' response/opinions	•
	•
	•
	•

EDITORIAL

School Tax Hike Does Not Merit Support

1   Voters go to the polls this week to decide on a proposed 5 percent hike in property taxes requested by the Springfield School District. School district trustees are asking for a $2.6 million increase in their annual revenues.

2   The district already levied a 6 percent tax increase five years ago, resulting in $3.1 million in additional revenues. The district added twenty-four staff positions and increased funding for music, art, physical education, and library programs.

3   Why is the district asking for more money now?

4   School trustees argue that the district's arts programs have been hard hit in recent years by state budget cuts. They want to spend $1.2 million—nearly half of the proposed tax revenue—to hire teachers in music, band, and art.

5   Meanwhile, our children fall farther behind in basic skills. The national average on the Acme standardized mathematics examination is 75 percent. In our district, students score an average of 62 percent.

6   Our school district must focus on essential core content such as mathematics, not waste more resources on less crucial subjects such as music. Our students deserve a quality education, but more money for the arts is not the key.

7   The community has rallied behind the school district in the past. This year, *Star Daily* is sending a simple message to voters: Enough, already. Tax dollars are critical for the ongoing operation of our schools, but it's time for the district to trim its budget just as we do in tight times.

8   Voters should say "no" to the proposed tax hike.

LISTENING

Listen to a conversation. Use the outline to take notes as you listen.

Main Idea: Two students apply the psychological theory of music and intelligence to their own lives and conclude that music enhances their spatial and analytical skills.

Anna's case

-
-
-
-

Sean's case

-
-
-

Study of children

-

SPEAKING

Speak on the following topic. Follow the steps below to prepare.

Debate the merit of arts education. What are its benefits? What are its disadvantages?

Step 1

- Work with a partner. Skim the reading and your notes from the reading and listening tasks (pages 170–172) to answer the following questions.

  1. What are the benefits of music and arts education?

  2. What are the disadvantages of having arts programs in schools?

  3. What counterarguments can arts opponents give for each argument in favor of arts education?

  4. What counterarguments can arts proponents give for each argument against arts education?

- Work in a group to discuss the arguments for and against arts education, as well as the counterarguments that can be made in response to each. Use your answers to the questions above to help you. Take notes on your ideas.

Step 2

With your partner, practice debating the ideas about arts education. Take turns advocating and refuting arts education. Then switch roles and debate again. Be sure to use the information in your notes to help you.

Step 3

Change partners. Debate the issue for two minutes. One student will advocate arts education, and one will refute it. Then switch roles and debate again.

To evaluate your partner's response, use the Speaking Evaluation Form on page 204.

4 Writing

INDEPENDENT TASK

Write on the following topic. Follow the steps below to prepare.

Explain the importance of music in your life.

Step 1

- As a class, brainstorm areas of life where you find music: as a player, listener, concert-goer, worshipper, shopper, and so on. Write ideas on the board.

- On your own, evaluate what you have heard. Are the ideas that your classmates suggested useful? Do they reflect your own relationship with music? Identify the areas of your life in which music is important. Why is music important to you?

- Organize your ideas by filling in the outline below. You may choose to expand the body of your essay to include more points.

Introduction—Thesis Statement: _____

_____

Body

    Point 1: _____

      Details: _____

    Point 2: _____

      Details: _____

Conclusion: _____

_____

Step 2

Write for 20 minutes. Leave the last 5 minutes to edit your work.

> To evaluate a partner's writing, use the Writing Evaluation Form on page 203.

5 Skill Focus

IDENTIFYING AND USING COHESIVE DEVICES

EXAMINATION

Look at the following items from the unit. Work with a partner and answer the questions about each item.

- How did you choose your answer? Did any words or ideas help you connect ideas?

- For Items 1 and 2, go back to the passage and mark any parts that helped you choose the correct answer.

- For Items 3 and 4, go back to your notes and mark any parts that helped you choose the correct answer. If necessary, listen again to the interview and the conversation and take notes on the parts that helped you.

Item 1 (Reading, p. 169)

Look at the four squares ☐ that indicate where the following sentence could be added to the passage. Where would the sentence best fit? Circle the letter that shows the point where you would insert this sentence.

> My body does not actually extend to the edges of my living space, but the sounds of my music reverberate from wall to wall, filling the room.

So that's what I do now with my cello. At least once a day I find time to tune it, close my eyes, and listen. **[A]** It's probably not going to lead to the kind of comeback I'd fantasized about for so long—years of playing badly have left scars on my technique, and, practically speaking, classical musicians returning from obscurity are almost impossible to promote—but I might eventually try giving a recital if I feel up to it. **[B]** Or better yet, I may play for Dr. Polk if our date at the concert goes well. $\boxed{C}$ Occasionally I feel a stab of longing, and I wish I could give just one more concert on a great stage before my lights blink off, but that longing passes more quickly now. I take solace in the fact that, unlike the way I felt before, I can enjoy playing for myself now. I feel relaxed and expansive when I play, as if I could stretch out my arms and reach from one end of the apartment to the other. $\boxed{D}$ A feeling of completeness and dignity surrounds me and lifts me up.

Item 2 (Reading, p. 168)

In paragraph 1, what does the word *it* refer to in the sentence, "I took off my shirt and tried it again."?
(A) Drawing the bow across the strings
(B) Turning off the lights in the studio
(C) Taking off the shirt
(D) Tightening the bow

Item 3 (Academic Listening, p. 164)

How does Begley explain the crucial brain functions that babies are born with?
(A) By presenting examples of essential bodily activities
(B) By contrasting the babies' abilities with those of adults
(C) By explaining the connection between music and the brain
(D) By describing the research of neuroscientists on babies

Item 4 (Campus Conversation, p. 163)

If necessary, listen again to part of the conversation.

> **Counselor:** The bottom line is if you want to be a jazz musician, you may also need to do other work to make ends meet. But that doesn't mean you can't continue your music. You just need to choose a career path that will provide time for music *and* steady employment. What about teaching? Do you like children?

Why does the counselor ask, "What about teaching? Do you like children?"?
(A) To start a discussion about the student's childhood
(B) To introduce an idea about a possible career
(C) To discourage the student from continuing her music
(D) To remind the student about her interest in children

Tips

To do well on the TOEFL, it is essential to learn how to identify and use cohesive devices. Cohesive devices are words and phrases that connect parts of a written or spoken text and signal the writer or speaker's organization or ideas.

- Look for the following cohesive devices within sentences, between sentences or paragraphs, or across larger parts of texts. When you speak or write, use the same types of cohesive devices.

  Repeated words: key words and word form variants repeated to link ideas in a text

  Specific and general words: general category words that refer back to specific words, such as *animal/cat*

  Synonyms: words with the same or similar meaning that connect parts of the text

  Pronouns: words that refer back to previous words or ideas

  Transition words: connecting words that show relationships between ideas, such as *in fact, for example, as a result, after,* or *but*

In **Item 1,** the inserted sentence makes reference to the cellist's *body* and *living space*. These ideas are introduced in the words *arms* and *apartment* just before point (D) in the reading. Thus, (D) is the correct place to insert the sentence.

To answer **Item 2,** you probably reread the sentences surrounding the word *it* and determined that this word was used to repeat the idea of drawing the bow across the strings—choice (A).

In **Item 3,** you probably took notes on the main point in this part of the interview and recognized that the speaker presented examples to clarify this point, using the phrase "things like that" to signal that she was including examples.

In **Item 4,** you probably recognized that the counselor's final questions suggested a career path that will provide time for music and steady employment, an idea that was previously mentioned in the conversation.

PRACTICE

1 *Read the passage on the next page. Use the tips from the previous section to help you complete the activities that follow.*

THE CELLIST OF SARAJEVO

By Paul Sullivan (from *Reader's Digest*)

1   On May 27, 1992, in Sarajevo, one of the few bakeries that still had a supply of flour was making and distributing bread to the starving, war-shattered people. At 4 P.M. a long line stretched into the street. Suddenly, a mortar shell fell directly into the middle of the line, killing 22 people and splattering flesh, blood, bone, and rubble.

2   Not far away lived a 35-year-old musician named Vedran Smailovic. Before the war he had been a cellist with the Sarajevo Opera, a distinguished career to which he patiently longed to return. But when he saw the carnage from the massacre outside his window, he was pushed past his capacity to absorb and endure any more. Anguished, he resolved to do the thing he did best: make music. Public music, daring music, music on a battlefield.

3   For each of the next 22 days, at 4 P.M., Smailovic put on his full, formal concert attire, took up his cello and walked out of his apartment into the midst of the battle raging around him. Placing a plastic chair beside the crater that the shell had made, he played in memory of the dead Albinoni's *Adagio in G minor*, one of the most mournful and haunting pieces in the classical repertoire. He played to the abandoned streets, smashed trucks and burning buildings, and to the terrified people who hid in the cellars while the bombs dropped and bullets flew. With masonry exploding around him, he made his unimaginably courageous stand for human dignity, for those lost to war, for civilization, for compassion and for peace. Though the shellings went on, he was never hurt.

4   After newspapers picked up the story of this extraordinary man, an English composer, David Wilde, was so moved that he, too, decided to make music. He wrote a composition for unaccompanied cello, "The Cellist of Sarajevo," into which he poured his feelings of outrage, love, and brotherhood with Vedran Smailovic.

2 *Find the following cohesive devices in the passage and write them below. How do these devices help to organize the text or show the writer's purpose?*

1. Cohesive transition words to connect the following paragraphs.

Paragraphs 2 and 3: _____

_____

Paragraphs 3 and 4: _____

_____

2. Words that refer to Vedran Smailovic: _____

_____

3. Repeated words (including word form variants): _____

_____

4. General/specific words that describe the war scenes: _____

_____

3 *Answer the questions. Work with a partner and discuss the cohesive devices that helped you choose your answers.*

1. Which of the following phrases most accurately reflects the significance of the duration of Smailovic's performances?
   (A) One day for every day that the shellings continued
   (B) One day for each person killed in the bakery line
   (C) One day for each year of Smailovic's life
   (D) One day for each neighbor who hid in cellars

2. Look at the four squares ☐ that indicate where the following sentence could be added to the passage. Where would the sentence best fit? Circle the letter that shows the point where you would insert this sentence.

   Unfortunately, the months of bombing had destroyed the city's music hall and had forced him to suspend that career indefinitely.

   Not far away lived a 35-year-old musician named Vedran Smailovic. **A** Before the war he had been a cellist with the Sarajevo Opera, a distinguished career to which he patiently longed to return. **B** But when he saw the carnage from the massacre outside his window, he was pushed past his capacity to absorb and endure any more. **C** Anguished, he resolved to do the thing he did best: make music. Public music, daring music, music on a battlefield. **D**

   For each of the next 22 days, at 4 P.M., Smailovic put on his full, formal concert attire, took up his cello and walked out of his apartment into the midst of the battle raging around him.

4 *Take notes on the main ideas of the passage. Then use your notes to prepare a one-minute summary of the passage. Include cohesive devices to connect ideas. Work with a partner. Take turns summarizing the passage.*

Freedom of Expression

| LISTENING |

Campus Conversation   A student editor and faculty advisor discuss running a controversial advertisement in their college newspaper.

Academic Listening   Journalism class lecture on television regulation

| READING |

Report   *The Web War: Lawmakers versus Librarians*

| WRITING |

Integrated Task: Read, Listen, Write   Discuss the conflicting opinions about censorship presented in a listening and a reading.

| SPEAKING |

Independent Task   State your opinion about government regulations of television, movies, or video games.

| SKILL FOCUS |

Identifying and Using Rhetorical Structure   Identifying and using rhetorical structure means you understand the relationships among facts and ideas in different parts of a spoken or written passage.

| TOEFL® iBT TARGET SKILLS |

- Identify and express main ideas
- Identify and express details
- Make inferences
- Complete a chart of important points and details
- Analyze the organization of a reading
- Prepare structured notes to present conflicting opinions

 For extra practice of TOEFL iBT skills, go to pages 242–259.

1 Listening

CAMPUS CONVERSATION

PRE-LISTENING VOCABULARY

Read the sentences. Guess the meaning of the boldfaced words and phrases. Write your ideas on the lines. Then match each word or phrase with a definition or synonym from the list on the next page. Work with a partner and compare your answers.

_____ 1. I'm writing a **term paper** on ancient methods of accounting. So far, my research has focused on the use of clay tablets and jars to record accounts in the Middle East.

_____

_____ 2. In English class, our professor explained the college rules on **plagiarism**. Then we practiced quoting and citing sources of information.

_____

_____ 3. College professors are concerned about **academic integrity**. They want to know that the work students do for grades is their own work, not copied from others.

_____

_____ 4. Some people believe that the government should **censor** Internet sites displaying content that is inappropriate for children, whereas others argue that the Internet should not be regulated.

_____

_____ 5. In 1996, the U.S. Congress passed the Communications Decency Act, which **bans** the communication of obscene or indecent material via the Internet to anyone under eighteen years of age.

_____

_____ 6. Our class time is almost over, so let me **wrap it up** by saying that the ownership of newspapers has shifted in recent years.

_____

_____ 7. Journalists must maintain a high standard of **ethics** in their profession. They must be honest and fair in gathering, reporting, and interpreting information.

_____

_____ 8. Student A: The food in the cafeteria has really gotten worse.
Student B: **I'm with you!** Let's write a letter to complain.

_____

_____ **9.** Unless you have a **compelling** excuse, such as a serious illness, I expect you to come to chemistry class on Wednesday with your finished lab report.

_____

_____ **10.** I believe we should have the right to speak out against the government. This is **where I stand** on freedom of speech.

_____

_____ **11.** Airline companies have kept their passenger lists private for many years, but recently, some airlines have been debating whether to start giving passenger information to the government or to maintain the **status quo**.

_____

_____ **12.** You make good points in favor of freedom of speech, but you need to **tone down** your language. Instead of calling book censorship *ridiculous*, use a less emotional word such as *unfair*.

_____

a. agree

b. being honest and having high principles in school work

c. convincing

d. examine material and remove any offensive parts

e. finish something

f. my opinion about

g. presenting someone else's words or ideas as your own

h. principles of behavior

i. prohibits

j. research report

k. soften

l. state of a situation at a particular time

Culture Note: Academic integrity is a serious issue at colleges and universities. The typical academic honesty policy, published in student handbooks and college catalogs, explains a school's policies on plagiarism and cheating (looking at another student's exam, taking notes into the exam room, and so on). Academic dishonesty has increased dramatically in the past few years, because the Internet makes it easy for students to buy term papers online and plagiarize them. Students found guilty of academic dishonesty face punishment ranging from warnings to expulsion from school.

FIRST LISTENING

Read the questions. Listen to a conversation between a student editor of a college newspaper and the newspaper advisor, a professor of journalism. Take notes as you listen. Share your notes with a partner. Then use your notes to answer the questions.

1. What are the professor and the student discussing?

   _____

2. What concern does the professor have about the newspaper?

   _____

3. What does the student say in reaction to the professor's concern?

   _____

SECOND LISTENING

Read the questions. Listen to the conversation again. Add details to your notes. Then use your notes to answer the questions. Work with a partner and compare your answers.

1. What is the conversation mainly about?
   (A) Writing a student editorial on freedom of the press
   (B) Printing a controversial advertisement in the school paper
   (C) Establishing stricter policies on plagiarism at a college
   (D) Analyzing the college's reaction to companies that sell essays

2. What problem does the faculty advisor find with the latest issue of the student newspaper?
   (A) The issue of the paper is not finished yet.
   (B) The editor does not have enough advertisements.
   (C) Some faculty may oppose an ad in the paper.
   (D) He does not like the student's idea for an editorial.

3. Which of the following is true about the college's new policy on plagiarism?
   (A) Student editors can be expelled for printing term paper ads.
   (B) The newspaper can be shut down if it runs term paper ads.
   (C) The student paper will lose money if it does not print ads.
   (D) Students can be expelled for turning in a purchased term paper.

Listen again to part of the conversation. Then answer question 4.

4. What is the faculty advisor's opinion of banning term paper advertisements?
   (A) It is an excellent way to reduce plagiarism.
   (B) It is not an effective way to decrease plagiarism.
   (C) It may reduce plagiarism if faculty talk about the issue.
   (D) It may increase the frequency of plagiarism on campus.

Listen again to part of the conversation. Then answer question 5.

5. What is the student editor's attitude toward the newspaper's need to advertise?
   (A) She is quite happy about it.
   (B) She is very angry about it.
   (C) She is unconcerned about it.
   (D) She is somewhat unhappy about it.

6. What does the faculty advisor suggest that the student editor do in the end?
   (A) Omit the term paper advertisement
   (B) Refuse to print any ads for term papers
   (C) Meet to decide whether to print the ad
   (D) Print the term paper advertisement

ACADEMIC LISTENING

FIRST LISTENING

Listen to a lecture by a journalism professor. Take notes to fill in the outline below. Work with a partner to combine your notes.

Main Idea: Government regulation of television has had limited success and will continue to be a challenge in the future.

Original problems/reasons for regulation

- watching TV violence leads to violent behavior
-
-

(continued on next page)

Solutions

Telecommunications Act

TV industry responsibility: _____

-
-
-

Manufacturer responsibility: _____

-
-

Continuing problems

V-chips

- ineffective
-
-
-

Ratings system

-
-
-

SECOND LISTENING

Read the questions. Listen to the lecture again. Add details to your notes. Then use your notes to answer the questions. Work with a partner and compare your answers.

1. What is the lecture mainly about?
   (A) The drawbacks of the TV rating system
   (B) The problems with the TV V-chip
   (C) The debate about the effectiveness of TV regulation
   (D) The contrast between TV and movie regulations

2. According to the professor, what was the main complaint that led to TV regulation?
   (A) Violence
   (B) Inappropriate language
   (C) Sexual content
   (D) Freedom of speech

Listen again to part of the lecture. Then answer question 3.

3. What is the professor's attitude when he says, "Most Americans don't even know their TV has a V-chip."?
(A) He is pleased.
(B) He is sympathetic.
(C) He is doubtful.
(D) He is troubled.

Listen again to part of the lecture. Then answer question 4.

4. What is the professor's attitude toward the TV stations' position on V-chips?
(A) He is amused.
(B) He is critical.
(C) He is nervous.
(D) He is apologetic.

5. How does the professor evaluate the TV ratings system?
(A) By giving examples of programming changes
(B) By comparing it to the movie ratings system
(C) By contrasting points of view about the ratings
(D) By explaining how it operates

ANALYSIS

It is helpful to know the purpose of a test item. There are three types of questions in the listening section.

1. Basic Comprehension

- main ideas
- details
- the meaning of specific sentences

2. Organization

- the way information is structured
- the way ideas are linked

3. Inference

- ideas are not directly stated
- speaker's intention, purpose, or attitude not explicitly stated

Go back to the listening questions and label each question with 1, 2, or 3. Then work with a partner to see if you agree. Check the Answer Key for the correct answers. Which questions did you get right? Which did you get wrong? What skills do you need to practice?

2 Reading

THE WEB WAR: LAWMAKERS VERSUS LIBRARIANS

PRE-READING

Work with a partner. Read the questions. Then preview the passage that follows to answer the questions. Read the title of the passage, the entire first paragraph, the first and last sentences of paragraphs 2 through 5, and the entire last paragraph.

1. What is the main organization type used in the passage?
   (A) Argumentation—argues or explains one or more viewpoints, presenting reasons to support the view(s)
   (B) Comparison/Contrast—implies that similarities and/or differences exist between two or more subjects; concludes that the subjects are either more similar or more different, or one is better than the other(s)
   (C) Cause/Effect—traces the causes and/or the effects of one subject on another
   (D) Problem/Solution—describes a problem or problems and the actual or possible solution(s)

2. What clues (words, phrases) in the passage helped you identify its overall organization?

   _____

   _____

   _____

READING

Read the passage on the next page and answer the questions. Then work with a partner and compare your answers. When you disagree, go back to the text to find helpful information.

The Web War:
Lawmakers versus Librarians

1   A censorship battle between protecting freedom of speech and protecting children from harmful Internet material is being fought on a rather unlikely field—the public library. In almost every city, town, and village in the United States there is a public library, and every one of them now has computer terminals for public use. On one side of the battle, the American Library Association (ALA) is opposed to content filters on library computers with Internet access. On the opposing side, the U.S. Supreme Court ruled that libraries must install filters to block indecent websites from library patrons under the age of eighteen. For the time being, the battle scene has stilled, but the ultimate winners in the all-out war for access versus control of the Web in public libraries have yet to be declared.

2   The debate first raged in the U.S. due to the enactment of the federal Children's Internet Protection Act (CIPA) in 1999. Public libraries—including school libraries—were forced to install content filters on Internet access terminals or lose certain federal funding. In response, the ALA started a legal battle to have the requirement reversed. In its 1943 Bill of Rights, the ALA said that libraries should present materials that represent many points of view on current and historical issues and not remove materials with unpopular viewpoints. At the same time, it is the responsibility of libraries to challenge censorship

if they suspect it. However, in 2003, the Supreme Court ruled that the filtering was constitutional, and the law should stand.

3   In its decision, the Supreme Court found that filters are "at least as effective" as government regulation of website operators. Earlier laws imposed criminal punishments on website operators for publishing harmful material. In contrast, CIPA places the burden on those who receive federal funds—public libraries and school districts—to ensure that children do not have access to obscene, pornographic, or other harmful images and text. According to supporters of the law, filters effectively keep out harmful Web content and do not have a negative impact on users.

4   Whereas some libraries such as the San Francisco library system oppose the law and have stated they will not abide by it, other libraries favor the filters and had even used blocking software on their computers before the law required it. In

1998, 15 percent of U.S. libraries used Internet filters, according to one survey. In the middle are libraries that have compromised by installing filters only on library terminals reserved for children.

5   Opponents rightly argue that legitimate research sites are being blocked by excessive and harmful filters. They point to numerous examples of harmless websites—such as home pages of religious and academic institutions—that are blocked by the filter software. Anti-filter groups also charge that the devices do not filter out a substantial portion of inappropriate Internet material. A recent study found that the filters failed to block the transmission of pornography, violence, and hate speech 25 percent of the time.

6   Dr. Martha McCarthy, an education professor at Indiana University, expects the Web war between lawmakers and librarians to continue to produce court battles. "Despite the Supreme Court decision, there may be challenges to the application of CIPA in some public libraries," said McCarthy. For instance, she said that adults may allege that it is too complicated to turn off the filters when they want to use the computers. She went on to say that the battle between freedom of speech and protection of children is likely to continue with regard to content on the Internet. Clearly, the government needs to find a more viable solution, or the free expression war will continue to rage.

1. What is the passage mainly about?
   (A) The reasons that libraries oppose Internet censorship
   (B) The effects of Internet censorship on children in libraries
   (C) The debate over blocking harmful Internet sites at libraries
   (D) The disadvantages of Internet blocking software in libraries

2. According to paragraph 2, what set off the argument about censorship in libraries?
   (A) The passage of the federal CIPA
   (B) The Supreme Court decision
   (C) The loss of federal funding
   (D) The battle to reverse the law

3. The word *enactment* in paragraph 2 is closest in meaning to
   (A) approval
   (B) passage
   (C) writing
   (D) announcement

4. In paragraph 3, the author's primary purpose is
   (A) To describe how public libraries use the Internet
   (B) To contrast the CIPA with earlier censorship laws
   (C) To identify the recipients of federal funding
   (D) To explain how earlier Internet censorship laws worked

5. In paragraph 5, why does the author mention religious and academic institutions?
   (A) To show how effective Internet blocking software can be
   (B) To illustrate that filters may fail to block harmful sites
   (C) To explain what types of research sites library patrons use
   (D) To show that the blocking software may target the wrong sites

6. The word *They* in paragraph 5 refers to
   (A) research sites
   (B) filters
   (C) examples
   (D) opponents

7. The word *substantial* in paragraph 5 is closest in meaning to
   (A) large
   (B) unimportant
   (C) decent
   (D) unacceptable

8. According to paragraph 2, what can be inferred about the ALA's position on Internet censorship?
   (A) The ALA has significantly changed its views.
   (B) The ALA continues to support censorship laws.
   (C) The ALA has a tradition of supporting freedom of speech.
   (D) The ALA does not take a strong stand on freedom of speech.

9. Which of the following statements about Internet censorship can be inferred from paragraph 6?
   (A) It illustrates the larger issue of freedom versus protection of minors.
   (B) It will become acceptable to most library users in the future.
   (C) It will not be argued in the future because of the Supreme Court decision.
   (D) It will probably be put into operation easily in public libraries.

10. Select the appropriate phrases from the answer choices below and match them to the group they characterize. ONE of the answer choices will NOT be used.

Lawmakers	**Librarians**
• _____	• _____
• _____	• _____
• _____	• _____

   (A) Oppose Internet access in public and school libraries
   (B) Believe that filters block legitimate research sites
   (C) Argue that filters do not negatively affect users
   (D) Supported CIPA through a court decision

(continued on next page)

(E) Required libraries to install Internet filters
(F) Want to present ideas with different points of view
(G) Challenge censorship when they believe it exists

11. Look at the four squares ☐ that indicate where the following sentence could be added to the passage. Where would the sentence best fit? Circle the letter that shows the point where you would insert this sentence.

> For example, between 1995 and 1999, at least thirteen U.S. states passed legislation that levied fines and other sanctions against websites displaying pornography, violence, and other harmful material.

In its decision, the Supreme Court found that filters are "at least as effective" as government regulation of website operators. [A] Earlier laws imposed criminal punishments on website operators for publishing harmful material. [B] In contrast, CIPA places the burden on those who receive federal funds—public libraries and school districts—to ensure that children do not have access to obscene, pornographic, or other harmful images and text. [C] According to supporters of the law, filters effectively keep out harmful Web content and do not have a negative impact on users.

[D] Whereas some libraries such as the San Francisco library system oppose the law and have stated they will not abide by it, other libraries favor the filters and had even used blocking software on their computers before the law required it.

12. Which of the following best expresses the essential information in this sentence from the passage?

> In contrast, CIPA places the burden on those who receive federal funds—public libraries and school districts—to ensure that children do not have access to obscene, pornographic, or other harmful images and text.

(A) The CIPA law ensures that only libraries and schools that get federal money are targeted.
(B) The law safeguards children from obscene or harmful information.
(C) CIPA wants to make sure that children have access to federal funds.
(D) The law makes libraries and schools ensure that children do not access harmful material.

3 Writing

INTEGRATED TASK: READ, LISTEN, WRITE

In this section, you will read a short passage and listen to an excerpt on a related topic. Then you will write about the relationship between the two.

READING

Read the passage. As you read, fill in the following summary chart.

IMPORTANT POINTS	DETAILS
Censorship statistics	• increasing in U.S.—35% increase in past year • •
Reasons behind censorship	• upholding community values • • •

Author's reaction to censorship	•
	
	•
	
	• disturbed by attacks against books that express ideas that censors disagree with:
	    •
	    •
	
	•
	
	•
	
	•

BOOK BANNING MUST BE STOPPED

By Marcia Cohen (adapted from an article in *Seventeen*)

1   Censorship of textbooks and other books in school libraries appears to be increasing in all parts of the country. People for the American Way, a Washington-based lobby group that recently conducted its fourth annual study of censorship, reports that incidents of censorship have increased 35 percent in the past year. In the past four years these incidents have more than doubled. Last July, the American Library Association published a list of more than five hundred books that have been banned, challenged, or removed from schools and public libraries around the country, ranging from *Harriet the Spy*, by Louise Fitzhugh (considered "dangerous" because it "teaches children to

lie, spy, back-talk, and curse"), to *The Merchant of Venice*, by William Shakespeare (purportedly anti-Semitic).

2   Often under the guise of upholding community values, censors attack books for profane or obscene language or for scenes of sex and violence. Apparently they believe that by shielding us, they will discourage us from adopting undesirable attitudes, speech, and behavior. The censors may mean well; however, I don't think teenagers encounter many words or details in books that they have not already been exposed to in real life. Besides, I am no more apt to swear after reading *Go Ask Alice* than I am to speak in blank verse after reading *Macbeth*.

3   Even more disturbing to me than attacks on so-called dirty books are those against books that express ideas with which censors—who are often political, social, or religious extremists— disagree. In Alabama, the state textbook committee rejected thirty-seven textbooks after various conservative groups had objected that the books failed to reflect certain "religious and social philosophies." In Oregon, environmentalists wanted to remove a social studies book because they believed it contained "pro-industry propaganda."

4   This kind of censorship alarms me because it resonates with intolerance. Why must our access to reading materials be denied simply because they violate some group's aesthetic, moral, religious, or political views? Why should one group be allowed to impose its views on an entire classroom, school, or state? By submitting to the demands of one group, don't we limit the freedom of another?

LISTENING

Listen to a radio interview. Use the outline to take notes as you listen.

Main Idea: Support for media censorship is increasing because many citizens think the media are contributing to a decline in family and moral values.

Current trends in media censorship

-
-

Reasons for stricter regulation

-
-

Concerns of a busy mother

-
-
-
-
-

Views of a parent of a tenth-grader

-
-
-
-
-

WRITING

Write on the following topic. Follow the steps below to prepare.

> Discuss the conflicting opinions about censorship presented in the listening and reading passages.

Step 1

- Work with a partner. Skim the reading and your notes from the reading and listening tasks (pages 191–193) to answer the following questions.

    1. What are the main reasons behind censorship, according to the reading?

    2. What reasons for censorship does the listening discuss?

    3. What reasons against censorship does the author of the reading passage give?

- Work in a group. Discuss reasons for and against censorship. Use your answers to the questions above to help you. Take notes to fill in the chart below.

REASONS FOR CENSORSHIP	REASONS AGAINST CENSORSHIP

- On your own, evaluate what you have heard. Which reasons on each side can you write about most effectively? Which details should you include to support these points?

- Organize your ideas by following the outline below.

Introduction—Thesis Statement

Introduce the situation, and briefly state the two sides of the issue.

Body

State the reasons on each side of the debate, and support the reasons with explanations and examples. Use one of these patterns:

Point-by-point pattern:

Present one pro-censorship reason and support it. Then, in the same paragraph, respond to this argument by presenting the anti-censorship position and supporting it. Repeat this pattern in the rest of the body paragraphs.

Block pattern:

Present the pro-censorship reasons in one body paragraph. Support the reasons. Present the anti-censorship reasons in another body paragraph. Add support.

Conclusion

Briefly summarize the debate and the two sides' reasons.

Possible concluding ideas:

Predict the future of the debate, or recommend solutions to the issues.

Step 2

Write for 20 minutes. Leave the last 5 minutes to edit your work.

To evaluate a partner's writing, use the Writing Evaluation Form on page 203.

4 Speaking

INDEPENDENT TASK

Speak on the following topic. Follow the steps on the next page to prepare.

State your opinion about government regulations of television, movies, or video games. Should these regulations exist? Do they work? How could they be improved?

Step 1

- Work in a group. Take turns discussing the regulations that you know about, how they work, and whether they could be improved. Include details to support your opinion. Take notes on ideas from your discussion.

- On your own, evaluate what you have heard. Do your group members consider TV, movie, and video game regulations effective? Could the systems for regulating these media be improved? Which ideas and details can you use in your response?

- Organize your ideas by filling in the chart below with the main points about the regulations that you will discuss. For each point, include details and your evaluation.

REGULATION OF _____

MAIN POINT	DETAILS	EVALUATION

Step 2

With a partner, take turns practicing a one-minute oral response to the topic. Be sure to use the information in your chart to help you.

Step 3

Change partners. Take turns giving a one-minute response to the topic again.

To evaluate your partner's response, use the Speaking Evaluation Form on page 204.

5 Skill Focus

IDENTIFYING AND USING RHETORICAL STRUCTURE

EXAMINATION

1 *Look at the following items from the unit. Work with a partner and answer the questions about the items.*

- How did you identify the organizational patterns and understand the relationships among ideas, information, and sections in the texts? Did you pay attention to the use of key words or expressions?

- For Item 1, go back to the pre-reading section (page 186) and review the clues that helped you find the correct answer.

- For Item 2, did you include key words and expression in your notes? Go back to your notes and mark the parts that helped you answer the item. If necessary, listen again to the lecture and take notes on the parts that helped you.

- For Item 3, mark the parts of the inserted sentence and the passage that helped you know where to insert the sentence.

Item 1 (Pre-reading, p. 186)

What is the main organization type used in the passage?
(A) Argumentation—argues or explains one or more viewpoints, presenting reasons to support the view(s)
(B) Comparison/Contrast—implies that similarities and/or differences exist between two or more subjects; concludes that the subjects are either more similar or more different, or one is better than the other(s)
(C) Cause/Effect—traces the causes and/or the effects of one subject on another
(D) Problem/Solution—describes a problem or problems and the actual or possible solution(s)

Item 2 (Academic Listening, p. 185)

How does the professor evaluate the TV ratings system?
(A) By giving examples of programming changes
(B) By comparing it to the movie ratings system
(C) By contrasting points of view about the ratings
(D) By explaining how it operates

Item 3 (Reading, p. 190)

Look at the four squares ☐ that indicate where the following sentence could be added to the passage. Where would the sentence best fit? Circle the letter that shows the point where you would insert this sentence.

For example, between 1995 and 1999, at least thirteen U.S. states passed legislation that levied fines and other sanctions against websites displaying pornography, violence, and other harmful material.

In its decision, the Supreme Court found that filters are "at least as effective" as government regulation of website operators. $\boxed{A}$ Earlier laws imposed criminal punishments on website operators for publishing harmful material. $\boxed{B}$ In contrast, CIPA places the burden on those who receive federal funds—public libraries and school districts—to ensure that children do not have access to obscene, pornographic, or other harmful images and text. $\boxed{C}$ According to supporters of the law, filters effectively keep out harmful Web content and do not have a negative impact on users.

$\boxed{D}$ Whereas some libraries such as the San Francisco library system oppose the law and have stated they will not abide by it, other libraries favor the filters and had even used blocking software on their computers before the law required it.

2 *Look at the following task from the unit. Work with a partner and answer the questions about the task.*

Item 4 (Independent Task, p. 194)

State your opinions about government regulations of television, movies, or video games. Should these regulations exist? Do they work? How could they be improved?

- How did you decide which appropriate rhetorical structure(s), or organizational pattern(s), to use to organize your response to the topic?

- How did you show the relationships among ideas in your response? Go back to your notes for the task and mark any expressions that you used to indicate these relationships. Show them to your partner and discuss your choices.

Tips

To do well on the TOEFL, it is essential to learn how to identify and use rhetorical structures. Rhetorical structures are the patterns used to organize a text. These structures help readers and listeners understand the relationships among ideas, information, and sections in the text.

Listening and Reading

- Look and listen for rhetorical structures in the entire text or large passages in a text. The following are common rhetorical structures:

  Argumentation: argues or explains one or more viewpoints, presenting reasons to support the view(s)

(continued on next page)

Comparison/Contrast: implies that similarities and/or differences exist between two or more subjects; concludes that the subjects are either more similar or more different, or one is better than the other(s)

Cause/Effect: traces the causes and/or the effects of one subject on another

Problem/Solution: describes a problem or problems and the actual or possible solution(s)

- Pay attention to how one statement or passage of a text fits into the surrounding text. A statement or passage may:

  introduce or conclude a topic

  present an example or other information about a topic

  shift to a different topic, or digress from the topic

- Be aware of transitional expressions that may provide clues about relationships among ideas and rhetorical structures.

  Transitional expressions: *as a result, another . . . , for instance, in contrast, first,* and so on.

In **Item 1,** you probably noticed that the author used the argumentation structure to organize the passage. Each paragraph presented the opinions on opposite sides of a debate, using expressions such as "On one side of the battle" and "On the opposing side . . ."

In **Item 2,** the organization between statements and the professor's remark that "ratings don't work as well for TV as for movies" probably helped you recognize that the professor was contrasting the two systems.

In **Item 3,** you probably read the entire passage and considered the use of the expressions "For example" and "In contrast" to determine how the inserted sentence would best connect with the other sentences in the passage.

Speaking and Writing

- Choose appropriate rhetorical structure(s) to suit your topic and purpose.

- Use transitional expressions to show relationships among ideas and rhetorical patterns.

To organize your oral response to the topic in **Item 4,** you should have chosen the rhetorical structure that best supported your opinion. For example, to state that there are many problems with the current government regulations and to offer ideas for improvements, you could have used a problem/solution pattern. Throughout your response, you should have used appropriate transitional expressions to signal your ideas and the relationships among them.

PRACTICE

1 *Read the passages. As you read, fill in the chart below. Write the number of the passage that corresponds to each rhetorical structure. Take notes on words or expressions that helped you to identify the rhetorical structure.*

PASSAGE	MAIN RHETORICAL STRUCTURE	WORD/EXPRESSION CLUES
	comparison/contrast	
	cause/effect	
	argumentation	

Passage 1: Free Expression for Students?

Since 1988, there has been a growing debate in the United States about the free speech rights of students under eighteen years of age. Some people are happy that, in 1988, the Supreme Court, the highest court in the United States, changed its previous 1969 ruling which had given students the same right to free speech that adults have. In 1988, the Supreme Court ruled that students could not print articles on teen pregnancy, drug addiction, and divorce in a school newspaper. Supporters of this decision insist that high school students are not mature enough to deal with such sensitive issues. However, others maintain that if students are not allowed to present their views on such issues in school newspapers, they will not be prepared to participate fully in a democratic society's free exchange of ideas when they are no longer in school. For these people, the 1988 ruling legalized a form of censorship. They believe that not allowing students to *write* about these issues will also prevent other students from being able to *read* about the issues. Looking to the future, they wonder when they will succeed in convincing people that students have rights, too.

Passage 2: Banning Books

The fear of unpopular ideas has led to the censorship of books in U.S. schools, libraries, and bookstores. In some areas, parents, educators, and religious groups have pressured schools and libraries to ban books that do not favor certain religious beliefs. For example, many state textbook committees have rejected textbooks that support "secular humanism," a belief that places people above God, and they have instead adopted textbooks that support religious views about the creation of humans and the earth. Libraries and booksellers have also banned books which they thought contained too much sexual or immoral content. As a result, many books, such as *The Grapes of Wrath* by John Steinbeck and the Harry Potter series by J. K. Rowling, have been banned. In 1905, the New York Public Library removed *Huckleberry Finn* by Mark Twain, now considered a masterpiece of American literature, because it said the book used vulgar language.

Passage 3: The United States Then and Now

Some of the difficulties in making laws to govern free expression arise because the United States of today is very different from the United States of 1789, when the nation's freedom of speech laws were first written. First, the United States in 1789 was a small society of 3.9 million people who agreed on most moral and political issues. For example, most people were religious and held the same ideas about right and wrong behavior, families, the institution of marriage, and other subjects. They mostly came from Europe, so they shared similar cultural backgrounds. Also, they were politically united because most had supported the U.S. fight for independence from Great Britain. Of course, Native Americans and African slaves lived in the United States, but at the time these two groups did not influence lawmakers.

In contrast, today's United States is a huge, populous nation whose citizens have many different moral, political, and ideological values. The United States is no longer confined to the states along the Atlantic Coast; its population of nearly 300 million is spread out in fifty states. Some of today's Americans descend from those first European settlers, but more recent immigrants, the descendents of slaves, and Native Americans now raise their voices in society. Their views vary because of their diverse racial, cultural, religious, and political backgrounds. Some practice a religion, while others do not. Some favor marriage between men and women; others do not. Some Americans prefer government control of many areas of society, but others want less government interference in their lives. In part, these differences between Americans then and now explain why it is difficult to reach a consensus about laws controlling free expression.

2 *Speak on the topic of students' freedom of expression. Use the tips from the previous section and the information in Passage 1 on the previous page to help you. Prepare and present two separate responses using different rhetorical structures. Follow the steps below to prepare.*

Step 1

- Work in a group. Take turns discussing the following topics. Take notes as you discuss.

Topic 1: Argumentation

Do you agree or disagree that students under the age of eighteen should have freedom of expression? Give arguments and reasons to explain your opinion.

Topic 2: Comparison/Contrast

How do students' rights of free expression in the United States compare and contrast with the rights of students in another country that you know? Describe the main similarities and/or differences.

- Work with a partner. Evaluate what you have heard. Which ideas and details can you use in your own responses to the topics?

Step 2

For each topic, make an outline of the main points that you will present in your oral response. Use your notes from Step 1 to help you organize your ideas. Share your outline with your partner.

Step 3

- Work with your partner. Take turns giving a one-minute oral response to the first topic (argumentation). Use the information in your outline to help you.

- Take turns giving a one-minute oral response to the second topic (comparison/contrast). Use the information in your outline to help you.

Evaluation Forms for Integrated and Independent Tasks

Exchange papers with a partner. Evaluate each other's writing using the grid below. Discuss strengths and weaknesses. Use the evaluation to revise and edit your writing. Write a second draft and give it to your teacher.

4 = always **3** = most of the time **2** = some of the time **1** = rarely or never

UNIT	1	2	3	4	5	6	7	8	9	10
CONTENT										
The response . . .										
addresses the topic.										
is organized.										
shows connections between ideas.										
LANGUAGE										
The writing incorporates . . .										
effective vocabulary.										
correct grammar.										
correct spelling and punctuation.										
TOTAL:										

SPEAKING

As you and your partner respond to the topic, evaluate each other's speaking using the grid below. Discuss strengths and weaknesses. Use the evaluation to improve your presentation.

4 = always   **3** = most of the time   **2** = some of the time   **1** = rarely or never

UNIT	1	2	3	4	5	6	7	8	9	10
CONTENT										
The response ...										
addresses the topic.										
covers the main points.										
contains good examples.										
has ideas that connect well.										
LANGUAGE										
The response ...										
is free of hesitations.										
exhibits clear pronunciation.										
incorporates effective vocabulary.										
incorporates correct grammar.										
TOTAL:										

Audioscript

UNIT 1: Addiction

CAMPUS CONVERSATION

PAGE 3, FIRST LISTENING

Student: Professor Babcock, can I, uh, can I talk to you for a minute?

Professor: Sure, Lisa, this is my office hour. What's up?

S: Well, OK, I'm working on that paper you assigned—the one on drug addiction—and, well, I was wondering . . . You said the paper should be two to three pages, but could I write one that's, like, six pages?

P: *That's* a request I don't get too often.

S: It's just that I've done all this Internet research and I've found so much stuff—all these interesting details—and, you know, I'd just hate to leave any of them out of my paper.

P: But this paper is supposed to be an overview of the topic, Lisa, not a description of every drug addiction that ever existed.

S: I know. But I've spent so much time looking up stuff . . .

P: How much time are you talking about?

S: Well, let's see . . . I started two days ago and, uh, I think I spent about a couple of hours that day. Then, yesterday, I really started finding some good websites, so it was probably about five hours. It's just amazing how much stuff there is out there.

P: That's a lot of time. You know, the Internet is a wonderful tool—I use it for my own research—but you have to be careful that you don't become addicted to it. You don't want it to start doing your thinking for you.

S: But you can learn so much—there are so many websites—

P: And some of them are a lot more reliable than others—so, you need to be discriminating in your research. But apart from the reliability issue, there's just a point where you need to stop accumulating information . . . where you need to start understanding it. This paper will be a good exercise for you—you'll need to take all that information you've gathered, and summarize it in two to three pages. You can't just copy over every detail that turns up.

S: Well, I would never just copy material. I know it needs to be in my own words.

P: I'm sorry, Lisa, I wasn't suggesting you'd do anything unethical. In fact, it's obvious you're very hardworking. What I'm trying to get at . . . Look, I'd like every student to know how to do research, but what really matters is this: can you communicate the information you uncover—in a genuinely meaningful way? Being able to grasp . . . being able to describe the key points is a lot more important than knowing a bunch of facts and details.

S: So, I can't write a longer paper. You're saying I just have to throw out all these interesting details.

P: Not all of them—select a few to illustrate your paper's main themes. Tell you what, why don't you plan a little talk for the class—say, about five minutes—and you can share some of what you've learned—after everyone's turned in their papers.

S: OK. I wonder if anyone else spent as much time on the Internet as I did.

P: Honestly . . . As I said, it's a great tool, but I don't want to create a bunch of Internet addicts in this class.

S: I'll remember that. Thanks, professor.

PAGE 3, SECOND LISTENING

Listen again to part of the conversation. Then answer question 5.

S: I wonder if anyone else spent as much time on the Internet as I did.

P: Honestly . . . As I said, it's a great tool, but I don't want to create a bunch of Internet addicts in this class.

What does the professor mean when he says, "Honestly"?

ACADEMIC LISTENING

PAGE 4, FIRST LISTENING

Warren Levinson: It's *Newsweek on Air*. I'm Warren Levinson of the Associated Press.

David Alpern: I'm David Alpern of Newsweek.

WL: David Brooks, you argue that we already live in an overcommunicated world that will only become more so in the next tech era. What exactly do you mean by that?

David Brooks: The problem is that we've developed technology that gets us so much information that we've got cell phones ringing every second, we've got computers and laptops, we've got personal organizers and it's just—we're just being bombarded with communication and every advance and technology seems to create more and more communications at us. I do believe at the end of the day it shapes our personality because we are sort of overwhelmed by the information flow.

DA: Seriously though, just last week we reported on research suggesting that all the multi-tasking may actually make our brains work better and faster, producing, as it's been reported, a world-wide increase in IQ up to 20 points and more in recent decades. Can you see any benefit in all these mental gymnastics we now have to go through?

DB: Yeah, I, I don't think we're becoming a race of global idiots, uh, but I think certain skills are enhanced and certain are not. You know, the ability to make fast decisions, to answer a dozen e-mails in five minutes, uh, to fill out maybe big SAT-type tests. That's enhanced. But creativity is something that happens slowly. It happens when your brain is just noodling around, just playing. When it puts together ideas which you hadn't thought of or maybe you have time, say, to read a book. You are a businessperson, but you have time to read a book about history or time to read a book about a philosopher and something that happened long ago or something or some idea somebody thought of long ago. Actually, you know, it occurs to you that you can think of your own business in that way, and so it's this mixture of unrelated ideas, ah, that feeds your productivity, feeds your creativity, and if your mind is disciplined to answer every e-mail, then you don't have time for that playful noodling. You don't have time for those unexpected conjunctions, so I think maybe we're getting smarter in some senses, but I think it is a threat to our creativity and to our reflection.

DA: So how wired or wirelessly are you tied into the new technology?

DB: A total addict. When I'm out there with my kids playing in our little league or something like that, I've got my cell phone in my pocket. I'm always wondering, "Gee, did I get a voicemail?" uh and that's why I think I'm sort of driven to write about this because I do see the negative effects it's having on my own brain patterns.

DA: Could be *Newsweek on Air* calling . . . David Brooks thanks a lot.

DB: Thank you.

PAGE 5, SECOND LISTENING

Listen again to part of the interview. Then answer question 4.

DA: Seriously though, just last week we reported on research suggesting that all the multi-tasking may actually make our brains work better and faster, producing, as it's been reported, a world-wide increase in IQ up to 20 points and more in recent decades.

Why does David Alpern say, "Seriously though"?

Listen again to part of the interview. Then answer question 5.

DA: Seriously though, just last week we reported on research suggesting that all the multi-tasking may actually make our brains work better and faster, producing, as it's been reported, a world-wide increase in IQ up to 20 points and more in recent decades. Can you see any benefit in all these mental gymnastics we now have to go through?

DB: Yeah, I, I don't think we're becoming a race of global idiots uh, but I think certain skills are enhanced and certain are not.

What does Brooks mean when he says, "I don't think we're becoming a race of global idiots."?

INTEGRATED TASK

PAGE 11, LISTENING

Teresa: Hi. I'm Teresa. I became a compulsive shopper almost overnight. My job had become just too stressful. So, to unwind after work, I'd head off to the mall. I started buying small things I really didn't need, but then I started spending more and more, and coming home later and later. It was "shop 'til you drop." My spending spun out of control until I was overwhelmed with debt.

Olivia: Sounds familiar, Teresa. Hi, everyone. I'm Olivia. For me, work was not problematic at all. Rather, my personal life was a mess. The guy I had been dating for twelve years suddenly left me for another woman. So I ended up feeling nervous and unsettled; I started having sudden anxiety attacks.

Maria: You mean headaches, rapid heartbeat, and sweaty palms?

Olivia: Yeah, those were the symptoms. But as soon as I pulled out my credit card, my best friend, I felt better, kind of energized. I felt strangely satisfied and enhanced.

Maria: I feel the same when I hold that little piece of plastic. Oh . . . sorry . . . I forgot to introduce myself. I'm Maria. Whenever I feel sad or depressed, charging a hundred bucks on my card just cheers me up. I've tried a bunch of different strategies to try to kick the habit, but so far I haven't found a way to do it. So, now here I am . . . hoping you all will help.

UNIT 2: Communities

CAMPUS CONVERSATION

PAGE 21, FIRST LISTENING

Student 1: Hey, Sam.

Student 2: Hi, Tamara. How's it going? Have you found a roommate yet?

S1: Yeah. Jen and I have decided to live together. We want to live off campus, but it's so difficult finding decent housing that isn't too expensive.

S2: How about looking in the Museum district? There are tons of reasons to live there: It's close to campus. You wouldn't even have to take a bus. I've seen a lot of for-rent signs. There's also so much to do there—museums nearby, and great shopping. And there's a twenty-four-hour supermarket and video store right in the center. And it's very safe. I always see people walking around late at night.

S1: Do you know how much apartments in the Museum district go for? It's ridiculous! A couple of my professors live around there. As a matter of fact, I already checked into a few apartments around there, and the rents are sky high. When you add utilities, well, they're way out of my league.

S2: Hmmm, let's see, what other options are there? I know. What about Fairmont? The rents are cheap, but I'm not so sure about that neighborhood.

S1: I definitely don't want to live there. Parties on every corner. They go on all night long.

S2: You know, Tamara, I live in Lawndale. I like it a lot—everyone is very friendly. And it's a pretty safe neighborhood. And the rent is reasonable, even with utilities. But it's really far from campus. I take two buses to get here—at the bus stop no later than 7:20, rain or shine! . . . an hour and a half on crowded buses, and I still have to run to make my 9:00 class! I'd take my own car, but the parking fees are outrageous—sixty dollars a term! And you know how plentiful parking spaces are at 8:45 in the morning!

S1: I know what you mean. We considered Lawndale, but—you're right—it's too far from everything. Both of us work downtown, so it would be a real pain to figure out the bus routes from home to school and then to work. I'm about to give up!

S2: Hey, what about using an apartment locator?

S1: No way. One company kept my friend's $200 deposit even though they didn't end up finding him a decent apartment.

S2: Well, what can I say? I've run out of ideas. The Museum district is too expensive, Fairmont is too noisy, Lawndale is too far, and using an apartment locator is a waste of money!

S1: Hmmm . . . Maybe we could rent a huge house, large enough for all of our friends!

S2: Great idea! So . . . where is this ideal house?

S1: It would be one block from campus—only a short walk away. A big brick house, two stories. With six huge bedrooms, a big, modern kitchen, a pool. . . .

S2: Right—keep dreaming. Let's go get some lunch and we'll look at the classifieds in the campus newspaper. Maybe we'll even find your dream house!

PAGE 22, SECOND LISTENING

Listen again to part of the conversation. Then answer question 3.

S2: I take two buses to get here—at the bus stop no later than 7:20 . . . rain or shine! . . . an hour and a half on crowded buses and I still have to run to make my 9:00 class! I'd take my own car, but the parking fees are outrageous—sixty dollars a term! And you know how plentiful parking spaces are at 8:45 in the morning!

What is the student's attitude when he says, "And you know how plentiful parking spaces are at 8:45 in the morning!"?

Listen again to part of the conversation. Then answer question 4.

S2: The Museum district is too expensive, Fairmont is too noisy, Lawndale is too far, and using an apartment locator is a waste of money!

What is the student's purpose in saying this?

Listen again to part of the conversation. Then answer question 5.

S1: Hmmm . . . Maybe we could rent a huge house, large enough for all of our friends!

S2: Great idea! So . . . where is this ideal house?

S1: It would be one block from campus—only a short walk away.

Why does the male student ask, "So . . . where is this ideal house?"?

ACADEMIC LISTENING

PAGE 23, FIRST LISTENING

Douglas Frantz, co-author: You know, they've tried to look backward at small-town America and take the best of those planning elements—you know, houses close together, sidewalks, front porches, tree-lined streets, easy, non-automobile-dependent access to the town center and to your neighbors and to the school and the other institutions that are vital. And they've tried to take some of those ideas and update them and come up with a livable, workable place where people can go and rekindle the sense of community that seems to be missing from suburbs all across the country.

Terry Gross, host: So give us a sense of how this new town, Celebration, was designed.

DF: Houses are all very close together. We were just 10 feet apart from our neighbors on either side of us, and that's pretty much the standard for the town. So, you have houses that are close together, houses that surround open areas. They have a lot of big parks, a lot of common areas. The theory is that you're willing to sacrifice your private yard space—you don't need a quarter of an acre or half an acre—if you have a public

area where you can go and enjoy the facilities there and, most importantly, you can interact with your neighbors. That helps to create this sense of community that's so important to many of these "new town" developments.

TG: You know, this whole sense of, like, "It's going to be a new town, but we're going to do it with a sense of nostalgia for the past so nothing can be designed past what existed in the 1940s"—it seems—it just seems a little contradictory, and some of the designs from the 1940s didn't really transfer that well into the '90s. Like, a lot of the houses had porches.

DF: . . . what Disney expected with these front porches, what the planners envisioned was it would create a "front porch culture"—that people would be out on their porches talking to their neighbors next door and to people walking down the street or people riding their bikes, and there would be this culture that, you know, either existed or existed in somebody's imagination, you know, 30, 40, 50 years ago.

But that really has been one of the failures that we observed during our two years in Celebration, and people don't spend very much time at all on their front porches. There are a couple of things going on. One is it's central Florida, and it's hotter than hell a good part of the year, and sitting on your front porch, even if you have a fan going, can be a very uncomfortable thing. People prefer to be inside in the air-conditioning.

PAGE 23, SECOND LISTENING

Listen again to part of the interview. Then answer question 5.

DF: But that really has been one of the failures that we observed during our two years in Celebration, and people don't spend very much time at all on their front porches. There are a couple of things going on. One is it's central Florida . . .

What does Frantz mean when he says, "There are a couple of things going on."?

INTEGRATED TASK

PAGE 30, LISTENING

Professor: OK, today we're going to continue to discuss urbanization, focusing on urban sprawl. So, can anyone define urban sprawl? Matt?

Student 1: When cities keep spreading out, getting bigger?

P: Yes. This is part of urban sprawl. Most people define it as the growth of cities in an unplanned manner.

Urban sprawl is low density, outward growth—mostly single-family residences—not upward, like a city with multi-family residences.

Many consider urban sprawl to be very harmful, including environmental groups like the Sierra Club, which calls sprawl "irresponsible," a "cancer," a "virus" on the land. Sprawl misuses land that should be preserved for wildlife, parks, farmland, and it's robbing us of our nature, they say.

Traffic is another negative effect of sprawl . . . traffic jams between cities and suburbs . . . especially during morning and evening commutes.

But some people see benefits to sprawl. Let's see . . . real estate development, home construction, new businesses, better schools, less noise and crime . . . all are considered positive features.

Now, which U.S. cities have the greatest sprawl? Any guesses? Let's see . . . Emily?

Student 2: Los Angeles? Maybe Houston, Texas? It's amazing how spread-out those cities are.

P: OK, good guesses! In the 1990s, big California cities like L.A. were booming and sprawling. But recently, southern cities have had the greatest sprawl. Atlanta, Georgia, is number one, with Houston, Texas, next.

So . . . many see sprawl as a problem. And is anything being done to stop it? Actually, several major anti-sprawl movements have emerged, including New Urbanism.

New Urbanism's first principle says that regionally we must create transportation systems and environment protections—like forbidding tree removal, water pollution, or animal habitat destruction.

And next, cities should provide housing and jobs that are close together.

And finally, neighborhoods should have single and multi-family housing where residents can walk to stores, or they need public transportation, parks. New Urbanists believe that parks and walking will make people actually connect socially.

So you know . . . New Urbanism may bring some changes to cities in years to come.

UNIT 3: Personality

CAMPUS CONVERSATION

PAGE 41, FIRST LISTENING

Student: Professor Boukhlif? Do you have a minute?

Professor: Hi, Katy. Yes, come on in . . . I've got a *few* minutes. Take a seat. I'm just grading this week's test. I didn't see yours. Wait, you weren't in class on Monday, were you?

S: No. I . . . um . . . wasn't. I thought . . . Well, to tell the truth, I didn't feel ready for the test. I'm really feeling overwhelmed by Arabic class.

P: Really? You always seem so enthusiastic, so willing to learn. Let's see. Your class grade is a C. Hmmm, you didn't do that well on the first test, did you? You got a fifty-five. But you can drop the lowest test grade. And we'll have at least ten more exams. You'll have lots of chances to bring up your grade. Why don't we make an appointment for you to make up the test? How about today at . . .

S: Professor Boukhlif, I feel really bad about this, but I think I should drop the class. I don't know how well I can do on this test. The problem is, I just don't understand it. Arabic is a lot harder than I thought. I mean, this is only beginning Arabic and I find it really hard. It's me, I know. Maybe I just can't learn it. It takes me hours just to memorize the vocabulary. And . . .

P: Katy, if it were someone else, I might agree, but you're a good student. You obviously have a gift for learning languages. You've studied Spanish and French and done well. What makes you think you can't learn Arabic, too?

S: My schedule is really tough this semester. When I realized how many projects and papers and tests were coming in such a short time, I got really nervous. I know I haven't spent enough time on Arabic and I feel as if I'm falling further and further behind.

P: Hmm . . . Let me think. If you got a tutor, maybe you wouldn't find it so difficult. As a matter of fact, there's a really good Arabic tutor in the Learning Lab this term. I know his

hours are flexible. You could make a standing appointment with him once or twice a week. And you can fit it into your schedule when it's convenient. And there's a great website—an Arabic online school. It's free for students. Here's the website. Try it. I really don't want you to drop. It's only the third week of classes. Katy, just give it another try.

I've got a meeting in ten minutes. Can you come back at two and we'll go over Chapters 1 and 2? Maybe I can help you with some of the material that's giving you trouble and you can get caught up. Then, we can reschedule the test.

S: I don't know . . . Well, I guess I could try.

P: Good!! You know, there are a couple of things I always tell my freshmen. It's important to have a positive attitude. Be confident. Tell yourself "I can do it!" And if you run into difficulties, ask for help.

S: Okay. I won't drop. I'll see you later—at two, right? And could you write down the name of that tutor? I'll drop by now and see if I can make an appointment.

P: Here. I'm glad you're willing to stick it out. I know you can do this.

S: Thanks for your support, Professor Boukhlif.

PAGE 42, SECOND LISTENING

Listen again to part of the conversation. Then answer question 3.

P: Why don't we make an appointment for you to make up the test? How about today at . . .

S: Professor Boukhlif, I feel really bad about this, but I think I should drop the class.

Why does the student say, "I feel really bad about this"?

Listen again to part of the conversation. Then answer question 4.

P: And there's a great website—an Arabic online school. It's free for students. Here's the website. Try it.

What can be inferred about the professor?

ACADEMIC LISTENING

PAGE 43, FIRST LISTENING

Host: If you're the sort to divide people into two groups, consider the division between those who always see the bright side and those who'd rather wallow in their misery.

Julie Danis tackles the Pollyanna syndrome in today's *Tale from the Workplace.*

Julie Danis: I'm Julie Danis with *Tales from the Workplace.*

Arriving at the office after a visit to the eye doctor with no diagnosis for my blurred vision, I was in a grouchy mood. "No time to be cranky," a co-worker said, "we have a project due." "Besides," she continued, "now you have a prescription to skip the mascara and rest your eyes, every two hours."

She'd done it again, I realized. She had made lemonade out of lemons. We all know people like this. They find the silver lining inside the darkest cloud . . . all the time . . . without fail . . . driving others to distraction with their "find the bright side" philosophy.

"Oh well," they say, "a stop-and-go commute is perfect for listening to language tapes while doing relaxation exercises, *mais oui*?"

They may emit an occasional, "Oh, no," when the computer crashes and the hold time on the 1-800-HELP line promises to be hours. But that is soon replaced by an, "Oh good, time to purge the files."

This optimistic outlook does have its merits. When you're snowed in with no hope of flying for 24 hours or more, take it as a sign you should catch up on some movies.

But don't get carried away. Nothing will take away the ache in your mouth or fill the void in your pocketbook from two root canals not covered by your company's health plan.

So, the next time someone says, "You can't cry over something that can't cry over you," assert yourself in the face of their sunny-side-up point of view. State firmly, "Yes I can, and I plan to do just that." Then go suck on some lemons and feel better in your own way.

I'm Julie Danis with *Tales from the Workplace*.

PAGE 43, SECOND LISTENING

Listen again to part of the commentary. Then answer question 3.

JD: Arriving at the office after a visit to the eye doctor with no diagnosis for my blurred vision, I was in a grouchy mood. "No time to be cranky," a co-worker said, "we have a project due." "Besides," she continued, "now you have a prescription to skip the mascara and rest your eyes, every two hours."

She'd done it again, I realized. She had made lemonade out of lemons.

What does the speaker mean when she says, "She had made lemonade out of lemons."?

Listen again to part of the commentary. Then answer question 4.

JD: We all know people like this. They find the silver lining inside the darkest cloud . . . all the time . . . without fail . . . driving others to distraction with their "find the bright side" philosophy.

"Oh well," they say, "a stop-and-go commute is perfect . . ."

What is the speaker's attitude toward the people she is describing?

Listen again to part of the commentary. Then answer question 5.

JD: So, the next time someone says, "You can't cry over something that can't cry over you," assert yourself in the face of their sunny-side-up point of view. State firmly, "Yes I can, and I plan to do just that." Then go suck on some lemons and feel better in your own way.

What does the speaker mean when she says, "Then go suck on some lemons and feel better in your own way."?

INTEGRATED TASK

PAGE 50, LISTENING

Student 1: Hi! Melissa, right?

Student 2: Yes, Chris.

S1: How did you know my name? We've never talked.

S2: Well, the professor . . . um, everybody knows you.

S1: Yeah, Dr. J's great. I really like our classmates, too. So . . . our assignment: "Find one theory from the personality chapter that applies to both of us. Write our own personal case studies." How about Zimbardo's theory about types of shyness? That one resonates with me. I've never really been shy, but I could write about situations that make me a little shy, like giving a speech in class.

S2: I could certainly describe shyness.

S1: Really? That profile sounds pretty depressing. I mean, well . . .

S2: No. It's okay.

S1: Please. Tell me why you said that.

S2: Well, I guess I've always been shy. I'm scared to say something stupid. That's why I sit by myself. It's not rational, but ever since I was eight . . .

S1: What happened?

S2: I really don't like to talk about it.

S1: Please?

S2: Well, I was in a school play . . . I was on stage in front of everyone—teachers, students, parents—and I completely forgot my lines. I just stood there frozen, and then ran off, crying. They laughed! Ever since, I've been afraid to socialize, afraid to make friends. I'm not like you . . .

S1: I'm really sorry about the school play and all, but you could try to make a friend, or say something in class.

S2: I know . . .

S1: Remember what our textbook says? Half the people out there are just as shy as you are.

S2: Yeah, still, it does make a good topic for me.

S1: For now, maybe. But don't be shy with me anymore. Let's meet for lunch tomorrow, and then type our case studies in the computer lab.

S2: Well, maybe . . .

S1: Come on. We're study partners!

S2: Well, OK.

S1: Noon? In the cafeteria?

S2: Alright.

MAKING INFERENCES

PAGE 53, EXAMINATION

Item 2:

JD: We all know people like this. They find the silver lining inside the darkest cloud . . . all the time . . . without fail . . . driving others to distraction with their "find the bright side" philosophy.

"Oh well," they say, "a stop-and-go commute is perfect . . ."

PAGE 54, TIPS

Example 1:
Yes, I can.
Example 2:
Yes, I can.

PAGE 55, PRACTICE

Activity 1:
1.
Version A: You're shy, aren't you?
Version B: You're shy, aren't you?
2.
Version A: Let's try it. It might help.
Version B: Let's try it. It might help.

3.
Version A: I have to live with myself.
Version B: I have to live with myself.

UNIT 4: Trends

CAMPUS CONVERSATION

PAGE 59, FIRST LISTENING

Student: Dr. Baird, excuse me, but do you have a minute? I just have a quick question.

Professor: Sure, Rezaan, I know the discussion today was challenging . . .

S: Well, actually I was able to follow today's discussion. But, I have another, um, personal matter I'd like your opinion on. It's sort of related to our marketing course, though.

P: What's on your mind?

S: Well, I've been looking all over for a decent used car—the bulletin boards, the student government office, the newspaper—but I haven't come across anything good. And then I heard from a friend who's in one of your other classes that you just bought a used car.

P: So, you heard about the car I bought on eBay?

S: Yeah. If you don't mind my asking, are you satisfied with it?

P: Oh, absolutely. It's a super little car . . . fairly low mileage, in pretty good shape. I got a great price.

S: But weren't you worried about buying a car online? I mean, I don't even like to buy books online because using a credit card can be so risky.

P: Sure, I know some people feel that way, but you know, online shopping has become so popular, so easy, and it's much safer than it ever used to be. eBay offers a bunch of different payment methods, so you don't necessarily need to use a credit card.

S: But what about the car? How did you know what you were buying without seeing it? What happens if what you buy turns out to be a lemon?

P: You get all kinds of information—vehicle history reports, photos, mileage—and a load of guarantees.

S: Well, I know that eBay is really reliable when you buy other things. Tons of my friends buy books, movies, CDs . . . And they're usually really happy with what they get, but I never heard of anyone buying a car online.

P: Listen. Do you remember the basic principles of marketing from our class last semester?

S: How could I forget? The four essential principles of marketing—creating, distributing, pricing, and promoting products . . .

P: Exactly. Well, eBay has caught on so fast because it simply follows those basic principles. So, first, the buyers and sellers create the products. It's really the "people's" shopping mall, with users deciding what products to offer.

S: OK . . .

P: Then, there's pricing. Price competition is what the auctions and bidding are all about. And eBay does a great job of promoting. Not only are there advertisements all over—in magazines, newspapers—but when you get right down to it,

their most valuable promotion tool is word of mouth. Everybody tells everybody else what a great experience they had buying or selling on eBay. Did you know that eBay has something like 125 million users worldwide?

S: Wow! That's incredible.

P: Yeah, and then, distributing—getting products from the sellers to the buyers as quickly as possible has been a key to eBay's phenomenal success.

S: Hey, this was really helpful, Professor Baird. I'm gonna check out what cars eBay has.

P: Good luck. I'll see you in class Friday.

PAGE 60, SECOND LISTENING

Listen again to part of the conversation. Then answer question 2.

S: Yeah. If you don't mind my asking, are you satisfied with it?

P: Oh, absolutely. It's a super little car . . . fairly low mileage, in pretty good shape. I got a great price.

S: But weren't you worried about buying a car online?

Why does the student ask, "But weren't you worried about buying a car online?"?

Listen again to part of the conversation. Then answer question 4.

P: Listen. Do you remember the basic principles of marketing from our class last semester?

S: How could I forget? The four essential principles of marketing—creating, distributing, pricing, and promoting products . . .

What can be inferred about the marketing principles?

ACADEMIC LISTENING

PAGE 60, FIRST LISTENING

Todd Mundt, host: Let's talk about a social condition that you wrote about then, there are a few that I want to touch on but the first one is the one I mentioned in the introduction, crime in New York City. Crime was a problem for a very long time in New York City and it was rising and rising and rising and then it started dropping and um, I suppose there could be a number of different reasons for it, but I can't really find that anybody really knows exactly for sure what caused it.

Malcolm Gladwell, author: Crime is so—is such a fundamentally contagious thing that once we reached a kind of tipping point and once certain influential people in communities hard hit by crime stopped behaving in that way, it was contagious, and there was a kind of sea change that happens all at once.

TM: Maybe we can go into those little triggers, because I find this really interesting because we're talking about such a big change that takes place uh, being triggered by very small things, uh, what do you think some of those were?

MG: Well, I'm very impressed by this idea called "the broken windows theory" which is an idea George Kelling has put forth in New England. He's argued for some time that criminals and criminal behavior is acutely sensitive to environmental cues and he uses the example, the broken window—that if you—if there is a car sitting on the street with a broken window, it is an invitation to someone to vandalize the car. Why? Because a broken window on a car symbolizes the fact no one cares about the car. No one's in charge, no one's watching, no one's . . . and if you think about it, this is a fundamentally different idea about crime than the kind of ideas that we've been carrying for the last 25 years. We have been told by conservatives over and over again that crime is the result of moral failure, of something deep and intrinsic within the hearts and souls and brains of criminals, that a criminal is by definition in the sort of conservative topology, someone who is insensitive to their environment, right? They just go out and commit crimes because that's who they are, they're criminals. Well, Kelling came along and said well no no, a criminal is like all of us, someone who is acutely sensitive to what's going on in the environment, and by making subtle changes in the environment, you can encourage and induce much more socially responsible behavior.

PAGE 61, SECOND LISTENING

Listen again to part of the interview. Then answer question 2.

MG: Crime is so—is such a fundamentally contagious thing that once we reached a kind of tipping point and once certain influential people in communities hard hit by crime stopped behaving in that way, it was contagious, and there was a kind of sea change that happens all at once.

What does Gladwell mean when he says this?

Listen again to part of the interview. Then answer question 4.

MG: We have been told by conservatives over and over again that crime is the result of moral failure, of something deep and intrinsic within the hearts and souls and brains of criminals, that a criminal is by definition in the sort of conservative topology, someone who is insensitive to their environment, right?

Why does Gladwell say "right?" at the end of this passage?

INTEGRATED TASK

PAGE 69, LISTENING

Professor: We've covered the basics about the U.S. Revolutionary War, so today I thought we'd delve a little deeper into the lives of some notable patriots. Let's begin with Paul Revere. His story is well-known . . . Surely someone recalls the poem about him . . .

Student: Oh, yeah . . . " . . . the midnight ride of Paul Revere . . . " Um, I don't remember much more . . .

P: Don't feel bad. OK, Revere rode from Boston to Lexington, Massachusetts, right, in 1775 to warn citizens about the British battle plans.

Now, of course you know that our textbook tells us the result of Revere's ride, but what I think is really interesting is the cause of Revere's success. You know, I've been reading a book by Malcolm Gladwell about trends and, um, what causes them. Gladwell thinks that new ideas catch on partly because socially connected people spread them. And, of course, this made me think about Revere . . .

Revere is what Gladwell calls a "connector," someone who knows everybody, who has a wide network of social connections—the type you always go to for the latest news. In fact, Revere learned about the British attack from several sources. After so many rumors came his way, naturally he jumped on his horse and took his legendary ride to Lexington. And the rest is history, literally. His news gave the colonial

army time to organize and meet the enemy with fierce resistance.

OK, so why was Revere's ride successful? Well, Revere lived his entire life in Boston, so he knew everybody. He had a social network from childhood, from business, from community work. Revere made friends among his business patrons. He owned a silver shop, he owned a printing press, an arms factory, even a dentistry. He belonged to almost every club and organization around—he was an officer in the Revolutionary Army . . . he was a member of the Freemasons . . . the Massachusetts Charitable Mechanics Association, so you can probably see that he connected with people everywhere. He was even a grand juror. Needless to say, Revere was very popular. In fact, when he died, it's reported that thousands of Bostonians attended his funeral.

So, as you can see, Revere had built such a wide circle of friends that he was the ideal person to spread a piece of critical news as far as possible. Consequently, Revere's tale, his word-of-mouth epidemic, if you will, is a legend told in every American history textbook today.

UNIT 5: Cross-Cultural Insights

CAMPUS CONVERSATION

PAGE 79, FIRST LISTENING

Student: Uh, excuse me, are you Mr. Vernon?

Counselor: Yes, you must be Luc.

S: Um, yes, I'm a little early for our appointment, so I can come back later if you're busy . . .

C: No, no. Please come in.

S: I've never been to the counseling center before. A friend of mine suggested I come.

C: Please, have a seat. You look a little stressed. Why don't you tell me what's on your mind?

S: Well, I'm really worried about my family. They're in Haiti . . . That's where I'm from.

C: Haiti, I see. Isn't that one of the places the recent hurricane hit? Is your family OK? I mean, were they affected by the hurricane at all?

S: No, no. I mean, no one was injured. I know that my parents and sisters are okay—I've been in touch with them—they're not in danger now. Their home was flooded, but they've already begun cleaning up. They're staying with my aunt temporarily. But I just feel so helpless, so irresponsible. I'm a wreck, being here so far away. I'm so upset that I haven't been attending classes this week. If this continues, I may flunk out!

C: Luc, what would you do if you could go home?

S: I'm not sure, but you see, I'm the oldest son. I'm supposed to take care of them.

C: But you said everyone is staying with your aunt. They're all in good health, and your parents are starting to repair the damage, right?

S: Yes, yes. But I still feel like I need to be there!

C: Luc, that's a normal reaction. Do they want you to go home?

S: Oh no, not at all. Well, maybe they do. I don't know. I know they're proud of me—that I'm here, in the U.S. studying, doing well. But, you see, in Haiti, families are very close. And parents can be kind of . . . well . . . strict. When I was in high school, my parents were always asking where I was going, who my friends' parents were . . . I knew that I wanted to come to the United States to study. My parents weren't exactly thrilled with the idea. And they definitely expect me to go home after I finish my studies here.

C: Do you want to go home?

S: Well, yes—and no. I love it here. But I also miss my family and my friends. My parents taught me to be proud of my heritage. I guess I'm confused . . .

C: Luc, I know that it must be very hard being far away from your family. It sounds as if you almost feel a little guilty being here while they are struggling to put their lives back together. But, for now, you need to face the fact that you aren't there physically. First and foremost, your family is okay. That's the most important thing. Now is there anyone in Haiti that you can call to go over and help your family?

C: Well, hmmmm, you know, I could call a couple of my friends. I have two really good friends who live about five miles from my parents. I'm sure they'd be willing to go over and help. Why didn't I think of that myself?

S: Luc, give yourself a break! It's natural not to be able to think clearly in the middle of a crisis. After all, the lives of your family were at stake. You know once you contact your friends, well, I think you'll feel much better.

C: Oh, thanks Mr. Vernon. I feel better already. I'm glad I came to talk to you about this.

S: I'm glad too, Luc. But before you leave, would you like to make another appointment? Maybe we could talk about some of the other things that are bothering you.

C: Yeah, that's probably a good idea. I'll make another appointment on my way out. Thanks again, Mr. Vernon.

PAGE 79, SECOND LISTENING

Listen again to part of the conversation. Then answer question 3.

S: Well, hmmmm, you know, I could call a couple of my friends. I have two really good friends who live about five miles from my parents. I'm sure they'd be willing to go over and help. Why didn't I think of that myself?

C: Luc, give yourself a break! It's natural not to be able to think clearly in the middle of a crisis.

Why does the counselor say, "Luc, give yourself a break!"?

ACADEMIC LISTENING

PAGE 80, FIRST LISTENING

Steve Scher: Kirsten Lagatree is our guest. Her book is *Feng Shui: Arranging Your Home to Change Your Life—A Room by Room Guide to the Ancient Chinese Art of Placement.* OK, so, I would like to walk into our newsroom, if we can, and have you just quickly kind of look at it and figure out what we can do for some of the people here who need a little help in their careers or their happiness. Any initial thoughts you have looking at this room?

Kirsten Lagatree: Umm . . . There are some very good things about this newsroom. For one thing, some of the writers are facing northeast. Northeast is the direction that governs mental ability, acuteness of thinking, scholarly success. So, those people in this newsroom, who are facing this, they not only get

an extraordinarily peaceful and beautiful view out the window, they are facing in the direction that's going to make them sharp, and make their writing better.

SS: OK, so this is my desk, over here, scattered with a barrel of monkeys, and they're red, so that's good . . . I'm facing east here, right? I'm facing east, almost to the southeast. Am I blocked up a little bit?

KL: Yeah, well, facing east, actually . . . when you face east you are facing the direction of growth, vitality, the color green. Health, vitality, youth: Those are the things that come with the direction. So maybe that's what makes you so peppy, Steve, and so young at heart. I'd like to say something about this southeast wall right here. That is your money corner. Southeast is the direction that governs money. You haven't done anything with this direction. You've got lots of equipment there . . . what you should have is the color purple, the number four.

SS: And a fish tank.

KL: Well, one thing at a time. The color purple and the number 4 go with that one direction, with the southeast. I'm glad you mentioned a fish tank . . . water flow symbolizes cash flow. There's a lot in feng shui that does word play, both in the Chinese language and in the English language, so, water flow equals cash flow. You walk in to some major corporate buildings nowadays, in New York or Los Angeles or Hong Kong, you are going to see fountains in the lobby. A lot of that. The fish that are in the tank . . . they symbolize abundance, as in "there are always more fish in the sea." What's your goal? You know . . . if your goal is to be a better writer, talk somebody into changing places with you here so that you can face northeast. If your goal is to become wealthy, do some enhancement there on your southeast wall, or do it at home. Say you want to get in a relationship in your life . . . at home, enhance a southwest wall with the color yellow and the number two. The southwest corner governs marriage, partnerships, motherhood. You pay attention to what, umm you know what, you can do to make something happen, and then you work with these outward symbols.

PAGE 81, SECOND LISTENING

Listen again to part of the interview. Then answer question 3.

SS: OK, so this is my desk, over here, scattered with a barrel of monkeys, and they're red, so that's good . . . I'm facing east here, right? I'm facing east, almost to the southeast. Am I blocked up a little bit?

Why does the host say, "Am I blocked up a little bit?"?

Listen again to part of the interview. Then answer question 4.

KL: You've got lots of equipment there . . . what you should have is the color purple, the number four.

SS: And a fish tank.

KL: Well, one thing at a time. The color purple and the number 4 go with that one direction, with the southeast.

Why does Lagatree say, "Well, one thing at a time."?

INTEGRATED TASK

PAGE 89, LISTENING

Professor: OK, so, let's see, we've seen how Japanese art influenced Western painters. Now we're going to explore Eastern influence on Western architecture as exemplified by one architect. Uh, let's see . . . who would you say was the most innovative American architect of the twentieth century? Uh . . . Maria?

Student: Frank Lloyd Wright?

Professor: Yes, that's right. Yes, indeed. Art historians consider him the premier Western architect of the 1900s. When you study his work closely, you see the Eastern influence, especially the philosophy of balance and energy flow in feng shui.

Let's consider "Fallingwater," Wright's famous home—built on a river in a forest and made of stone, wood, and glass. The influence of Chinese feng shui is quite evident. First, the Chinese believed in *yin* and *yang*—balance in everything. Fallingwater has simple interiors, large spaces, lots of light (the yin) . . . balanced by low ceilings (the yang). Fallingwater also balances objects in rooms with empty space . . . open areas and occupied areas. That's another principle of feng shui. There are also the five Chinese elements (fire, water, wood, earth, and metal). So, Wright balanced his use of materials—wood, metal, and forest surroundings.

Uh, finally, another important part of feng shui is the idea of energy flow. Wright's open, bright spaces encouraged the flow of *chi'i*, or energy. No cluttered spaces, no tight corners . . . large windows to allow plenty of light . . . All of these contribute to energy flow. Some say that Wright incorporated feng shui into his design by building a waterfall onto the rear of the Fallingwater home, thus incorporating a large amount of rushing chi'i—negative energy—into his plan.

So, you might say that Wright was innovative in adopting Eastern ideas . . . though, of course, the principles of feng shui existed 2,000 years before Wright. Still, in the West, feng shui is a new and increasingly popular concept.

USING CONTEXT CLUES

PAGE 95, PRACTICE

Activity 2

My mother says I'm becoming "English." This hurts me, because I know she means I'm becoming cold. I'm no colder than I've ever been, but I'm learning to be less demonstrative. I learn this from a teacher who, after contemplating the gesticulations with which I help myself describe the digestive system of a frog, tells me to "sit on my hands and then try talking." I learn my new reserve from people who take a step back when we talk, because I am standing too close, crowding them. Cultural distances are different, I later learn in a sociology class, but I know it already. I learn restraint from Penny, who looks offended when I shake her by the arm in excitement, as if my gesture had been one of aggression instead of friendliness. I learn it from a girl who pulls away when I hook my arm through hers as we walk down the street—this movement of friendly intimacy is an embarrassment to her.

Listen again to part of the passage. Then answer question 1.

My mother says I'm becoming "English." This hurts me, because I know she means I'm becoming cold. I'm no colder than I've ever been, but I'm learning to be less demonstrative.

What does the speaker's mother mean by "becoming English"?

Listen again to part of the passage. Then answer question 2.

I'm learning to be less demonstrative. I learn this from a teacher who, after contemplating the gesticulations with which I help myself describe the digestive system of a frog, tells me to sit on my hands and then try talking.

Why does the teacher tell the student to sit on her hands and then try talking?

UNIT 6: Faith

CAMPUS CONVERSATION

PAGE 99, FIRST LISTENING

Student: Hi, Professor Kelly.

Advisor: Hi, Tom. How's it going?

S: Have I caught you at a bad time?

A: No, no. Please, come in.

S: Thanks. Well, I need some advice. I really respect your point of view. It's about summer session. I registered for a biology class and a psychology class. I wanted to get the last of my core classes out of the way, but now I'm having second thoughts.

A: Why?

S: Well, you know about my interest in Buddhism. I've told you a little about my meditation . . .

A: Yes, I remember our conversation.

S: Well, lately I haven't been able to make any time to meditate. I had tried to arrange my schedule so that I'd have time in the mornings, but sometimes, after a late night or a stressful day, I just turn off the alarm and go back to sleep. Meditating helps me relax and see things more clearly. I know if it weren't for my meditation, I wouldn't be in the honors program, but I'm having a really hard time now balancing my school work with my need to have personal time.

A: Hmmm. Well, I can understand that. You have a very heavy course load this semester. And I know you're involved in a lot of extracurricular activities as well. Aren't you the editor of the school newspaper?

S: Yes, it's very time-consuming, but I love the work—and the people.

A: You know, Tom, it's difficult to make time for a spiritual life, especially with our busy schedules. But I'm not sure I understand how your summer schedule fits into this. You'll only be taking two courses, right? So you should have more personal time.

S: Well, I'm wondering whether I should spend the summer at a retreat, instead of taking summer classes. I've been to this retreat twice before and it was such an incredible experience. There was a group of about thirty of us. We lived as a community for four weeks. We meditated together, ate together, studied together . . . We did chores . . . People composed and shared poetry and songs . . . We could really communicate with each other, even during the silent periods. As the weeks passed, the sense of community grew deeper and more significant . . . I'm just worried that if I attend the retreat, I'll fall behind in my academics.

A: Tom, I've known you for three years now. You are one of the most dedicated students I've ever met. You always strive to achieve your best work. So whether or not you decide to go on that retreat, I know what a positive effect meditation has on your studies.

S: Thanks for your support, Professor Kelly. I'll think some more about going on that retreat. Maybe if I go home and meditate, I'll be able to see things more clearly! Thanks, Professor Kelly. I just needed to talk about it.

A: My door is always open, Tom. Now, I expect you to come by and tell me all about your summer!

PAGE 100, SECOND LISTENING

Listen again to part of the conversation. Then answer question 3.

S: I know if it weren't for my meditation, I wouldn't be in the honors program, but I'm having a really hard time now balancing my school work with my need to have personal time.

A: Hmmm. Well, I can understand that. You have a very heavy course load this semester. And I know you're involved in a lot of extracurricular activities as well. Aren't you the editor of the school newspaper?

Why does the advisor mention the student's extracurricular activities?

Listen again to part of the conversation. Then answer question 5.

A: Tom, I've known you for three years now. You are one of the most dedicated students I've ever met. You always strive to achieve your best work. So whether or not you decide to go on that retreat, I know what a positive effect meditation has on your studies.

What can be inferred from the advisor's response?

ACADEMIC LISTENING

PAGE 101, FIRST LISTENING

Alex Beam: Was this an . . . Was this an . . . sort of an intellectual fact-finding journey or was this a spiritual quest for you?

William Claassen, author: It was a number of things. It was a . . . certainly it was a project that I took on as a journalist, as a writer. It was also a spiritual journey for me because it allowed me to continue my journey in monastic traditions, uh, and what I might find there and how that might apply to my life and what I could communicate about what I had witnessed in these various communities.

AB: I want to draw you out on the subject of the work of the monastery. Why don't you briefly talk about the work of that monastery, which is in a sense the easiest to illustrate.

WC: Sure. Although Wat Tham Krabok is part of this forest monastic tradition, it was different in the sense that they were working on issues that were outside of the monastery. They had taken on efforts of working with AIDS patients and also providing assistance with Hmong villagers who were refugees out of Laos who had begun gathering in that area where the monastery was located. So, actually, a great deal of their time was spent in this work, the AIDS work, and also the work with the refugees, which, uh, created a little different situation in terms of their daily schedule, in terms of how rigorous their chanting schedule was, in terms of the solitude of the community because there were a lot of people coming in, children as well as adults, as well as Westerners, coming in to view this program for the AIDS patients, also for drug addicts. They also worked in that area. So, there was a lot of movement in and out of the community, which made it a different situation than what I experienced in other forest monasteries.

AB: What um . . . were you ever . . . um . . . I am going to use a term—not totally flattering, but this notion of the monastic day tripper, the visitor. Were you . . . I know that at sometimes you were sort of greeted with a bit of suspicion. Isn't that fair to say?

WC: I think so. I talk in the book about a term that I learned on Mt. Athos—the two-legged wolf, the idea of an individual being on pilgrimage, but really more interested in the uniqueness of what this community is . . . and sort of the temporary visitor. There were certainly times when there was suspicion about my time in those communities.

AB: The two-legged wolf obviously refers to sort of tourists who are kind of visiting the beaches in Thailand and the monks of Mt. Athos, kind of joy riders. But what specific impact have the two-legged wolves, had, say, on Mt. Athos?

WC: Well, on Mt. Athos, for example, at one time, there was maybe a seven- or ten-day period that men could make a pilgrimage on the peninsula. Because of the numbers of men that are wanting to be on Mt. Athos, they've reduced that period of time to four days. Actually, four days was five or six years ago, so they may have even reduced it further than that. But it creates a demand on the land, and it also creates a time demand on the part of the communities.

PAGE 101, SECOND LISTENING

Listen again to part of the interview. Then answer question 3.

WC: So, actually, a great deal of their time was spent in this work, the AIDS work, and also the work with the refugees, which, uh, created a little different situation in terms of their daily schedule, in terms of how rigorous their chanting schedule was, in terms of the solitude of the community because there were a lot of people coming in, children as well as adults, as well as Westerners, coming in to view this program for the AIDS patients, also for drug addicts.

What does Claassen suggest about the work of the Wat Tham Krabok monks?

Listen again to part of the interview. Then answer question 4.

AB: What um . . . were you ever . . . um . . . I am going to use a term—not totally flattering, but this notion of the monastic day tripper, the visitor. Were you . . . I know that at sometimes you were sort of greeted with a bit of suspicion. Isn't that fair to say?

Why does the interviewer say, "Isn't that fair to say?"?

INTEGRATED TASK

PAGE 109, LISTENING

Philosophy professor: Let's continue our discussion of monastic communities by focusing on one practitioner. Now, I'm going to use the example of Thomas Merton. He was a well-known figure in monastic tradition.

Now, Merton was one of the most famous Roman Catholic monks of the twentieth century, and he was best known for his writings on spirituality. So, how did Merton become a monk? In one of his books, Merton describes sitting in a church one day, mysteriously feeling drawn to God . . . so intensely that he decided at that moment to commit himself to the Catholic faith. He did volunteer work for a while but didn't feel quite spiritually complete. So in 1941, he became a Trappist monk and joined Our Lady of Gethsemani monastery in Kentucky.

It wasn't easy for Merton to adapt to life as a monk . . . the loneliness, the rigors of monastic life. I mean, he'd been an active, outgoing young man. Now, suddenly, he had to give up smoking, drinking, and speaking and live an ascetic life of fasting, silent meditation, and prayer.

At first, the change made Merton somber, and his fellow monks worried about him. But eventually, he developed a gift for writing. For the next twenty years Merton "talked" by writing about his life, his faith and the human issues that he considered important. His 1948 autobiography, *The Seven Storey Mountain,* sold more than a million copies.

Merton also wrote about the ascetic life of a monk. About fasting, he said, and I quote, "The goal of fasting is inner unity. This means hearing but not with the ear; hearing, but not with the understanding; it is hearing with the spirit, with your whole being." So, Merton found inner unity from fasting and other ascetic practices. Fasting helped him to understand things that, well, he could not understand with his ears or his mind.

Through his ascetic life, Merton gained understanding of non-religious issues, too. He wrote for the general public, against nuclear weapons, in support of peace and non-violence. Legislators in Congress quoted from Merton's writing to support civil rights legislation. He also met the Dalai Lama, which resulted in a deeper understanding between Christians and Buddhists throughout the world. For twenty years, Merton donated all his money from his books to his monastery, so his contributions to a better world were financial as well as philosophical . . .

SUMMARIZING

PAGE 116, PRACTICE

Activity 2:

Dreifus: Many people get a sense of God by observing nature. What will religions be like in a hundred years if there is little nature left on earth?

Dalai Lama: The world itself is nature. The sun, the moon, they are nature. Even if there were no more animals, nature would still be here. For those religions that believe in a creator, they would have to find reasons to explain why our beautiful blue planet became a desert.

If you ask me whether it's good or bad, of course it's bad. But in the Buddhist tradition, something like that would not change our attitude. We believe the whole world will come and disappear, come and disappear—so eventually the world becomes desert and even the ocean dries up. But then again, another new world is reborn. It's endless.

UNIT 7: The Workplace

CAMPUS CONVERSATION

PAGE 119, FIRST LISTENING

Student: Uh, excuse me, are you Mrs. Hawes—the person I should see about the work-study opening?

Library supervisor: Yes, yes. Come in.

S: Thank you. I was really happy when I saw the sign posted that you need a work-study student. I've always wanted to work in a library.

L: Well, that's wonderful. And a bit unusual! So many students don't even use the library, let alone want to work in it! With the Internet and all, libraries aren't used half as much as they used to be. You know, some students might even be surprised to learn that the library is really very high-tech. We have Internet access and a bank of computer terminals where students can search for information here very efficiently.

S: Well, I'm quite familiar with the library. I come here often.

L: Good. Well, you know we can only accept students who are qualified to receive work-study funding. Unfortunately, I can't interview you unless you've filled out the work-study authorization form and had it signed by a financial aid officer.

S: Oh, I've done that already. Here's my form.

L: Well, everything looks in order. Great. Let me explain the position. We need someone who can perform multiple tasks—shelving books, keeping the stacks in order, replenishing paper in the computer printers—there's a myriad of jobs involved. You wouldn't normally need to deal with the students, but there may be an occasion when you might be called on to provide reference help. Of course, there would be a training period, so you'd be familiar with all that. Do you have any experience working in a library or an office . . . you know, work that might've gotten you some experience with some of these tasks?

S: Hmm, well, I did work one summer in a bookstore. I reshelved books, took inventory, and sometimes filled in as a cashier when the store was really busy.

L: That's great experience. You must be an organized person to be able to handle various jobs at once.

S: Yes, I didn't have any trouble multitasking. Oh, and I got along very well with everyone.

L: Well, it sounds like you meet our criteria. Do you have any questions?

S: Yes, what are the hours?

L: Well, the work-study guidelines require that you work twelve hours every week, but the hours are flexible. We might need you to fill in on occasional nights and weekends. And it's important to be on time. If you're due here at 2 P.M., that means 2 P.M., not 2:10. Would that work for you?

S: I understand. I'm always on time to my classes. I can't stand it when students come in late.

L: Well, then . . . You sound like a promising candidate. I do have to consult with my colleagues before I can make the final decision, but I think your chances are pretty good.

S: Terrific! I'm ready to start today!

L: Great. I'm glad to see you're enthusiastic. Let me just check with my colleagues and I should know by 10 A.M. tomorrow. Can you come back then?

S: Sure . . . Great! Thanks for your help!

PAGE 119, SECOND LISTENING

Listen again to part of the conversation. Then answer question 2.

S: I was really happy when I saw the sign posted that you need a work-study student. I've always wanted to work in a library.

L: Well, that's wonderful. And a bit unusual! So many students don't even use the library, let alone want to work in it!

Which sentence best expresses how the supervisor probably feels?

Listen again to part of the conversation. Then answer question 4.

S: I'm always on time to my classes. I can't stand it when students come in late.

L: Well, then . . . You sound like a promising candidate. I do have to consult with my colleagues before I can make the final decision, but I think your chances are pretty good.

What does the supervisor mean when she says, "I do have to consult with my colleagues before I can make the final decision."?

ACADEMIC LISTENING

PAGE 120, FIRST LISTENING

Host: More and more companies today are keeping an eye on employees as they work, and we'd like to hear what's happening at your workplace. Our first caller is Bob from Tallahassee, Florida. Hello, Bob. You're on the line with *Talk of the Town.*

Caller 1: Hi, I just wanted to say that I have a sneaking suspicion that there's a lot of secret watching of employees in our office, but I don't always know when and how it's done. Sometimes our boss scans our office with video cameras to see whether we're doing a good job. I mean, talk about authorities watching, right? I mean, snooping into our private lives is really outside the range of responsible business. I mean, really, the thing we need to look at is why companies want to control our lives and restrict our freedom.

Host: Thanks, Bob. That's an interesting point. Some say the technological ease of monitoring workers is responsible for this increase in monitoring . . .

Caller 1: You don't know the half of it! Do you know how easy it is to hook up a few cameras . . . I mean, it's really easy, OK? Then all the bosses have to do is sit back and watch us. Something has to be done about this!

Host: I understand your concern. But, there are few laws that address workplace privacy. Why don't we hear from Mary from Minneapolis.

Caller 2: Hello. Thanks for taking my call. I love your show. OK, I had a similar experience as your previous caller. I used to work in a company where they watched workers constantly. They kept a record of all outgoing long-distance and local calls of each employee. You know, in this suspicious atmosphere, it was impossible to have a sense of pride and dignity in my work. I felt insulted. I just felt they didn't respect me. My boss had no lawful reason to know who I called. It was a clear invasion of my privacy. You know, the point I want to make is that employers have gone too far.

Host: A record of all your phone calls! Well, that does seem a bit excessive. Thank you for your call. Let's go to Louis. Hello. You're on *Talk of the Town.*

Caller 3: Good afternoon. I'm calling from my cell phone on the New Jersey turnpike. I can't understand what's causing this increase in employee monitoring. It's unfair. Employers just listen to employee phone calls whenever they want, listening to both personal and business calls. They also do drug testing unpredictably, without warning, and for no good reason. I mean, you'd have to agree our privacy deserves some protections.

Host: Hmmm. It sounds as if you've had some first-hand experience of this. OK. I think we have time for one more call . . . Susan from Little Rock, Arkansas.

Caller 4: Hello. Great show! I am the owner of a company that manufacturers highly sophisticated computer chips. There's nothing harmful or evil about these monitoring practices. Look, as an employer, I have the right to know how my employees are using their time. And on top of that, we have a lot of expensive equipment in our offices. I use the video cameras to prevent theft. And in addition, my managers and directors use e-mail to handle a great deal of business, so I have sophisticated monitoring equipment to check their e-mail to watch for any abusive language or insulting comments about a person's race. And this is for the employees' own protection.

PAGE 121, SECOND LISTENING

Listen again to part of the program. Then answer question 4.

Caller 2: I used to work in a company where they watched workers constantly. They kept a record of all outgoing long-distance and local calls of each employee. You know, in this suspicious atmosphere, it was impossible to have a sense of pride and dignity in my work. I felt insulted. I just felt they didn't respect me.

What can be inferred about Mary (Caller 2)?

Listen again to part of the program. Then answer question 5.

Host: Thanks, Bob. That's an interesting point. Some say the technological ease of monitoring workers is responsible for this increase in monitoring . . .

Caller 1: You don't know the half of it! Do you know how easy it is to hook up a few cameras . . . I mean, it's really easy, OK? Then all the bosses have to do is sit back and watch us. Something has to be done about this!

What is Bob's (Caller 1's) attitude toward the radio host's comment about monitoring?

Listen again to part of the program. Then answer question 7.

Caller 3: Employers just listen to employee phone calls whenever they want, listening to both personal and business calls. They also do drug testing unpredictably, without warning, and for no good reason. I mean, you'd have to agree our privacy deserves some protections.

Why does Louis (Caller 3) say, "I mean, you'd have to agree our privacy deserves some protections."?

INTEGRATED TASK

PAGE 129, LISTENING

Elaine Korry: That's all well and good, says Rebecca Locketz, the legal director of the ACLU's Workplace Rights Project. She concedes there are legitimate uses of monitoring programs. But too often, says Locketz, surveillance practices demean workers for no good reason.

Rebecca Locketz: You certainly do not need to monitor key strokes. When you give someone fifty reports to key into a computer, and you see that they have only completed twenty by day's end, you don't need to count key strokes. They only finished two-fifths.

EK: Locketz argues that employees should not have to leave their human dignity at the workplace door. And she says they're entitled to a few safeguards in this area. First, the ACLU says employees should always be informed when they're monitored. And second . . .

RL: There should be no monitoring whatsoever in purely private areas.

EK: Yet, so far there is only one state—Connecticut—that forbids surveillance in areas such as locker rooms or the employee lounge. In other states, employers do secretly videotape private places if they suspect theft or criminal activities such as drug dealing. There's only one federal statute, the 1986 Electronic Communications Privacy Act, that safeguards employee privacy. But according to Larry Finneran with the National Association of Manufacturers, the scope of the act is limited to eavesdropping on private telephone calls.

Larry Finneran: There are specific rules. An employer listening for content of personal phone calls . . . an employer can . . . can limit duration of personal phone calls. An employer can say, "no personal phone calls." But under the Electronic Communications Privacy Act, an employer cannot listen for content. And that . . . they are already protected to that degree.

UNIT 8: Perspectives on War

CAMPUS CONVERSATION

PAGE 139, FIRST LISTENING

Recruiter: Hi! Welcome to the Job Fair. Interested in an ROTC scholarship?

Student: I don't know. I don't know very much about ROTC. I had thought about the military for a time, in high school. Can you tell me a little bit about it?

R: Well sure, ROTC is a program sponsored by the U.S. Army. It's the Reserve Officer Training Corps. We provide scholarships to students who are interested in leadership opportunities in the military. What's your major?

S: Nursing.

R: Really? The Nursing Corps is an important branch of the army! Here's how it works: You continue your required classes in nursing, you take an ROTC leadership training course over the summer, and we take care of your college tuition. Then, you're commissioned as a Second Lieutenant in the army and you embark on specialized training. It's a great way to complete your education and get job training, all with financial support!

S: Well, I don't know. It does sound interesting, I guess . . .

R: In the Nursing Corps, you'd be an officer—training staff, teaching courses, working in a hospital or other medical facilities.

S: Hmmm. I see. But what about my nursing courses? I've nearly finished two years of my nursing program already.

R: Well, like I said, you'd continue with the courses required for your nursing degree. You'd just add the ROTC training course. Army ROTC is one of the nation's top leadership programs. It trains you to become a leader and a manager.

S: What are the requirements for a scholarship?

R: OK, well, the ROTC would provide you with tuition for the remaining two years of college. You need to be between seventeen and twenty-seven, and it looks like you'd meet the physical standards, right?

S: Yes, I'm twenty, and I'm in really good shape. I work out at least three times a week.

R: You'd also need to maintain a 2.5 GPA.

S: I already have a 3.0 average.

R: Excellent. Are you a U.S. citizen?

S: Yes, I am.

R: Well, think about it. If you sign up, you could be on the road to getting your tuition paid. It's important to know as well, that after graduation, you're committed to serving two years in active duty, the Reserves, or the National Guard. And because you've already done two years of your nursing curriculum, you could do the ROTC training in the summer.

S: Well, it sounds interesting. You've given me a lot to think about.

R: Excellent. Well listen, we're having an orientation meeting on campus at 4 P.M. next Monday where you can find out more about the program. We'll be meeting in the Student Life Building, Room 401.

S: OK. Thanks a lot. I'll think about it.

R: Thank you.

PAGE 140, SECOND LISTENING

Listen again to part of the conversation. Then answer question 2.

R: If you sign up, you could be on the road to getting your tuition paid. It's important to know as well, that after graduation, you're committed to serving two years in active duty, the Reserves, or the National Guard. And because you've already done two years of your nursing curriculum, you could do the ROTC training in the summer.

Why does the recruiter say, "It's important to know"?

Listen again to part of the conversation. Then answer question 3.

R: Hi! Welcome to the Job Fair. Interested in an ROTC scholarship?

S: I don't know. I don't know very much about ROTC. I had thought about the military for a time, in high school. Can you tell me a little bit about it?

What is the student's attitude when the recruiter asks about the scholarship?

Listen again to part of the conversation. Then answer question 4.

R: In the Nursing Corps, you'd be an officer—training staff, teaching courses, working in a hospital or other medical facilities.

S: Hmmm. I see. But what about my nursing courses? I've nearly finished two years of my nursing program already.

Why does the student ask, "But what about my nursing courses?"?

ACADEMIC LISTENING

PAGE 141, FIRST LISTENING

Terry Gross: In your article about the Red Cross in *The New Yorker*, you wrote that witnessing the Red Cross, and traveling to all these war zones, challenged your views on antiwar culture. What do you mean by that?

Michael Ignatieff: Well, I'm a Canadian; I was very involved in the antiwar, anti-Vietnam protests that were centered in Toronto during the 60's because Toronto was an antiwar center because so many draft evaders and draft resisters ended up there. I grew up in the antiwar culture of my generation . . . I think what I discovered in the Red Cross's approach is an alternative ethic, which is that, you know, you cannot abolish war, you can't do without war.

And war in fact is a natural, necessary, and sometimes, dare I say it, even desirable way to solve certain social conflicts between ethnic groups. Oppressed groups sometimes can only use war to free themselves. Well, if that's the case, if we can't abolish war from human culture, then we'd better find some way to tame it.

And that's the ethic that the Red Cross lives by, and I think the simple rules that the Red Cross tries to enforce, which is: You don't shoot prisoners, you don't make war on noncombatants, you try and stay away from civilian targets, you kill people, you don't torture or degrade their bodies. You know, just very very simple rules of humanity are an important addition to civilization.

PAGE 141, SECOND LISTENING

Listen again to part of the interview. Then answer question 3.

MI: And war in fact is a natural, necessary, and sometimes, dare I say it, even desirable way to solve certain social conflicts between ethnic groups. Oppressed groups sometimes can only use war to free themselves. Well, if that's the case, if we can't abolish war from human culture, then we'd better find some way to tame it.

Why does Ignatieff say, "dare I say it"?

Listen again to part of the interview. Then answer question 4.

MI: And that's the ethic that the Red Cross lives by, and I think the simple rules that the Red Cross tries to enforce, which is: You don't shoot prisoners, you don't make war on noncombatants, you try and stay away from civilian targets, you kill people, you don't torture or degrade their bodies. You know, just very very simple rules of humanity are an important addition to civilization.

What is Ignatieff's attitude toward the Red Cross ethic?

INTEGRATED TASK

PAGE 149, LISTENING

Host: Our next guest, Dr. David Chan, will give us a different perspective on relief organizations during wartime. He is a physician with Doctors Without Borders.

Dr. Chan, I know you're familiar with the principles of the International Red Cross. Recently we spoke with Dr. Sandra Martino, an ICRC physician who explained the idea of the warrior's honor and the Geneva Conventions as ways to protect war victims. What is your view of the warrior's honor?

Chan: As a physician working for Doctors without Borders, I too have seen the devastating effects of war going on in volatile war zones. I agree with the ICRC that soldiers must try to obey "codes of honor," or rules of war. I do not equate war with barbarism and savagery. However, we members of Doctors without Borders disagree with the ICRC in an important way: We do not believe that a soldier's aggression can be tamed and controlled, since war by its nature unleashes instincts and behavior that cannot always be restrained. It's simply unrealistic to think that soldiers will always live by rules of war, simple common-sense rules that tell them how to behave.

Host: And what about the ICRC's ethic of neutrality? Do you think relief workers and others can remain neutral when they observe war?

Chan: No, I don't think that's realistic, either. War is much more than that. As doctors, we see the horrific after-effects of war. So, we do much more than just disseminate basic health-care information or bandage up the wounded. There are times when we cannot and will not be neutral. And we don't hesitate to denounce human rights violations.

PARAPHRASING

PAGE 156, PRACTICE

Activity 2:

Volunteer: Hello. How are you doing? I'm here to collect messages for your family.

POW: Thanks so much. But I have a question. Can I attach photos to my message?

V: Yeah, you can. However, I gotta warn you: You must protect them with something so they don't get damaged.

POW: Oh. Then, does that mean I can staple a little plastic bag to the message?

V: Well, this is the first time anybody has ever asked me that question. Let me think. Yeah, I guess it's all right with me. I can't imagine the prison censor would object. But what exactly are you going to put in this bag? Because, you know, plastic bags are against prison rules.

POW: Please, please, trust me. Don't worry. But I have to tell you: It's not for photos. It's for something more special than that. You see, I've been working in the prison gardens this year. I grew the greatest azaleas in the world. I want to send some of the seeds to my wife. It's as simple as that.

UNIT 9: The Arts

CAMPUS CONVERSATION

PAGE 162, FIRST LISTENING

Counselor: Hi, Gina! You're right on time. I was opening the career software so that you could get started.

Student: Thanks, Ms. Bryant. As I told you on the phone, I'm studying music, and I'm interested in getting some facts about jobs in the music industry, salaries, that kind of stuff. I'm really interested in performing.

C: Right. Well, OK. I've done a bit of research on this already and, um, I probably don't have to tell you that music is not usually a very stable career. Part-time schedules . . . freelance employment . . . the U.S. labor statistics bureau doesn't paint a pretty picture.

S: Yes, I know it's going to be tough. But I'm determined. If a person has talent and determination, she can do anything! I've loved music since I was a child. My dream is to become a jazz pianist.

C: I'm sure you are very talented, and I can tell that you really want to do this, but you also have to be realistic. And the reality is that not many successful jazz musicians can earn a living at it because the competition is so keen. Most musicians supplement their income with earnings from other sources.

Here, let's look at this data on job trends in music. It says most musicians work only part-time in that field. You know, the stress of constantly looking for work leads many musicians to accept day jobs to pay the bills. Then they moonlight as musicians.

S: Well, I'm sure I can get a job playing in a restaurant or something. I know it won't be easy at first.

C: No, I don't think it will be easy. Gina, I don't think you should give up your music or your dream. But, for now, I'd recommend that you also consider alternatives that might offer a more stable income and combine your love of music with something else. Perhaps you could do a double major in music and another field . . . or major in something else and minor in music. You could have a stimulating career and still make time for music.

S: I don't like that idea at all. My music is more than a hobby to me. It's my life. It's all I want to do.

C: All I'm asking is that you consider alternatives. You never know what might come of it.

S: Well, I guess I could just look into other fields. I understand your point about having some stability.

C: The bottom line is if you want to be a jazz musician, you may also need to do other work to make ends meet. But that doesn't mean you can't continue your music. You just need to choose a career path that will provide time for music *and* steady employment. What about teaching? Do you like children?

S: As a matter of fact, I love kids. I volunteered in an elementary school, tutoring, when I was in high school. Maybe I could do a double major in music and in elementary education?

C: Sounds promising!

PAGE 162, SECOND LISTENING

Listen again to part of the conversation. Then answer question 3.

S: Thanks, Ms. Bryant. As I told you on the phone, I'm studying music, and I'm interested in getting some facts about jobs in the music industry, salaries, that kind of stuff. I'm really interested in performing.

C: Right. Well, OK. I've done a bit of research on this already and, um, I probably don't have to tell you that music is not usually a very stable career. Part-time schedules . . . freelance employment . . . the U.S. labor statistics bureau doesn't paint a pretty picture.

What is the counselor's attitude toward the student's career choice?

Listen again to part of the conversation. Then answer question 5.

C: Here, let's look at this data on job trends in music. It says most musicians work only part-time in that field. You know, the stress of constantly looking for work leads many musicians to accept day jobs to pay the bills. Then they moonlight as musicians.

S: Well, I'm sure I can get a job playing in a restaurant or something. I know it won't be easy at first.

Which sentence best expresses how the student probably feels?

Listen again to part of the conversation. Then answer question 6.

C: The bottom line is if you want to be a jazz musician, you may also need to do other work to make ends meet. But that doesn't mean you can't continue your music. You just need to choose a career path that will provide time for music and steady employment. What about teaching? Do you like children?

Why does the counselor ask, "What about teaching? Do you like children?"?

ACADEMIC LISTENING

PAGE 163, FIRST LISTENING

Warren Levinson: "Your Child's Brain" is the subject of this week's cover story in *Newsweek*. To discuss it we have science editor Sharon Begley. Thanks for joining us again, Sharon.

Sharon Begley: Hi, Warren.

WL: What parts of an infant's brain are already physically set at birth?

SB: Really the only things that a baby is born with are the circuits that do things absolutely crucial for life . . . keeping the heart beating . . . breathing . . . controlling temperature . . . reflexes . . . things like that . . . and of course a baby can see and hear. A baby has the primary senses when he or she comes into the world. But the rest of it is still a "work in progress."

WL: I was fascinated by some of the research on music and the relationship to other kinds of reasoning, particularly mathematics. Like, I had always assumed that musical talent and mathematics kind of went together because they had something to do with each other . . . um . . . in terms of filling puzzles . . . and in terms of . . . you have mathematics involved in setting out the beats to various kinds of music.

SB: That's right. Yes . . . music itself is highly mathematical, and that made some neuroscientists think that somehow the patterns of firing in neural cells were similar, as in mathematical abilities and logical thinking and spatial reasoning. So what they did is give two- and three-year-old little preschoolers lessons in singing and in piano, and after several weeks of this the children were much better at solving mazes on pieces of paper and copying geometric shapes, so it seems again that these circuits were sort of primed to be wired up, and music somehow did it.

WL: But it also turns out that they tend . . . the wiring for both of those things tend to be right next to each other . . .

SB: They're in the same part of the brain . . . this old right side of the brain that we've heard about for years . . . yeah.

WL: I have to say, though, that in your reporting . . . there . . . as a father of children, I get two reactions: One fills me with excitement that I really have a very significant role to play in how my children grow up to be able to solve things and to be able to live their lives, but the other reaction . . . and it's a little bigger . . . it's sort of scary . . . the notion that so many windows are closed so early, that by the ages of three and seven, I may have already blown it in so many areas.

SB: Well I feel the same way . . . mine are ten and seven . . . and I look at all these missed opportunities and think . . . Oh God . . . I should've been doing this or that . . . or whatever. You know, I think we should not panic parents.

Listen again to part of the interview. Then answer question 3.

WL: I was fascinated by some of the research on music and the relationship to other kinds of reasoning, particularly mathematics. Like, I had always assumed that musical talent and mathematics kind of went together because they had something to do with each other . . . um . . . in terms of filling puzzles . . . and in terms of . . . you have mathematics involved in setting out the beats to various kinds of music.

Why does the host say, "I had always assumed that musical talent and mathematics kind of went together because they had something to do with each other"?

Listen again to part of the interview. Then answer question 5.

WL: I have to say, though, that in your reporting . . . there . . . as a father of children, I get two reactions: One fills me with excitement that I really have a very significant role to play in how my children grow up to be able to solve things and to be able to live their lives, but the other reaction . . . and it's a little bigger . . . it's sort of scary . . . the notion that so many windows are closed so early, that by the ages of three and seven, I may have already blown it in so many areas.

What does the host mean when he says, "it's sort of scary"?

INTEGRATED TASK

Student 1: Hey, Sean. Have you finished the psyche take-home exam?

Student 2: Almost, Anna. I'm stuck on the last question—about writing a case study to apply a theory in psychology to our own lives. I'm thinking of writing on the theory of music enhancing intelligence . . .

S1: Wow, seriously?! That's the topic *I* chose. I thought it was a pretty cool question.

S2: Yeah? So what did you write about it?

S1: Well, I said the theory was true, based on my experiences. When I was a kid, my mom insisted that I take piano lessons, and now that I'm studying architecture, the courses seem fairly easy.

S2: Really? So exactly how did music help?

S1: Well, we take a lot of design courses—structural, urban, architectural design . . . plus physical and environmental systems. When I create designs, I have to be able to visualize how systems work together and analyze the human, technical, and economic factors. So here's what I wrote—"I think musical training strengthened the parts of my brain that perform spatial and analytical tasks."

S2: Huh! That's amazing! Maybe I *will* write on that idea. I've had a similar experience.

S1: Did you take music lessons as a child?

S2: Well, no, but I do listen to music when I do my calculus homework. It helps me concentrate, and I can actually do the problems faster. I've aced all the tests in calculus, and I'm the only student who doesn't have to take the final!

S1: Wow, I'm impressed. You know, it's just like that study of children that we read about, where musical training made them score higher on analytical reasoning tests.

S2: OK. So, there's my topic! I'm going to go type up my exam right now.

S1: Don't forget to put some music on while you're working . . . You know, to, like, stimulate your brain circuits.

IDENTIFYING AND USING COHESIVE DEVICES

Item 4:

Counselor: The bottom line is if you want to be a jazz musician, you may also need to do other work to make ends meet. But that doesn't mean you can't continue your music. You just need to choose a career path that will provide time for music *and* steady employment. What about teaching? Do you like children?

UNIT 10: Freedom of Expression

CAMPUS CONVERSATION

Faculty advisor: Hi, Tasha! How's this week's issue coming?

Student editor: Hi, Dr. J. It's going fine—we're almost ready to wrap it up. We've got a lead story on the new college e-mail system . . . Oh, and we also have another full-page ad. It's from a Web-based company that sells term papers.

FA: Hmmm. Can I see the ad?

SE: Yeah. I'm just about to insert it on page five. Here it is.

FA: That's a great looking ad, but, you know, it might pose a bit of a problem.

SE: Really? Why? I thought we'd had advertisements for essays in the paper before.

FA: Yes, that's true, but right now it's a hot topic. You know, Tasha, the English department just approved a tough new plagiarism policy, and it's going before the Faculty Senate next week. Students may be expelled if they turn in one of these essays with their own name on it.

SE: I think every student knows the risks. But what about our ad? Isn't it unconstitutional to censor it? I mean, what about our right to freedom of the press? We should be allowed to print what we want! That's what you teach us in law and ethics class!

FA: Calm down, Tasha. I'm not saying that we can't print the ad. I'm just concerned about the campus reaction. A lot of faculty and administrators have been talking about plagiarism, and many of them are in favor of banning these ads. I guess they figure a ban on ads from these companies would reduce the number of plagiarized essays.

SE: Well, you know Dr. J., everyone already knows where you can download papers, even for free. And our professors are so quick to tell us how they can just Google a sentence from our paper to catch plagiarism. And isn't that why the college newspaper staff decided fifteen years ago to give up school funding . . . so that they could retain their editorial independence? Of course, that means we have to rely on advertising.

FA: You know, Tasha, I think you may have a law career ahead of you. You certainly make compelling arguments. But you don't have to convince me. You know where I stand on editorial independence. I'm with you.

SE: So does that mean we get to go with the ad? We really need that $500.

FA: Alright, why don't we have an editorial team meeting this afternoon? We'll weigh our options and come up with a decision and a plan.

SE: OK—I'll get everyone together. You know, I was wondering what my editorial would be this week. Now I have it! I'll defend the status quo . . . oppose the advertising ban proposal and defend freedom of speech!

FA: Just remember to tone down your language. Support your arguments with facts, Tasha, and I think that will make a great editorial.

SE: Thanks, Dr. J. I Gotta go to class now. See you this afternoon.

PAGE 182, SECOND LISTENING

Listen again to part of the conversation. Then answer question 4.

FA: Calm down, Tasha. I'm not saying that we can't print the ad. I'm just concerned about the campus reaction. A lot of faculty and administrators have been talking about plagiarism, and many of them are in favor of banning these ads. I guess they figure a ban on ads from these companies would reduce the number of plagiarized essays.

What is the faculty advisor's opinion of banning term paper advertisements?

Listen again to part of the conversation. Then answer question 5.

SE: And isn't that why the college newspaper staff decided fifteen years ago to give up school funding . . . so that they could retain their editorial independence? Of course, that means we have to rely on advertising.

What is the student editor's attitude toward the newspaper's need to advertise?

ACADEMIC LISTENING

PAGE 183, FIRST LISTENING

Journalism professor: Hello everyone. OK, so, today we're going to continue our discussion of media censorship by looking at television. Since government regulation of television is fairly new in the United States, there's still plenty of debate about whether or not regulation should exist and how effective it is.

Concerns about the effects of TV on children have existed, well, almost since the birth of television. Most research has shown that watching violent TV shows often leads to more violent behavior in children. One study proved that the average American child will have watched 8,000 murders on television by the age of twelve. It's no wonder, then, that many people believe that the amount of violence shown on TV should be decreased.

In 1996, Congress responded to these concerns by passing the Telecommunications Act. Uh, this law ordered the TV industry to establish a ratings system based on the system used to rate movies. The TV ratings are those "signs" on your screen that alert you about program content. You've seen them, right? Like, for instance, "TV-14" means "parents strongly cautioned." The content may be unsuitable for viewers under the age of fourteen. Or, um, "TV-MA" means "mature audience only." Oh, and details about the content are listed, too: S stands for sex, V for

violence, L for language. You get the idea. The FCC—Federal Communications Commission—is the government agency that controls the TV ratings and it issues stiff fines when networks air programs with inappropriate content.

Now, the Telecommunications Act also required TV manufacturers to install blocking devices in all new sets. These blocking devices are called V-chips—violence chips—and what they do is they allow parents to program the TV to block out inappropriate channels or programs. The FCC regulates and monitors V-chips too, by the way.

So, the question is: Has the Telecommunications Act lived up to its goals of cleaning up television programming? The answer is mixed, depending on which side of the debate you're on.

OK, on one side, parents, educators, and religious leaders complain that V-chips have been ineffective. Most Americans don't even know their TV has a V-chip. Most people don't use them, and when they do, many children find it easy to undo the blocking. And parents and others complain that children can still see sex and violence on TV at all hours.

And on the other side, the TV industry, which opposed the V-chip when it first came out, well, they've been promoting it recently. TV stations are probably reacting to the FCC's clamping down and issuing huge fines for recent violations. But, you know, the networks' response isn't as noble as it might seem. I mean after all, the V-chip gives TV stations an excuse to offer any kind of programs they want, and they can just say, "Well, look, if you don't like a program, just use your V-chip."

TV ratings have been more effective than V-chips. But even Richard Heffner, the creator of the movie ratings system, he warns that ratings don't work as well for TV as for movies because there's an important missing piece—the box office. There's no box office on a television, of course, so there's no intermediate point where someone is checking to see the ratings are being followed. If parents don't monitor their children's TV viewing, then I'm afraid the ratings don't work.

So, TV regulation is still a work in progress. In coming years, the regulation of TV and other media that come into homes— with no box office intermediary—will continue to challenge us all.

PAGE 184, SECOND LISTENING

Listen again to part of the lecture. Then answer question 3.

Journalism professor: Ok, on one side, parents, educators, and religious leaders complain that V-chips have been ineffective. Most Americans don't even know their TV has a V-chip. Most people don't use them, and when they do, many children find it easy to undo the blocking.

What is the professor's attitude when he says, "Most Americans don't even know their TV has a V-chip."?

Listen again to part of the lecture. Then answer question 4.

Journalism professor: And on the other side, the TV industry, which opposed the V-chip when it first came out, well, they've been promoting it recently. TV stations are probably reacting to the FCC's clamping down and issuing huge fines for recent violations. But, you know, the networks' response isn't as noble as it might seem. I mean, after all, the V-chip gives TV stations an excuse to offer any kind of programs they want, and they can just say, "Well, look, if you don't like a program, just use your V-chip."

What is the professor's attitude toward the TV stations' position on V-chips?

INTEGRATED TASK

PAGE 192, LISTENING

Host: Welcome to *Media Issues*. Today we're discussing the increasing support for media censorship. Our guest is Dr. Wallace Mills, professor of religious studies at Edwards State University.

Dr. Mills, recently we've noticed that more citizens are voicing their support for media censorship. And, increasingly, states and schools are passing laws and policies that support censorship. So, what do you see as the reasons behind the move towards stricter media regulation?

Wallace Mills: Well, you know, many people today, especially parents, educators, and religious leaders, feel that the media are contributing to a decline in family values and moral principles. And they're making strong cases for their views with state legislatures and school districts.

So, if you look at it from the viewpoint of parents—and parents are the main group supporting censorship—the media are formidable forces. A busy mother is concerned about violence and sex on TV shows and movies, and the books her children read, the music they listen to, and, of course, the Internet with its adult content. Now, she can restrict the amount of time her children spend with different media, but can she really restrict what they see, read, or listen to? It's not easy, as we all know, so parents are fighting back against what they see as inappropriate media content.

H: Yeah, like the recent case at Springfield High School?

WM: Yes, exactly. Indeed. In that case, parents were upset about their children reading the novel *Ordinary People* in a tenth-grade class. One parent in particular, Mrs. Elizabeth Jones, told the school board that she didn't want her daughter reading a novel that uses bad language and portrayed a dysfunctional family and a teenaged son's intimate relationships.

This Mrs. Jones said her daughter was too young and immature to be able to handle this material responsibly. And she also felt school lessons should reflect the community's values. Now, at school, her daughter was reading about sex and family breakdowns, while at home, Mrs. Jones and her husband were trying to teach their children to value family life and moral behavior.

So, you know, it's no wonder that parents like Mrs. Jones are distressed about the media. Clearly, many people like her would like to see the media clean up their acts.

Answer Key

UNIT 1

CAMPUS CONVERSATION
Pre-listening Vocabulary, page 2

1. d   3. e   5. c   7. h
2. f   4. b   6. a   8. g

First Listening, page 3

1. They are discussing a research project for a class.
2. She wants to turn in a longer paper than the professor specified.
3. The student may be spending too much time on Internet research.

Second Listening, page 3

1. C   3. D   5. A
2. C   4. B

ACADEMIC LISTENING
First Listening, page 4

POSITIVE	NEGATIVE
• multi-tasking makes brain work faster • IQ up 20+ pts. • ability to make fast decisions • answering emails quickly • test taking	• bombarded & overwhelmed • no time for playful/creative noodling • no reflection • obsessed with checking voicemail

Second Listening, page 5

1. C   3. B   5. C
2. C   4. C

MICK'S TOUGHEST INNING
Reading, page 6

1. D   4. B   7. D   10. A
2. A   5. C   8. B   11. B, E, F
3. C   6. C   9. A

Analysis, page 9

1. Basic Comprehension: 1, 2, 4, 10, 11
2. Organization: 3, 9
3. Inference: 5
4. Vocabulary and Reference: 6, 7, 8

INTEGRATED TASK
Reading, page 10

Lifestyle	• work or school performance affected • spending a lot of time online
Relationships	• different relationships over the Net than face-to-face • we lose relationship skills
Feelings	• anxious, depressed, empty, lonely when off the Net • look forward to being online, connecting with others

Listening, page 11

Reasons for compulsive shopping:
- job too stressful
- problems in personal life: guy leaves for another woman
- sad or depressed

Effects of compulsive shopping:
- Lifestyle: come home late
- Financial: overwhelmed with debt
- Emotional: energized, satisfied, enhanced, cheered up

Speaking, page 12

EFFECTS OF INTERNET ADDICTION	EFFECTS OF COMPULSIVE SHOPPING
• Spend too much time online • Work or school performance affected • Lose relationship skills; develop Net relationships—very different from face-to-face relationships • Feel anxious, depressed, lonely when not online	• Spend time shopping, come home late • Spend too much money • Shopping = substitute for bad relationships • Reduces anxiety, depression, but becomes addictive

SIMILARITIES	DIFFERENCES
• take time • affect/substitute for relationships • habits relieve anxiety at first, but then cause problems	• Net addiction affects work, school • compulsive shopping costs a lot of money

SKILL FOCUS: COMPARING AND CONTRASTING

Practice, page 16

1. a. Mantle's success and Mantle's private life full of problems

   b. line between paragraphs 3 and 4

   c. (But)

2. contrast

3. *Suggested outline:*

Topic 1: Mickey Mantle—one of the greatest baseball players

   Details: played for the Yankees in their years of glory
   symbolized hope, prosperity, & confidence
   of America
   was a fast, powerful player; won many
   games and championships
   American dream—handsome country boy,
   son of poor miner

Topic 2: Mantle's private life full of problems

   Details: constant pain from injuries
   lived to fulfill father's dream; drank to
   forget father's death
   addiction destroyed his body—cirrhosis,
   liver cancer
   he turned away from old life, but died at 63

UNIT 2

CAMPUS CONVERSATION

Pre-listening Vocabulary, page 20

1. g	4. a	7. i	10. j
2. b	5. d	8. h	
3. f	6. e	9. c	

First Listening, page 21

1. They are discussing the difficulties in finding good housing.

2. The choice is difficult because some neighborhoods are expensive, some are noisy, and others are far from their school.

3. The idea to rent a huge house large enough for a group of friends is proposed.

Second Listening, page 22

1. A	3. C	5. B
2. B	4. B	

ACADEMIC LISTENING

First Listening, page 23

1. The topic is living in a planned community.

2. Examples:

houses close together, sidewalks, front porches, tree-lined streets, easy access to town center, houses around open areas, big parks, common areas, small private yards

3. He has a negative feeling about Celebration.

Second Listening, page 23

1. C	3. A	5. A
2. D	4. B	

Analysis, page 24

1. Basic Comprehension: 1, 3, 4

2. Organization: 2

3. Inference: 5

MAKING ENDS MEET

Reading, page 25

1. D	4. C	7. B	10. C
2. C	5. D	8. A	11. B, C, E
3. B	6. A	9. A	

INTEGRATED TASK

Reading, page 28

1. Social and civic interaction

   a. Central Market Street district

   Details:

   - reduces traffic
   - encourages social contact
   - compact downtown—people walk, meet neighbors
   - events—art festivals
   - narrow, traffic calm streets with slower speed limits to encourage bicycling, walking

   b. Housing to encourage socializing

   Details:

   - single- and multi-family residences
   - apartments close to downtown
   - houses built close together with small yards
   - lobbies, porches

2. Environmental preservation

   a. Town location and design

   Details:

   - 4,900 acres, with 4,700 acre greenbelt
   - greenbelt, parks, common areas accommodate animals, plants

   b. High-rise office, apartment buildings

   Details:

   - high-density space in small geographic area—reduces urban sprawl

- energy-efficient systems, materials: insulated glass, cooling towers, low-wattage lamps.

Listening, page 30

Definitions of *urban sprawl*

General definition: the growth of cities in an unplanned manner

Description: cities spreading outward, not upward

Effects of urban sprawl

Negative

- robbing us of nature
- increased traffic

Positive

- new homes, businesses
- better schools
- less noise, crime

Solutions to urban sprawl—New Urbanism principles:

Regions

- transportation systems
- environmental protections

Cities

- housing, jobs close together

Neighborhoods

- single- and multi-family housing
- walk to stores, public transportation, parks

Writing, page 31

Urban sprawl problem

Suburban cities grow outward, use land that should be left natural.

> **New Urbanism solutions**
>
> build towns and cities that don't harm environment
>
> don't cut down trees
>
> don't pollute water
>
> protect animal habitat
>
> **Celebration's features**
>
> 700-acre greenbelt, parks, common areas save wildlife, provide animal habitats
>
> offices use energy-efficient cooling and electric systems and materials: insulated glass, cooling towers, low-wattage lamps

Urban sprawl problem

Single-family homes cause sprawl.

> **New Urbanism solution**
>
> build single- and multi-family residences
>
> **Celebration's features**
>
> multi-family residences

high-density apartment buildings close to downtown

houses built close together, with small yards

Urban sprawl problem

Traffic jams to and from suburbs and cities

> **New Urbanism solutions**
>
> develop transportation systems by region
>
> provide housing and jobs so people don't live far from work
>
> create walkable neighborhoods: walk to stores, public transportation, parks, etc.
>
> **Celebration's features**
>
> "traffic calming"—narrow streets, slower speed limits— slows traffic, encourages walking, bicycling
>
> central downtown district: close to housing, can be reached on foot or by bicycle

Urban sprawl problem

No social interaction

> **New Urbanism solution**
>
> increase social interaction: parks, walkable neighborhoods
>
> **Celebration's features**
>
> compact district encourages foot travel, social interaction
>
> special events like art festivals bring residents together
>
> houses built close together
>
> lobbies, front porches

SKILL FOCUS: USING DETAILED EXAMPLES

Practice, page 36

1

Passage 1

General topic: Looking for housing in the Museum district

> Example: It's close to campus
>
> > Detail: wouldn't have to take bus
>
> Example: There's lots to do
>
> > Details: museums, shopping, market; video store
>
> Example: Safety
>
> > Detail: people walking at night

Signal punctuation: colon (:)

Passage 2

General topic: Most people consider urban sprawl to be very harmful.

> Example: Sierra Club says sprawl is "irresponsible," "cancer," "virus on land"
>
> > Details: misuses land that should be preserved for wildlife, parks, farmland; robbing us of nature

Signal words: *including, like*

Passage 3

General topic: Author took two jobs to make ends meet:
Weekend job at nursing home + full-time job at house
   cleaning service

    Example: Merry Maids

       Details: customer pays $25/hr, cleaner gets $6.65/hr

Signal punctuation: long dash (—), colon (:)

Signal phrase: "as follows"

UNIT 3

CAMPUS CONVERSATION

Pre-listening Vocabulary, page 40

1. j	4. g	7. c	10. e
2. a	5. i	8. f	
3. e	6. b	9. h	

First Listening, page 41

1. She has come to tell the professor that she wants to drop the course.

2. The professor is surprised. She tells the student not to drop.

3. She suggests the student get a tutor and study online. She offers to go over the difficult material with the student. She advises the student to keep a positive attitude, to be confident, and to ask for help when she needs it.

Second Listening, page 42

1. C	3. D	5. B
2. D	4. B	

ACADEMIC LISTENING

First Listening, page 43
Second Listening, page 43

PROBLEM	POLLYANNA REACTION
Visit to eye doctor	• "no time to be cranky" • skip mascara, rest eyes
Stop-and-go commute	• perfect for listening to language tapes and doing relaxation exercises
Computer crashes, hold time on help line is hours	• "Oh, no" • "Oh good, time to purge files"
Snowed in with no hope	• catch up on movies

1. B	3. D	5. B
2. A	4. A	

KEEPING YOUR CONFIDENCE UP

Reading, page 44

1. D	4. C	7. D	10. B
2. B	5. D	8. D	
3. C	6. B	9. D	

Analysis, page 48

1. Basic Comprehension: 1, 8, 9

2. Organization: 10

3. Inference: 3, 4, 5

4. Vocabulary and Reference: 2, 6, 7

INTEGRATED TASK

Reading, page 48

SITUATIONAL SHYNESS	CHRONIC SHYNESS
• shy, awkward if object of attention at social gathering • common, temporary • caused by particular situation • blind date • may experience if not prepared for a situation, performing in public • feel arousal, negative thoughts, tension	• can mark lives • carried around • less popular • fewer friends • less social support • lower self-esteem • less money • fewer leadership skills • more boring life • more likely to be depressed • more inclined to be lonely

Listening, page 50

MALE STUDENT— CHRIS	FEMALE STUDENT— MELISSA
• everybody knows him • likes professor, classmates • situations make him shy • outgoing: gives Melissa advice; invites her to lunch, computer lab	• has always been shy • scared to say something stupid • sits by self • school play: forgot lines, froze, ran off crying • afraid to socialize, make friends

Speaking, page 50

Zimbardo's definition

Situational Shyness: common, temporary feeling caused by a particular situation

Chronic Shyness: dispositional shyness that can mark people's lives; carried around, ready to emerge

Which student fits in this category?

Situational Shyness: Chris

Chronic Shyness: Melissa

How does the student in this category relate to others?

Situational Shyness: Everybody knows him. He likes his professor, classmates.

Chronic Shyness: She's afraid to socialize, makes few friends.

How does the student in this category act in class?

Situational Shyness: The professor, everyone in class knows him, so he probably talks to students a lot, asks the professor questions during class.

Chronic Shyness: She's scared to say something stupid. She sits alone. She probably doesn't socialize with classmates or ask many questions.

What kinds of situations make the student in this category shy?

Situational Shyness: He says he's not really shy, but admits that some situations—like a class speech—make him a little shy.

Chronic Shyness: Any social situation with people she doesn't know probably makes her feel shy, though she seems more comfortable in one-on-one conversation. School play experience made her afraid of being center of attention.

How does the student in this category deal with the other student?

Situational Shyness: He tells Melissa not to be shy with him. He tells her half of people are shy. He invites her to lunch, computer lab.

Chronic Shyness: She's shy, but opens up to Chris by sharing her past experience. She's reluctant when he invites her to lunch, but accepts.

SKILL FOCUS: MAKING INFERENCES

Practice, page 55

1
  1. B   2. A   3. A
     A   B   B

3
  1. A
  2. A
  3. B

UNIT 4

CAMPUS CONVERSATION

Pre-listening Vocabulary, page 58

1. e	4. i	7. d
2. c	5. b	8. g
3. h	6. f	9. a

First Listening, page 59

1. He asks the professor about buying a used car.
2. He is concerned about using a credit card online and about the risk of buying a "lemon."
3. Reasons for eBay's success:

   buyers and sellers create products; price competition; promotion in magazines, newspapers and by word of mouth; distributing products quickly

Second Listening, page 60

1. B	3. C	5. B
2. A	4. D	

ACADEMIC LISTENING

First Listening, page 60

1. It dropped.
2. Gladwell uses the example of a car with a broken window.
3. Cues from the environment can cause criminals to commit crimes.

Second Listening, page 61

1. C	3. D	5. C
2. B	4. D	

Analysis, page 62

1. Basic Comprehension: 1, 5
2. Organization: 3
3. Inference: 2, 4

THE STORY OF SILENT SPRING

Pre-reading, page 62

Suggested answers:

MASS MOVEMENT	POSSIBLE TRIGGERS
Nazism—a movement led by Adolf Hitler in Germany in the 1930s-40s	• global economic depression • unemployment • belief in racial superiority
English as an international language—the current movement to have English function as the common "world" language	• increased movement of people between countries = need for common language
Anti-gun movement—current movement to ban or restrict the sale and use of guns in United States	• increase in gun-related crimes • increase in gun-related deaths, including accidental deaths involving children • more guns and gun-related action shown in movies, other media

Reading, page 63

1. A	4. D	7. C	10. B
2. C	5. C	8. C	11. C
3. A	6. A	9. A	12. B, E, F

INTEGRATED TASK
Reading, page 67

CATEGORY	DEFINITION	DETAILS
Mavens	type of people who have specialized knowledge	• people rely on mavens when deciding where to shop or dine, or which movies to see, etc.
Connectors	kind of people who know everybody	• have extraordinary social ties • powerful in generating word-of-mouth epidemics—can spread information five or six times
Salesmen	able to persuade people to adopt a new idea	• have natural ability to win people over, to get hold of an idea and make it go a long way

Listening, page 69

Paul Revere's ride

- rode from Boston to Lexington to warn of British attack
- learned of attack from several sources
- news gave colonial army time to organize and resist enemy

Revere's social connections

- was a "connector": knew everybody, the type you go to for news
- lived entire life in Boston
- had network from childhood, business, community
  - businesses: owned silver shop, printing press, arms factory, dentistry
  - clubs and organizations: Army officer, Freemason, Charitable Association
  - grand juror
- very popular
- thousands came to his funeral

Writing, page 70

A CONNECTOR...	REVERE'S ACTIVITIES/ CHARACTERISTICS
...knows everybody	He knew everybody, lived entire life in Boston, thousands attended his funeral.
...has social ties	Strong social ties came from his childhood, businesses (silver, printing, arms manufacturing, dentistry), his clubs, political activity (Army, Freemasons, etc.), etc.
...is able to spread word-of-mouth epidemics	Wide circle of friends enabled him to receive and spread news.

SKILL FOCUS: IDENTIFYING AND USING MAIN IDEAS AND DETAILS
Practice, page 75

Introduction—Thesis Statement (main idea of passage): New ideas spread like viruses through person-to-person communication.

Topic Sentence (main idea of paragraph): Companies can transmit ideas in the same way that viruses spread.

Detail 1: Hotmail illustrates a "virusworthy" idea.

Detail 2: Everyone knows Hotmail because the name appears on its e-mail messages.

Topic Sentence (main idea of paragraph): The people who disseminate information can be called "sneezers."

Detail 1: Oprah Winfrey is an example of someone who spreads ideas.

Detail 2: Viewers follow Winfrey's recommendations about books.

UNIT 5

CAMPUS CONVERSATION
Pre-listening Vocabulary, page 78

1. g	3. b	5. h	7. d
2. f	4. c	6. e	8. a

First Listening, page 79

1. They are discussing the student's worries about a family crisis.
2. The student is upset because he is far away and can't help his family.
3. The counselor suggests that the student contact friends who can aid his family.

Second Listening, page 79

1. A   3. B   5. B
2. C   4. D

ACADEMIC LISTENING

First Listening, page 80

1. He asks her to look at the newsroom and suggest what can be done for people who need help in careers, happiness.

2. She says there are some very good things about the room.

3. Some writers face northeast (good); Northeast = mental ability, peaceful view, makes writing better; East = growth, vitality, green, youth; Southeast = money, purple, 4; Southwest = marriage, partnerships, motherhood, yellow, 2

Second Listening, page 81

1. B   3. C   5. B
2. A   4. A   6. D

READING

Pre-reading, page 82

1. *sagas* = stories, tales. The paragraph tells about the stories of the students.

2. *fleeing* = escaping, running away. Many immigrants escape or run away from wars and dictatorships.

Reading, page 82

1. B   4. B   7. D   10. D
2. C   5. A   8. D   11. D
3. B   6. A   9. A   12. B, D, E

Analysis, page 86

1. Basic Comprehension: 1, 5, 7, 10, 12
2. Organization: 2, 11
3. Inference: 3, 4
4. Vocabulary and Reference: 6, 8, 9

INTEGRATED TASK

Reading, page 87

FEATURES OF VICTORIAN DESIGN	DETAILS AND EXAMPLES
Filled spaces	• bareness is a sign of poor taste • fill spaces with as many objects as possible Peninsula Hotel: • ornate wood furniture • tabletops, walls adorned with decorative objects, art • size, number of elements give it impressive, elegant atmosphere
Use of rich fabrics	• cloth is a primary material in Victorian rooms • thick, rich drapery compensates for lack of light • fabric on furniture • plush carpets, rugs Peninsula Hotel: • thick draperies on windows
Decoration of walls	Peninsula Hotel: • molding, wallpaper, paint • moldings add texture, depth to already complicated interiors • results: rooms that overflow with decorative, elegant elements

Listening, page 89

Balance	Energy Flow
• Chinese believe in yin, yang: balance in everything • Fallingwater: yin—simple, large interiors, lots of light • yang—low ceilings • balance of objects, empty spaces; open, occupied areas • balanced use of 5 Chinese elements: fire, water, earth, wood, metal	• Wright's open, bright spaces encouraged energy flow • energy = chi'i • no clutter, tight spaces • large windows allow light • waterfall = negative energy

SKILL FOCUS: USING CONTEXT CLUES

Practice, page 94

1
1. C
2. houses
3. the direction—south
4. C
5. B

2

CULTURAL DIFFERENCE	DETAILS
Being less demonstrative	Teacher says to sit on hands while describing frog digestive system
Cultural distances	People step back when she talks, she's standing too close
Arm-shaking gesture	Penny is offended, thinks gesture means aggression, not friendliness
Walking arm-in-arm	Friend is embarrassed when speaker hooks arms while walking

1. B   3. C
2. B   4. A

UNIT 6

CAMPUS CONVERSATION

Pre-listening Vocabulary, page 98

1. h   4. d   7. i   10. j
2. b   5. g   8. f
3. c   6. e   9. a

First Listening, page 99

1. The student must choose whether to attend a summer retreat or take courses.

2. He wants to attend the retreat because he hasn't had time to meditate lately, and it was an incredible experience before.

3. The advisor says that the students is very dedicated and that meditation obviously has a positive effect on his studies.

Second Listening, page 100

1. D   3. A   5. D
2. C   4. B   6. C

ACADEMIC LISTENING

First Listening, page 101

1. Types of work: work with AIDS patients, work with Hmong villagers/refugees, chanting, program for drug addicts

2. The work creates a different daily schedule—less chanting and solitude.

3. "Day trippers" and "two-legged wolves" are tourists or temporary visitors to the monastery.

Second Listening, page 101

1. C   3. B   5. C
2. D   4. D   6. B

Analysis, page 102

1. Basic Comprehension: 1, 2, 5

2. Organization: none

3. Inference: 3, 4, 6

RELIGION

Reading, page 103

1. D   4. B   7. B   10. A
2. C   5. A   8. C   11. C
3. D   6. B   9. D   12. C

INTEGRATED TASK

Reading, page 107

IMPORTANT POINTS ABOUT FASTING	DETAILS
Roots of fasting in religions	• Judaism, Christianity, Islam: roots = ancient prophets • Eastern religions: roots = ancient yogic, ascetic traditions
General purpose of fasting	• increase spirituality • come closer to the divine
Benefits of fasting	Eck: • breaks attachment to material things • speaks out against consumption, materialism Ahmed: • vital to spiritual well-being • replenishment of the soul • without it, people become spiritually exhausted • helps people pull back from daily lives

Listening, page 109

Merton's struggle to follow ascetic practices

- felt drawn to God, committed himself to Catholic faith
- did volunteer work, but felt spiritually incomplete
- became a Trappist monk
- suffered through loneliness, rigors of monastic life
- had to give up smoking, drinking, talking
- ascetic life: fasting, silence, prayer

Merton's rich life as a monk

- made him somber
- developed a gift for writing
- for 20 years, "talked" by writing about life, faith, human issues

- autobiography *The Seven Storey Mountain* sold 1 million copies, 1948
- wrote about ascetic life
- found inner unity and understanding through fasting, ascetic practices
- wrote against nuclear weapons, for peace, non-violence
- legislators quoted him to support civil rights legislation
- met Dalai Lama, brought deeper understanding between Buddhists and Christians
- donated money from his books to monastery

Writing, page 110
Suggested outline:

Introduction—Thesis Statement (fasting and spirituality): Fasting is a means of breaking away from day-to-day needs and getting in touch with one's beliefs, as is demonstrated by the life of Thomas Merton.

Topic Sentence (Merton's ascetic practices): Merton lived a rigorous life as an ascetic Catholic monk.

Details: gave up smoking, drinking, talking; ascetic practices included fasting, silence, prayer

Topic Sentence (impact of Merton's ascetic practices): Though he struggled at first, Merton benefitted from fasting, leading him to make a great impact on the world.

Details: gained spirtuality, inner unity, understanding; wrote influential books; donated money

Conclusion: Merton's life demonstrates the power of fasting as a way to "step back" from everyday life and focus on spiritual beliefs.

SKILL FOCUS: SUMMARIZING
Practice, page 115

1. B, D, E
2. *Suggested summary:*
   There are thoughtless people in the world, but most people want wars and violence to end, according to the Dalai Lama. The religious leader believes that people are not so focused on a single nation's interests as in the past, and he says people today pay more attention to the world around them. Moreover, the Dalai Lama thinks that because of the information revolution, there is no longer a possibility for large, national wars.

2

Suggested summary:
The Dalai Lama says that in 100 years, even if there is not much nature left on earth, there will still be religion. He thinks people will need religions to help explain why the earth became a desert. But

Buddhists believe the world will come and disappear in an endless cycle. The world may become a desert, but it will be reborn.

UNIT 7

CAMPUS CONVERSATION
Pre-listening Vocabulary, page 118

1. j	4. f	7. a	10. b
2. g	5. e	8. d	
3. i	6. c	9. h	

First Listening, page 119

1. They are discussing a work-study position in the library.
2. Kinds of work: shelving books, keeping stacks in order, replenishing paper in computer printers, providing reference help
3. The supervisor decides to consult her colleagues to see if the student will get the job.

Second Listening, page 119

1. B	3. D	5. B
2. A	4. A	

ACADEMIC LISTENING
First Listening, page 120

Caller 1—Bob
1. Employee
2. Employers are secretly watching employees in his office. He thinks this is outside the range of responsible business.

Caller 2—Mary
1. Employee
2. She worked in an office where the company watched workers constantly. She thought her boss had no reason to do this. Employers have gone too far.

Caller 3—Louis
1. Employee
2. He doesn't understand what's causing the increase in employee monitoring. He thinks workers' privacy deserves protections.

Caller 4—Susan
1. Employer
2. She thinks there's nothing harmful about these monitoring practices. As an employer, she has the right to know how her employees are using their time. She uses monitoring to prevent theft and protect her employees.

Second Listening, page 121

1. D		3. A		5. B		7. B	
2. B		4. C		6. A		8. D	

COCA-COLA THINKS INTERNATIONAL

Pre-reading, page 123

1

1. Paragraph 1; 160 countries
2. Paragraph 1; 300 employees
3. Paragraph 2; Roberto Goizueta, Cuba
4. Paragraph 4; overseas

2

Coca-Cola's approach to human resource management is a significant factor in the company's international success.

Reading, page 123

1. B
2. D
3. A
4. A
5. B
6. D
7. D
8. HRM Strategies: A, D, F
   Recruitment Strategies: C, E
9. D
10. A
11. B
12. C, D, E

Analysis, page 127

1. Basic Comprehension: 1, 8, 9, 10, 12
2. Organization: 2, 3, 4, 11
3. Inference: 5, 6
4. Vocabulary and Reference: 7

INTEGRATED TASK

Reading, page 128

Tools for workplace surveillance	• video cameras • audio recorders • computer software
Things that companies monitor	• e-mail • Internet • phone • computer files
Reasons that companies monitor	• to protect themselves and employees legally; to detect legal violations • to measure productivity • to deter theft

Listening, page 129

Problems with workplace surveillance

- often demeans workers
- overmonitoring (counting key strokes)
- secret monitoring
- monitoring in private areas

Recommendations about workplace surveillance

- protect workers' dignity
- inform employees when they're monitored
- do not monitor in purely personal areas
- establish specific rules about listening to private calls

Speaking, page 130

Suggested list:

- Explain the reasons behind the monitoring to maintain employees' dignity.
- Don't monitor employees when they are in private areas at the work site (bathrooms, break rooms, cafeterias).
- Notify employees of how, when, and where they will be monitored.
- Use video cameras to deter theft in areas where equipment and supplies are kept.
- Monitor e-mail, phone, and Internet activities to ensure that no legal violations occur.
- Monitor Internet activity to ensure that employees are not wasting time.

INDEPENDENT TASK

page 131

Sample notes:

Description of job job title, type of work, duties	ESL professor at U.S. university teach ESL reading, writing, listening, speaking develop courses and materials work on special projects related to field
Workplace inside/outside, atmosphere, hours, colleagues/managers	work inside a building, in pleasant surroundings work full time, have flexible hours, get summers off have collegial relationships with colleagues have minimal supervision
Compensation salary, benefits	earn $50,000+ a year have good health benefits for self, family have educational benefits

SKILL FOCUS: SKIMMING AND SCANNING

Practice, page 133

Answers will vary.

1. Paragraph 1: The success of Michael Dell, who started Dell Computer company as a college student, illustrates that entrepreneurial skill is not only found in experienced businesspeople.

   Paragraph 2: Dell was interested in business at an early age.

Paragraph 3: Dell started selling computers from his dorm room at a university.

Paragraph 4: Dell's method of selling custom-made computers was very successful.

Paragraph 5: Dell's strategy of building computers only when orders came in has made his company into a vast empire.

2. Dell started his business in college, in 1984.

   When he finished his freshman year in college in 1984, he told his parents he wanted to leave school to start his own computer company.

3. Dell built computers only when the orders came in.

   Michael Dell's way of tackling the problem of cost was to build the computers only when the orders came in. This reduced inventory and allowed him to use upgraded and cheaper components as soon as they were available.

4. "his decision" = Dell's decision to quit college and start his own business

5. *tackling* = dealing with, handling

UNIT 8

CAMPUS CONVERSATION

Pre-listening Vocabulary, page 138

1. a   3. g   5. f   7. c
2. d   4. h   6. e   8. b

First Listening, page 139

1. They are discussing the possibility of the student's participation in ROTC.

2. Information the recruiter gives:

   • ROTC = Reserve Officer Training Corp—sponsored by U.S. Army

   • Provide scholarships for students interested in leadership opportunities in military

   • Nursing Corps—important branch of army

   • Continue required nursing classes, take ROTC training course in summer, ROTC pays tuition

   • Commissioned as 2nd Lieutenant in army

   • Complete education, get job training, financial support

   • Nursing Corps officers train staff, teach courses, work in hospital

   • Continue with courses required for degree

   • ROTC training—one of top leadership programs

   • Requirements: Age 17-27, physical standards, 2.5 GPA, U.S. citizen

   • After graduation, committed to serving 2 years in active duty, Reserves, or National Guard

   • Orientation—4 P.M. next Monday, Student Life Building, Room 401

Second Listening, page 140

1. B   3. B   5. D
2. D   4. C   6. A

ACADEMIC LISTENING

First Listening, page 141

IMPORTANT POINTS	DETAILS
Toronto in the 1960s	• antiwar center, many draft evaders & resisters there • Ignatieff grew up in antiwar culture of his generation
Ignatieff's views of war; Red Cross ethic	• You cannot abolish war, you can't do without war. • War is a natural, necessary and sometimes even desirable way to solve social conflicts • If we can't abolish war, we'd better find some way to tame it.
Red Cross rules of war	• Don't shoot prisoners. • Don't make war on noncombatants. • Stay away from civilian targets. • Kill people, but don't torture or degrade their bodies.

Second Listening, page 141

1. B   3. C   5. A
2. C   4. D

Analysis, page 142

1. Basic Comprehension: 1, 5

2. Organization: 2

3. Inference: 3, 4

ASMARA JOURNAL: IN PEACE, WOMEN WARRIORS RANK LOW

Pre-reading, page 143
Suggested paraphrases:

Excerpt 1

In times of peace, women soldiers have a low status.

Excerpt 2

Sometimes Nuria Mohammed Saleh misses war, because she misses being treated like a man. However, she doesn't miss feeling afraid, or even excited or part of a group.

Excerpt 3

Most female former soldiers, including Saleh, have trouble functioning in the society of their youth because it is traditional and male-oriented.

Excerpt 4

Maybe women soldiers thought if they fought in the war, they would have a higher rank in Eritrean society, but they were wrong.

Reading, page 144

1. C	5. D	9. C	13. D
2. C	6. B	10. D	14. A, D, E
3. A	7. A	11. C	
4. B	8. A	12. C	

INTEGRATED TASK

Reading, page 148

IMPORTANT POINTS	DETAILS
Why Martino joined the ICRC	• drawn to the idea of doing relief work • studied the ICRC and Geneva Conventions; fascinated by neutrality ethic
Barriers to joining the ICRC	• wondered if she could do her job: see misery, have no comforts, stay neutral • parents opposed her decision to join • parents urged her to join Doctors Without Borders
ICRC's principles and work	• we all share moral tradition: warrior's honor • warriors must tame, control aggression • Geneva Conventions remind people to follow warrior's honor • physicians provide medical services, disseminate information

Listening, page 149

Chan views of war and the warrior's honor

- soldiers must try to follow rules of war
- does not equate war with barbarism, savagery
- a soldier's aggression can't always be tamed
- unrealistic to think that soldiers will follow rules of war

Chan's views of neutrality

- not realistic for observers to be neutral
- doctors see horrific after-effects of war
- doctors do more than disseminate information, bandage wounded

- sometimes they can't and won't be neutral
- they don't hesitate to denounce human rights violations

Writing, page 150
Suggested outline:

Introduction—Thesis Statement: The ICRC believes in neutrality and the warrior's honor, but Doctors without Borders believes in a soldier's natural aggression and taking sides in a war.

The warrior's honor

ICRC: Warriors can be trained to follow rules of humane behavior.

Doctors without Borders: Aggression is natural. Behavior can't always be restrained.

Neutrality

ICRC: Bystanders, doctors, relief workers must remain neutral during war.

Doctors without Borders: Health care workers cannot and will not remain neutral. Human rights violations will be denounced.

Conclusion: The two international health care organizations have very different views about the nature of war.

SKILL FOCUS: PARAPHRASING

Practice, page 154

1
1. A, E, F
2. D

2

MAIN POINTS	NOTES
General situation	A Red Cross volunteer talks to a POW
POW's question about photos	Can I attach photos to my message?
Volunteer's warning about photos	Protect them so they don't get damaged.
POW's question about a bag	Can I staple a plastic bag to the message?
Volunteer's response and further questions	Yes. What are you going to put in the bag?
POW's explanation about the bag	I want to send seeds to my wife.

Suggested paraphrase:

An ICRC volunteer visited a POW to collect messages. The POW asked if he could attach photos to his letter. The volunteer said "yes," but warned the man to protect the photos with something. The POW then asked if he could attach a plastic bag to his message. The volunteer decided it was okay, but he wanted to know what the man planned to put in the bag. The POW admitted that he didn't want to send photos. He finally confessed that he wanted to send his wife azalea seeds.

UNIT 9

CAMPUS CONVERSATION

Pre-listening Vocabulary, page 160

1. e	4. k	7. a	10. f
2. h	5. d	8. c	11. g
3. i	6. l	9. j	12. b

First Listening, page 162

1. They are discussing the student's possible career in music.

2. Information from counselor:

   • Music—not a stable career

   • Part-time schedules, freelance employment

   • Statistics don't paint a pretty picture.

   • Not many musicians can earn a living; they supplement income with earnings from other sources.

   • Most musicians work part-time in that field; they work day jobs, moonlight as musicians

3. The counselor suggests that the student consider alternatives that offer more stable income and combine her love of music with something else. She recommends double majoring in music and another field or majoring in something else and minoring in music. She suggests teaching.

Second Listening, page 162

1. A	3. C	5. D
2. C	4. D	6. B

ACADEMIC LISTENING

First Listening, page 163

IMPORTANT POINTS	DETAILS
Brain at birth	• baby born with circuits that do crucial things: • heartbeat • reflexes • breathing • seeing • temperature • hearing
Music and math	• music/math related • math involved in musical beats • music is mathematical • neuroscientists: similar patterns in math, logical/spatial reasoning
Insights from preschooler study	• two- and three-year-olds got music lessons • became better at solving mazes, copying geometric shapes • music caused circuits to be wired up • wiring for both things is in same side of brain • host is excited, but scared he blew it with his kids • guest agrees, but says "don't panic parents"

Second Listening, page 164

1. D	3. C	5. A
2. A	4. B	

THE SOLOIST

Pre-reading, page 165

Answers will vary.

Excerpt 1

(After improvising for a while)

Before: The cellist was improvising—playing whatever came to his mind.

After: He continued to play the D minor Bach suite in the dark.

Excerpt 2

(For the first time) (again)

Before: Previously, the cellist worried about how his music sounded to others.

After: He regained his ability to hear the music himself.

Excerpt 3

(After an hour or so) (again)

Before: The cellist had been playing for a while, not paying attention to his surroundings. He had not played for an audience for some time.

After: He continued to play to his audience—the cat.

Reading, page 166

1. C	4. A	7. D	10. A
2. A	5. D	8. A	11. D
3. A	6. B	9. C	12. B, C, E

Analysis, page 170

1. Basic Comprehension: 1, 2, 6, 10, 12
2. Organization: 5, 11
3. Inference: 3, 7, 8
4. Vocabulary and Reference: 4, 9

INTEGRATED TASK

Reading, page 170

IMPORTANT POINTS	DETAILS
What the schools want	• 5 percent hike in property taxes • $2.6 million increase in revenues
Why they want it	• arts programs have been hard hit by state budget cuts • want $1.2 million to hire music, band, art teachers
Editors' response/ opinions	• children falling behind in basic skills: national math exam average: 75; district average: 62 • district trustees must attend to essential core courses like math, not waste more time/money on arts • district must trim budget • vote "no" on tax hike

Listening, page 172

Anna's case

- mom insisted she take piano lessons as a child
- now, architecture courses seem easy
- takes a lot of design courses: has to visual design and analyze factors
- musical training enhanced her spatial/analytical skills

Sean's case

- listens to music while doing calculus
- music helps him concentrate, work faster
- aced tests, doesn't have to take final

Study of children

- musical training improved analytical test scores

INDEPENDENT TASK

page 173

Sample outline:

Introduction—Thesis Statement: Music complements my moods, stimulates my thoughts, and relaxes me.

Body

Point 1: Music is an accompaniment to my moods.

Details: Lively music—celebratory; slow music—meditative

Point 2: Music helps me concentrate.

Details: Music without lyrics—focuses thoughts while studying, working.

Point 3: Music calms me.

Details: Daily stress—music transports my mind to other places.

Conclusion: Music plays an important role in my life and gives me many benefits.

SKILL FOCUS: IDENTIFYING AND USING COHESIVE DEVICES

Practice, page 176

2

1. Paragraphs 2 and 3: Not far away . . .
Paragraphs 3 and 4: After newspapers picked up the story . . .
2. musician, he, cellist, his
3. musician/music, cello/cellist, war, played, shell/shellings
4. flesh, blood, bone, rubble, carnage, massacre, battlefield, battle raging, crater, shell, abandoned streets, smashed trucks, burning buildings, terrified people who hid in the cellars, bombs dropped, bullets flew, masonry exploding, shellings went on

3

1. B
2. B

4

Suggested summary:

On May 27, 1992, in Sarajevo, twenty-two people were killed by a mortar shell while standing in line to buy bread. Nearby, a cellist, Vedran Smailovic, saw the massacre. Because he was so affected by it, he decided to play his cello on the spot where the people were killed. He played a very mournful song for twenty-two days at 4 P.M. The bombing continued, but he wasn't hurt. Later, newspapers reported the cellist's wartime concert, and a composer wrote a song in Smailovic's honor.

UNIT 10

CAMPUS CONVERSATION

Pre-listening Vocabulary, page 180

1. j	4. d	7. h	10. f
2. g	5. i	8. a	11. l
3. b	6. e	9. c	12. k

First Listening, page 182

1. They are discussing an advertisement for term papers.

2. He is concerned that the college administration may want to ban this kind of ad.

3. She thinks the student newspaper has the right to reprint the ad.

Second Listening, page 182

1. B	3. D	5. D
2. C	4. B	6. C

ACADEMIC LISTENING

First Listening, page 183

Original problems/reasons for regulation

- watching TV violence leads to violent behavior
- average child will see 8,000 murders on TV by age 12
- people want less violence on TV

Solutions

Telecommunications Act

TV Industry responsibility: ratings system

- based on movie rating system
- signs indicate content (TV-14, TV-MA, etc.)
- FCC controls ratings, issues fines for violations

Manufacturer responsibility: V-chips

- blocking devices—parents program TV to block inappropriate material
- FCC regulates and monitors

Continuing problems

V-chips

- ineffective
- people don't know their TVs have them, don't use them
- children can undo the blocking
- children can still see sex and violence on TV
- give TV stations an excuse to show any programs they want

Ratings system

- more effective than V-chips
- doesn't work as well as movie ratings—no box office
- If parents don't monitor TV viewing, ratings don't work

Second Listening, page 184

1. C	3. D	5. B
2. A	4. B	

Analysis, page 185

1. Basic Comprehension: 1, 2

2. Organization: 5

3. Inference: 3, 4

THE WEB WAR: LAWMAKERS VERSUS LIBRARIANS

Pre-reading, page 186

1. argumentation

2. battle; On one side . . ./On the opposing side . . . ; all-out war; debate raged; supporters of the law; Whereas some libraries . . . oppose, other libraries favor . . . ; Opponents argue; war will continue to rage

Reading, page 186

1. C	6. D	11. Librarians: B, F, G
2. A	7. A	12. B
3. B	8. C	13. D
4. B	9. A	
5. D	10. Lawmakers: C, E	

INTEGRATED TASK

Reading, page 191

IMPORTANT POINTS	DETAILS
Censorship statistics	- increasing in U.S.—35% increase in past year - in past four years, incidents have doubled - 500+ books banned in schools, public libraries: *Harriet the Spy*, *The Merchant of Venice*
Reasons behind censorship	- upholding community values - profane language - sex, violence scenes - discouraging undesirable attitudes, speech, behavior

Author's reaction to censorship	- censors mean well, but teenagers exposed in real life to things in banned books
	- not apt to swear after reading *Go Ask Alice*
	- disturbed by attacks against books that express ideas that censors disagree with:
	  - Alabama textbooks banned for not following religious, social philosophies
	  - Oregon environmentalists wanted to ban textbook for "pro-industry propaganda."
	- censorship = intolerance
	- Why is access denied because it violates moral, aesthetic, religious, or political views?
	- submitting to one group = limiting freedom of others

Listening, page 192

Current trends in media censorship

- more citizens voicing support for censorship
- states and schools passing laws and policies that support censorship

Reasons for stricter regulation

- people feel media are contributing to decline in values
- people making strong cases with legislatures and school districts

Concerns of a busy mother

- violence, sex on TV/movies
- books her children read
- music they listen to
- Internet—adult content
- can restrict time, but not what her kids see, read, etc.

View of a parent of a tenth-grader

- upset because daughter had to read *Ordinary People*
- novel had bad language, portrayed dysfunctional family and intimate relationships
- felt daughter was too young, immature to handle material
- felt lessons should reflect morals of community
- at school, daughter read about sex, family breakdown; at home, parents teaching family, moral values

Writing, page 193

REASONS FOR CENSORSHIP	REASONS AGAINST CENSORSHIP
• protect children • uphold family and community values • too much violence, sex, profanity on TV, Internet, and in books	• freedom of press—censorship infringes on others' rights • need to present all sides of issues • censorship methods ineffective

INDEPENDENT TASK

page 194
Sample notes:

REGULATION OF TELEVISION		
MAIN POINT	**DETAILS**	**EVALUATION**
TV ratings don't work	Ratings appear on TV screens, but they are meaningless because no one abides by them.	• Parents need to block inappropriate programs. • TV stations should air inappropriate programs after 10 P.M.
TV v-chips don't work.	Children can undo parents' blocking.	• TV manufacturers must redesign v-chips so that blocked channels or programs cannot be unblocked by children.

SKILL FOCUS: IDENTIFYING AND USING RHETORICAL STRUCTURE

Practice, page 199

1

PASSAGE	MAIN RHETORICAL STRUCTURE	WORD/EXPRESSION CLUES
3	comparison/contrast	very different from the same ideas similar cultural backgrounds In contrast different . . . values no longer . . . some practice/others do not less these differences
2	cause/effect	has led to because as a result
1	argumentation	a growing debate Supporters . . . insist/However, others maintain . . . when will they succeed in convincing . . .

2

Sample outline for Topic 1:

Main Idea: Students under the age of eighteen should have freedom of expression.

Point 1: They are not adults, but they already have many responsibilities.

Details: They can drive a car in many countries. They work.

Point 2: They are human beings who should have rights just like adults.

Details: Universal rights—freedom of expression, religion, movement, etc.

Conclusion: Let students have the right to express themselves.

Sample outline for Topic 2:

Main Idea: Students' rights of free expression are very different in the United States than they are in China.

   Point 1: Students can view any Internet sites in the U.S., but not in China.

      Details: U.S.—libraries, schools may put filters on Internet computers, but students' home computers are free from censorship. China—citizens' Internet access is censored. Many sites have been blocked by the government.

   Point 2: Students can demonstrate peaceably in the U.S., but not in China.

      Details: Students in U.S. protested the recent war in Iraq. In China, students have been imprisoned for protesting.

Conclusion: Students in these two countries have different levels of freedom of expression.

ETS Practice Sets
for the TOEFL® iBT

LISTENING

Listen to the conversations and lectures. Answer the questions based on what is stated or implied by the speakers. You may take notes while you listen. Use your notes to help you answer the questions. (Check the Answer Key on pages 265–266.)

CONVERSATION 1

1. What are the two speakers mainly discussing?
  (**A**) How to use graphs effectively in a class presentation
  (**B**) Where the professor posts class information on the Internet
  (**C**) The way the student requests information from the professor
  (**D**) What the student needs to do to meet a deadline for a paper

2. According to the professor, e-mail communication is useful in certain situations. What two examples does the professor mention? **Choose TWO answers.**
  (**A**) Obtaining more details on class work with imminent deadlines
  (**B**) Providing the professor with copies of student presentations
  (**C**) Sharing information about research sources for class papers
  (**D**) Asking follow-up questions about a lecture the professor has given

3. What does the professor imply about discussion groups on the Internet?
  (**A**) They are not as effective as discussion groups that meet in person.
  (**B**) They do not always provide accurate information for participants.
  (**C**) They are not adequate substitutes for attending her seminar.
  (**D**) They do not make use of the professor's lectures on the course material.

4. What does the professor ask the student to do?
  (**A**) Take better notes
  (**B**) Talk more in class
  (**C**) Write longer papers
  (**D**) Send more e-mails

Listen again to part of the conversation. Then answer question 5.

5. Why does the professor say this?
(**A**) To give an example of the benefits of electronic communication
(**B**) To explain why she has added more office hours for students
(**C**) To express some frustration with a current social norm
(**D**) To remind the student to check his e-mail frequently

CONVERSATION 2

1. What is the conversation mainly about?
(**A**) The student's job performance
(**B**) The student's social skills
(**C**) The manager's recruiting plans
(**D**) The manager's computer problems

2. What type of full-time job does the student want after graduation?
(**A**) Hospitality management
(**B**) Software programming
(**C**) Customer service
(**D**) Computer sales

3. What is the student's attitude toward interviewing for full-time jobs?
(**A**) He wants to become better at presenting himself.
(**B**) He finds the process very informative.
(**C**) He believes it will be easy to find the job he wants.
(**D**) He thinks that interviewers have treated him unfairly.

4. How does the manager offer to help the student?
(**A**) By giving him time off for interviews
(**B**) By writing him a letter of recommendation
(**C**) By assigning him new job responsibilities
(**D**) By setting up a meeting for him with a recruiter

Listen again to part of the conversation. Then answer question 5.

5. What does the manager mean when she says this?
(**A**) That the student needs to do more studying
(**B**) That the student is good at working with people
(**C**) That the student will be successful in his new job
(**D**) That the student will need to work hard to acquire a skill

LECTURE 1

1. What aspect of the nineteenth century is the lecture mainly about?
(**A**) Differences between British and American utopian ideals
(**B**) The introduction of free public education
(**C**) An attempt to develop a utopian community
(**D**) Economic reform movements in the United States

2. According to the professor, what did Robert Owen believe about human behavior?

(**A**) Society benefits from human beings' tendency to be competitive.

(**B**) Childhood circumstances are the most significant influence on behavior.

(**C**) Children learn better behavior when educated by their parents at home.

(**D**) A life of hard work will improve an individual's character.

3. Why does the professor mention Owen's views on the use of technology?

(**A**) To show a difference between Owen's beliefs and those of other reformers

(**B**) To describe how Owen became successful managing textile mills

(**C**) To illustrate Owen's unhappiness with industrialization in Great Britain

(**D**) To explain how New Harmony was built in such a short period of time

4. According to the professor, why did some people join the New Harmony community? **Choose TWO answers.**

(**A**) They saw an opportunity to achieve greater social and economic equality.

(**B**) They were unhappy with their lives in England.

(**C**) They agreed with Owen's ideas on science and education.

(**D**) They were attracted by the promise of owning private property.

5. What does the professor imply about the name of the community?

(**A**) It was originally the name of a similar community in England.

(**B**) It was later used by other utopian communities in the United States.

(**C**) It was not an accurate reflection of the situation in the community.

(**D**) It was not chosen by the people in the community.

6. What is the professor's opinion of the New Harmony experiment?

(**A**) She agrees with those who view it as a complete failure.

(**B**) She believes that it was more successful than other utopian experiments of the period.

(**C**) She wants to conduct more research before reaching any conclusions.

(**D**) She thinks that elements of the experiment had an effect on society as a whole.

LECTURE 2

CD2 TRACK 39

1. What is the professor mainly discussing?
  (**A**) The effectiveness of a particular type of marketing
  (**B**) The role of technology in a successful marketing effort
  (**C**) The risks associated with unconventional advertising tactics
  (**D**) The difficulties involved in marketing products to college students

2. Why does the professor ask the students about movies they have recently seen?
  (**A**) To examine how college students typically spend their leisure time
  (**B**) To point out the way some people make decisions about how they spend their money
  (**C**) To find out what types of movies are popular among college students
  (**D**) To demonstrate different ways that advertisements are used to promote movies

3. The professor discusses some of the benefits of word-of-mouth marketing. Identify whether each of the following is a benefit. **Check the correct boxes.**

	A benefit	Not a benefit
(**A**) Receiving discounted prices		
(**B**) Making fewer bad purchases		
(**C**) Getting personally relevant advice		
(**D**) Finding product details quickly		
(**E**) Obtaining objective information		

4. According to the professor, how can a business take advantage of the process of word-of-mouth marketing?
   (A) By paying experts to write reviews of their products
   (B) By encouraging people who are known and respected to try their products
   (C) By advertising their products in as many places as possible
   (D) By having their employees criticize the products of competitors

5. What does the professor think about the way some restaurant managers address customer complaints?
   (A) They are mistaken in thinking that free food is an acceptable response.
   (B) They should be more understanding of how easy it is for an employee to make a mistake.
   (C) They do not realize that some people will complain no matter what the circumstances.
   (D) They do not appreciate the potential benefits of handling complaints properly.

Listen again to part of the lecture. Then answer question 6.

6. Why does the student say this?
   (A) To emphasize her unhappiness with a recent purchase
   (B) To express disagreement with the professor's comment
   (C) To move the class discussion in a different direction
   (D) To find out if the professor understands her point of view

READING

Read the passages and answer the reading comprehension questions. (Check the Answer Key on pages 265–266.)

READING 1

Utopians and Education

1   The Greek word *utopia* has been used by those who envision a perfect world. The social reformers of the eighteenth and nineteenth centuries, like the British industrialist Robert Owen and the French theorist Charles Fourier, are considered Utopians because they believed in impossibly ideal conditions of social organization. Convinced that they possessed the truth, Utopians often exhibited a sense of mission by which they tried to persuade the unbeliever to accept the truth of their visions. Nonviolent but persuasive, Utopians relied heavily on providing unbelievers with information to convert them to the Utopian vision so that they joined the cause. Utopians relied on informal education to make their messages known to an ever-widening audience. Owen and Fourier, for example, were tireless writers who produced volumes of essays and other publications. In particular, Owen was a frequent lecturer and organizer of committees designed to advance his Utopian beliefs.

2   Education was designed to create a popular movement for joining the Utopian cause. In this journalist or lecture stage, Utopian education consisted of two elements. First, it mentioned the ills of society and suggested how they might be remedied. Second, it presented a picture of life, often minutely detailed, in the new society.

3   Utopians believed that modern industrialism had caused individuals to lose interest in the values of both family and the larger society, resulting in personal and social disorganization. To overcome this sense of alienation, Utopians sought to create perfectly integrated communities. Like the ancient Greek city-state, the new community would be a totally instructive environment. Work, leisure, art, and social and economic relationships would reinforce the sense of community and cultivate communitarian[1] values. Fourier's form of communal organization, the phalanstery, consisted of 2,000 members and was organized into flexible groups that provided for production, education, and recreation. In addition to communal workshops, kitchens, and laundries, the phalanstery would also provide libraries, concert halls, and study rooms for its members.

4   Utopian theorists, especially Owen, emphasized the education of the young in institutes and schools. The child, they reasoned, held the key to continuing the new society. Rejecting older concepts of child depravity and inherited human weakness, Utopians believed that human nature can be

---

[1] communitarian—marked by membership or support of a social organization in small, collectively controlled communities

molded . Owen and other Utopians advocated beginning children's education as early as possible. Young children, they reasoned, were free of the prejudices and biases of the previously established social order. If they were educated in community nurseries, they would be free from the contaminating ideas of those who had not yet been cured of the vices of the established society. They could be shaped into the desired type of communitarian human being. Community nurseries and infant schools performed a second function: freeing women from the burdens of child rearing and allowing them to have full equality with the male residents of Utopia.

5   According to Fourier, the family and the school in the previously established social order were agencies used to criticize and correct children. Fourier intended to replace them with associative or group-centered education in which peer friends would correct negative behavior in the spirit of open friendship. Fourier's associative form of education involved mutual criticism and group correction, which was a form of character molding that brought about community social control and conformity. Fourier believed that children, like adults, had instincts and interests that should be encouraged rather than repressed. He envisioned a system of miniature workshops in which children could develop their industrious instincts.

6   His associative education was also intended to further the children's complete development. First, the body and its senses were exercised and developed. Second, cooking, gardening, and other productive activities would cultivate the skills of making and managing products. Third, mental, moral, and spiritual development would incline the child to truth and justice.

7   Schooling in the Utopian designs of Owen, Fourier, and others rejected learning that was highly verbal, rigidly systematic, and dominated by classical languages. Because of its concern for forming character, it often led to pioneering insights in early childhood education. It was intended, however, to bring about a sense of conformity to group norms and rules. While immersion in the group diminished the personal alienation caused by industrial society, it also restricted the opportunity to develop individual difference and creativity.

1. Which of the sentences below best expresses the essential information in the following sentence from paragraph 1? Incorrect choices change the meaning in important ways or leave out essential information.

Convinced that they possessed the truth, Utopians often exhibited a sense of mission by which they tried to persuade the unbeliever to accept the truth of their visions.

(**A**) Because they felt they were right, Utopians convinced unbelievers to accept their point of view.

(**B**) Utopians had a sense of purpose and truth that unbelievers did not accept.

(**C**) The belief that they were right gave Utopians a strong sense of purpose in persuading others.

(**D**) Unbelievers often changed their minds once they realized that the Utopians thought that they possessed the truth.

2. According to paragraphs 1 and 2, what was the main method that Utopians used to spread their beliefs?
- **(A)** They formally educated students in schools.
- **(B)** They expressed their ideas to audiences in writing and speaking.
- **(C)** They challenged non-Utopians to public debates.
- **(D)** They organized groups of Utopians to meet in people's homes.

3. Why does the author mention "the ancient Greek city-state" in paragraph 3?
- **(A)** To contrast ancient Greek culture with Fourier's vision of Utopian culture
- **(B)** To suggest that both Greek and Utopian communities were organized for educational purposes
- **(C)** To emphasize that both Greek and Utopian communities encouraged individual expression
- **(D)** To illustrate the superiority of Greek moral values to those of Utopians

4. Paragraph 3 suggests that according to Utopian belief, modern industrialism harmed people by
- **(A)** causing personal and social disorganization
- **(B)** increasing their desire for social activity
- **(C)** restricting their economic relationships
- **(D)** encouraging too much leisure activity

5. The word **_integrated_** in paragraph 3 is closest in meaning to
- **(A)** managed
- **(B)** instructed
- **(C)** informed
- **(D)** unified

6. The word **_molded_** in paragraph 4 is closest in meaning to
- **(A)** understood
- **(B)** shaped
- **(C)** confused
- **(D)** grouped

7. According to paragraph 5, how did Fourier believe that children should be educated?
- **(A)** They should learn from their interactions with other children.
- **(B)** Their behavior should be supervised by older adults.
- **(C)** They should be instructed primarily by the individual family unit.
- **(D)** They should receive criticism from both adults and children.

8. According to paragraphs 5 and 6, what was one purpose of associative learning?
- **(A)** It taught children how to develop strong critical abilities.
- **(B)** It enabled children to live harmoniously in a group setting.
- **(C)** It taught children to control their natural instincts.
- **(D)** It demonstrated the superiority of spiritual over physical development.

9. The word **cultivate** in paragraph 6 is closest in meaning to
   (**A**) separate
   (**B**) require
   (**C**) develop
   (**D**) organize

10. The word **It** in paragraph 7 refers to
    (**A**) Utopian schooling
    (**B**) verbal, rigidly systematic learning
    (**C**) concern for forming character
    (**D**) early childhood education

11. The word **immersion** in paragraph 7 is closest in meaning to
    (**A**) expansion
    (**B**) variation
    (**C**) involvement
    (**D**) imagination

12. According to the passage, all of the following are advantages of a Utopian education EXCEPT:
    (**A**) Children are not affected by the prejudiced beliefs of adults.
    (**B**) Women are freed from the obligations of raising children.
    (**C**) Children learn to work hard naturally in groups.
    (**D**) Personal creativity is emphasized.

13. Look at the four squares ☐ that indicate where the following sentence could be added to the passage. Where would the sentence best fit? Circle the letter that shows the point where you would insert this sentence.

    In this way, both sexes would advance as far as they were able within the Utopian community.

    Young children, they reasoned, were free of the prejudices and biases of the previously established social order. **A** If they were educated in community nurseries, they would be free from the contaminating ideas of those who had not yet been cured of the vices of the established society. **B** They could be shaped into the desired type of communitarian human being. **C** Community nurseries and infant schools performed a second function: freeing women from the burdens of child rearing and allowing them to have full equality with the male residents of Utopia. **D**

14. Read the first sentence of a summary of the passage. Then complete the summary by circling the THREE answer choices that express the most important ideas in the passage. Some sentences do not belong in the summary because they express ideas that are not presented in the passage or are minor ideas in the passage.

Utopians viewed education as the most important way to build an ideal society.

(**A**) The Utopian Robert Owen saw schools for the very young as critical to shaping human character.

(**B**) The importance of adult authority was not emphasized in Utopian education.

(**C**) Utopians believed that certain studies were more appropriate for men than women.

(**D**) Family loyalty was emphasized over community loyalty in Utopian society.

(**E**) Utopian education encouraged open, instructive relationships between children.

(**F**) Utopian schooling had an influence on traditional early childhood education.

READING 2

The Endangered Species Act

1   In colonial days, huge flocks of snowy egrets inhabited coastal wetlands and marshes of the southeastern United States. In the 1800s, when fashion dictated fancy hats adorned with feathers, egrets and other birds were hunted for their plumage. By the late 1800s, egrets were almost extinct. In 1886 the newly formed Audubon Society began a press campaign to shame feather wearers and end the terrible folly. The campaign caught on, and gradually, attitudes changed and new laws followed.

2   Florida and Texas were the first states to pass laws protecting such birds. Then, in 1900, the United States Congress passed the Lacey Act, forbidding interstate commerce to deal in illegally killed wildlife, making it more difficult for hunters to sell their kill. Since then, numerous wildlife refuges have been

established to protect the birds' feeding habitats. With millions of people visiting these refuges and seeing the birds in their natural locales, attitudes have changed significantly. Today the thought of hunting these birds would be abhorrent to most people, even if official protection were removed. Thus protected, egret populations were able to recover substantially. In the meantime, the Lacey Act has become the most important piece of legislation protecting wildlife from illegal killing or smuggling.

3   Congress took another major step when it passed a series of acts to protect endangered species. The most comprehensive and recent of these acts is the Endangered Species Act (ESA) of 1973 (reauthorized in 1988). An endangered species is a species that has been reduced to the point where it is in imminent danger of becoming extinct if protection is not provided. The act also provides for the protection of threatened species, which are judged to be in jeopardy but not on the brink of extinction. When a species is officially recognized as being either endangered or threatened, the law specifies substantial fines for killing, trapping, uprooting (plants), or engaging in commerce in the species or its parts. The legislation forbidding commerce includes wildlife threatened with extinction anywhere in the world.

4   The ESA requires the United States Fish and Wildlife Service (USFWS), under the Department of the Interior, to draft recovery plans for protected species. Habitats must be mapped and a program for the preservation and management of critical habitats must be designed, such that the species can rebuild its population.

5   Some critics of the ESA believe that the act does not go far enough. A major shortcoming is that protection is not provided until a species is officially listed as endangered or threatened by the USFWS and a recovery plan is established. Species usually will not make the list until their populations have become dangerously low. Over the past years, the USFWS has been working intensely on listing species and developing recovery plans for them. One of the species recently removed from the list, and an amazing recovery story, is that of the American peregrine falcon. The bald eagle also is scheduled to be removed from the list soon.

6   Both the peregrine falcon and the bald eagle were driven to extremely low numbers because of the use of DDT as a pesticide from the 1940s through the 1960s. Carried up to these predators through the food chain, DDT caused a serious thinning of the birds' eggshells that led to nesting failures in the two species and in numerous other predatory birds. By 1975 a survey indicated that there were only 324 pairs of nesting peregrines in North America. DDT use was banned in both the United States and Canada in the early 1970s, and the stage was set for recovery of the bird. Working with several nonprofit captive-breeding institutions such as the Peregrine Fund, the USFWS sponsored efforts that resulted in the release of some 6,000 captive-bred young falcons in 34 states over a period of 23 years. There are now about 1,600 known breeding pairs in the United States and Canada—well above the targeted recovery population of 631 pairs.

1. According to paragraph 1, what almost caused egrets to become extinct?
   (A) The hunting of egrets for their feathers
   (B) The Audubon Society's lack of interest in protecting birds
   (C) A slow drying of the wetlands and marshes that formed the egrets' habitat
   (D) A campaign by the press to reduce the number of egrets in the southeastern United States

2. It can be inferred from paragraph 1 that after 1886 the influence of the Audubon Society caused
   (A) a new interest in coastal wetlands
   (B) a change in what was considered fashionable
   (C) an increase in the hunting of birds
   (D) an increase in the use of feathers for hats

3. Which of the sentences below best expresses the essential information in the following sentence from paragraph 2? Incorrect choices change the meaning in important ways or leave out essential information.

   With millions of people visiting these refuges and seeing the birds in their natural locales, attitudes have changed significantly.

   (A) Many people have changed the way they think about birds as a result of visiting bird refuges.
   (B) Birds have become accustomed to having millions of people come to their natural locales.
   (C) Birds have changed the way they live because of the millions of people who come to see them.
   (D) Millions of people now want to observe birds living in habitats that are natural and safe.

4. What does paragraph 2 indicate would happen if laws like the Lacey Act were removed?
   (A) Many people would begin to hunt birds.
   (B) More bird refuges would have to be created.
   (C) Most people would continue to oppose the hunting of rare birds.
   (D) Bird populations in some natural locales would decline.

5. The word *comprehensive* in paragraph 3 is closest in meaning to
   (A) common
   (B) complete
   (C) convenient
   (D) controversial

6. What is the function of paragraph 3's discussion of the terms "endangered species" and "threatened species?"
   (A) To argue that government officials need more information when making laws
   (B) To identify which animals need to be protected and which do not
   (C) To suggest that legal terminology continues to change over time
   (D) To provide the legal definitions of species that are protected by the law

7. Which of the following is NOT mentioned in paragraph 3 as an illegal activity when a species is officially recognized as endangered?
(**A**) Selling the animal anywhere in the world
(**B**) Keeping the animal in captivity
(**C**) Catching the animal in a trap
(**D**) Killing the animal

8. What is the purpose of paragraph 4?
(**A**) To explain the benefits of the ESA legislation compared with the legislation described in paragraph 3
(**B**) To provide specific examples of critical habitats that the USFWS has successfully managed
(**C**) To outline the procedures established under the ESA that enable endangered species to rebuild their populations
(**D**) To compare the ESA legislation with an alternate recovery plan

9. The word *shortcoming* in paragraph 5 is closest in meaning to
(**A**) influence
(**B**) weakness
(**C**) request
(**D**) discussion

10. Which of the following can be inferred from paragraph 5 to be the reason some people are critical of the ESA?
(**A**) The ESA list of endangered species has gone too far and become too long.
(**B**) The ESA rules have protected only those species that have great commercial value.
(**C**) The ESA protection of species should begin earlier than it does under the current act.
(**D**) The ESA rules permit species to be removed from the list before they have been able to fully recover their populations.

11. According to paragraph 6, how did peregrine falcons and bald eagles became endangered?
(**A**) Predatory birds began eating the eggs of falcons and eagles.
(**B**) The use of DDT reduced the amount of food available in the falcon and eagle habitat.
(**C**) Falcons and eagles could no longer find materials to build their nests when the use of DDT was discontinued.
(**D**) Falcons and eagles that had consumed food containing DDT laid eggs with defective shells.

12. The word *banned* in paragraph 6 is closest in meaning to
(**A**) prohibited
(**B**) analyzed
(**C**) resumed
(**D**) accepted

13. Look at the four squares ☐ that indicate where the following sentence could be added to the passage. Circle the letter that shows the point where you would insert the sentence. Where would the sentence best fit?

Using this powerful law in 1997, 134 wildlife crimes were prosecuted and punished, and by 1999 special agents of the Fish and Wildlife Service were investigating 1,500 violations of Lacey.

With millions of people visiting these refuges and seeing the birds in their natural locales, attitudes have changed significantly. **A** Today the thought of hunting these birds would be abhorrent to most people, even if official protection were removed. **B** Thus protected, egret populations were able to recover substantially. **C** In the meantime, the Lacey Act has become the most important piece of legislation protecting wildlife from illegal killing or smuggling. **D**

14. Read the first sentence of a summary of the passage. Then complete the summary by circling the THREE answer choices that express the most important ideas in the passage. Some sentences do not belong in the summary because they express ideas that are not presented in the passage or are minor ideas in the passage

The once endangered egret serves as an example of how a species can be prevented from becoming extinct.

(A) The Audubon Society began a campaign in the newspapers to encourage people to wear fancy hats made with beautiful bird feathers.

(B) The social attitudes that once endangered birds changed, and important laws were passed to protect birds from being killed.

(C) Congress passed a number of acts designed to preserve endangered species and their habitats so that populations could rebuild themselves.

(D) Recently, laws such as the Lacey Act and the ESA were reviewed and strongly criticized by the Department of the Interior and the United States Fish and Wildlife Service.

(E) Unfortunately, the peregrine falcon and bald eagle can now be bred only in captivity and no longer live in their natural habitats where their numbers had become dangerously low.

(F) The populations of two endangered species of birds have recovered after laws were passed making the use of the pesticide DDT illegal.

WRITING

For this task, you will read a passage about an academic topic and you will listen to a lecture about the same topic. Then you will write a response to a question that asks you about the relationship between the lecture you heard and the reading passage. You should allow 3 minutes to read the passage. Then listen to the lecture. Then allow 20 minutes to plan and write your response.

INTEGRATED WRITING TASK 1

READING

Read the passage.

Easter Island

1   Easter Island, a small, remote island in the Pacific Ocean, was once home to a flourishing culture. But about 500 years ago (A.D. 1500), its society went into a steep decline. History teaches us that events like this are often caused by outside influences. So it is not unreasonable to consider whether there are facts about the decline of Easter Island's society that would be explained by a hypothesis of an invasion.

2   One such fact has to do with trees. Most Pacific island societies have managed to find an ecologically balanced way of living by using—but not overexploiting—natural resources such as trees. Most Pacific islands, therefore, remain lush—but not Easter Island. Although it was once densely forested, most of its trees had disappeared by about 500 years ago. Environmental destruction of this sort has often been caused by invaders who deplete an area's natural resources without any concern for the future.

3   Facts about the large stone statues on Easter Island could also support the idea of an invasion. There are about 900 of these statues on the island; the largest is over 20 meters tall. The native society clearly placed a great deal of importance on their production. Yet at about the same time that the island became deforested, islanders stopped making these huge statues. An invasion would help explain why this traditional practice came to a sudden end.

4   Furthermore, we know that around the time these other changes were taking place, a new religion developed on Easter Island: the "Birdman" worship. There is no convincing evidence that the Birdman religion existed before 1500, which suggests that this new religious practice may have been introduced by outsiders.

LISTENING

 CD2 TRACK 41

Now listen to an excerpt on the same topic.

WRITING

Summarize the points made in the lecture, being sure to specifically indicate how they challenge explanations offered in the reading passage.

INTEGRATED WRITING TASK 2

READING

Read the passage.

External versus Internal Hiring

1   When a company needs to hire someone for a managerial position, there is often a choice between promoting an employee who is already working inside the company or bringing in a person from outside. Hiring a qualified outsider is often to a company's advantage for several reasons.

2   An important reason for hiring outsiders as managers is that they bring a new perspective. This contributes to the diversity of ideas and allows company practices to be seen in a new light. Often, an outside hire will ask, "What's the reason for doing things this way?" This question may lead to a reevaluation of practices that are actually inefficient but have become so much a part of the routine that it's difficult for insiders to question them.

3   Another major factor to be considered is the cost of on-the-job training. Hiring outsiders allows a company to look for people who already have the particular skills and experience required for the job. The company will not have to spend time and money training an internal employee for the new job—something that has to be done when, for example, an employee is promoted from a technical position to a managerial one. In such a case, usually the employee would be sent to classes to help learn needed managerial skills.

4   Finally, managers hired from the outside will often have business contacts with suppliers, customers, and technicians that they have developed in their previous job. Clearly these contacts can be a valuable asset for the company that hires managers from the outside.

LISTENING

Now listen to an excerpt on the same topic.

WRITING

Summarize the points made in the lecture, being sure to specifically explain how they cast doubt on points made in the reading passage.

SPEAKING

INTEGRATED SPEAKING TASK 1

Read the short text below. Then listen to a talk on the same topic. You will then answer a question about what you have read and heard. You may take notes as you listen. You may use your notes to help you prepare your response. You will need to combine appropriate information from the text and the talk to provide a complete answer to the question. (Check the Answer Key on pages 265–266.)

READING

Northern University's professors have made a request of the university's student association. Read the following article in the student newspaper describing the request and the student association's response to it. You will have 45 seconds to read the announcement. Begin reading now.

> The student association has rejected a request by the university's professors to stop publishing the Professor Ratings Survey. This popular report, which the student association publishes each year, gives students the opportunity to evaluate their professors by filling out questionnaires, which the student association then collects. Based on these questionnaires, the professors are assigned ratings. The professors say that the survey is irresponsible, because the ratings are inaccurate and unfair. The student association says it disagrees strongly and claims that the professors want to impose censorship.

LISTENING

Now listen to an excerpt on the same topic.

SPEAKING

Speak on the following topic.

The student discusses his opinion of the professors' request. Explain what the professors want and why the student agrees or disagrees with their request.

INTEGRATED SPEAKING TASK 2

Read the short text below. Then listen to a talk on the same topic. You will then answer a question about what you have read and heard. You may take notes as you listen. You may use your notes to help you prepare your response. You will need to combine appropriate information from the text and the talk to provide a complete answer to the question. (Check the Answer Key on pages 265–266.)

READING

Now read a passage about the right to free speech. You have 45 seconds to read the passage. Begin reading now.

Although the First Amendment of the U.S. Constitution guarantees free speech, this right is not absolute in all places. The government can, if it chooses, ban free speech from some types of government-owned property. Specifically, it can ban free-speech activities from places called *nonpublic forums*. Nonpublic forums include places intended for the exercise of official government functions where protesting could disrupt important essential services. In contrast, the government may not ban free speech from *traditional public forums*. These are areas open for anyone's use, like parks, which the government owns but which are not designed for official government business.

LISTENING

Now listen to an excerpt on the same topic.

SPEAKING

Speak on the following topic.

Using the example from the talk, explain what is meant by *nonpublic forums* and *traditional public forums*.

Audioscript

LISTENING

PAGE 242, CONVERSATION 1

Professor: Hi, Sam, thanks for coming in to see me.

Student: No problem. I got your e-mail. What did you want to see me about?

P: Well, actually, it was your e-mail—or e-mails I should say—that I wanted to talk about. You know, you've sent me quite a few this semester.

S: Aren't we supposed to use e-mail when we have questions?

P: Up to a point, sure. But I don't have time to read a lot of e-mails, so they really need to be about things that are urgent. For example, if you need to clarify something about an assignment that's due soon.

S: Like when I asked about, uh, using graphs in our papers?

P: Exactly. That made me realize I needed to let the whole class know—and quickly—that using graphs would be an excellent idea, since you were comparing population growth rates in different countries.

S: What about, um, when I asked you about railroads and population growth—you know, the connection between them?

P: That was fine, too, because I'd already covered that topic—though I wish you'd asked the question in class—but, anyway, that let me know I hadn't been as clear as I thought I'd been, or wish I'd been, in my presentation—so I spent some more time on that point in the next class.

   Look, there's no question e-mail can be a great tool for communication, but you can't get so dependent on it that you never communicate any other way. Like your last e-mail: you asked about the implications of climate changes on population growth. Now, that's a fascinating topic—but it's so broad I couldn't possibly cover it all in an e-mail. That's something we should talk about during an office hour—or, better yet, it's a great question for our seminar. That way everyone can be involved in the discussion.

S: Couldn't we have that discussion on e-mail?

P: I think that discussion groups on the Internet serve a useful purpose if people live far away from each other, but I don't like to …If I can talk to a student, I'd much rather do that. And I want students to talk to me—and to each other. You'll get plenty of chances to practice your writing skills—with tests and papers, but I want everyone …I want you to learn how to express your opinions …your ideas in real live discussions and class debates.

S: It's just, sometimes I think of questions when we're not in class, when you don't have office hours—and I hate to wait.

P: You know, that's one of the things about modern technology—we've begun to expect that everybody should be available all the time. I know twenty-four-hour communication sounds good …but most things actually can wait.

S: I get it. I'll, uh, stop and think before I send any more e-mails.

P: You know, you ask great questions—I just want you to ask more of those questions in class, OK?

S: OK.

Listen again to the part of the conversation. Then answer question 5.

P: You know, that's one of the things about modern technology—we've begun to expect that everybody should be available all the time. I know twenty-four-hour communication sounds good …

Why does the professor say this?

PAGE 243, CONVERSATION 2

Manager: Hi, Dave, you wanted to see me?

Student: Yeah, uh, Ms. Carpenter, I wanted to talk to you about my job.

M: Is there a problem?

S: Not exactly. I mean the job's great. Working on software applications for the computer systems …it's really interesting, and it's a fantastic way to use what I've learned in my computer science major, but …it's just that …I'll graduate in the spring and, while it's only October, I've already had a few interviews for jobs. Mostly to get some experience interviewing.

M: How did they go?

S: OK. Well, actually, not great. I'm looking for a job with a big computer company—in some kind of client support area—something where I can help people …customers with their computer problems, technical stuff.

M: You ought to be good at that.

S: I'm pretty sure I would be, but the problem is …It's just that I'm not that comfortable talking to people when I don't know them—like corporate recruiters. I'm fine when they're asking me about technical stuff, but they don't just wanna talk about computer skills, they wanna ask a lot of, uh, business-type questions. I don't know what to say 'cause I don't have that much, uh, business experience. So I give these really short answers.

M: A lot of people feel a little awkward, a little shy with strangers. You shouldn't feel too bad about that.

S: But it's not good in an interview. I just need to get better at, uh, some of these social types of situations. I have no trouble talking to friends, so I'm sure I can learn to do better in business situations.

M: So how can I help?

S: Well, I was thinking that if I could do something here that involved working with people—more than I do now—I'd learn to, uh, learn how to seem more professional, more confident.

M: Did you have anything particular in mind?

S: Well, I saw this job posted at the conference center—it says they need someone to help with computer problems. Would that mean working with people?

M: It sure would. We get all these visitors—like recruiters—and a lot of them have problems with the computer equipment they want to use for a presentation. Anyway, the meeting coordinator—that's Simon—gets all kinds of calls for help and he doesn't always have someone around who knows how to fix the problem. Most of the students who work in the center are majoring in hospitality management, so their computer skills are pretty basic. But, you…

S: That sounds great!

M: Now, remember, a lot of these folks are completely stressed at the thought that there might be a problem with their big, important presentation. Of course, if you can learn how to handle these folks—successfully—well, you should have no trouble persuading a company that you've got the people skills for whatever job they might have.

S: I'd like to try it. It might make a big difference when I start interviewing seriously next semester.

M: OK, then. I'll find someone to take over your current job, and you can report to Simon starting next week.

S: Thanks, Ms. Carpenter, I really appreciate this.

Listen again to the part of the conversation. Then answer question 5.

M: Of course, if you can learn how to handle these folks—successfully—well, you should have no trouble persuading a company that you've got the people skills for whatever job they might have.

What does the manager mean when she says this?

PAGE 243, LECTURE 1

Professor: One of the interesting things that we haven't covered yet is the significant increase in the number of model … of utopian communities that were established in the first half of the century. By most counts, there were at least a hundred. Rather than trying to discuss a lot of them, I'd like to spend some time focusing on just one of those utopian communities—one that I think is pretty typical in its ambitions—and its problems.

The example I have in mind is Robert Owen and the community he established in New Harmony, Indiana. Owen was a successful industrialist in Great Britain, who achieved quite a bit of fame for some of his reforms of the traditional textile mill environment. Things like improved working conditions, shorter hours and better pay, and, most significantly, schools for children. But Owen had grander schemes—beyond labor reforms. He had a vision of the ideal community … in other words, a utopian community.

Owen envisioned a community where all property was shared. He saw science and technology as a way to improve people's lives. He saw an important role for education and schools in improving … as a way to improve society. For example, Owen believed that the way people … that people behave the way they do because of their environments—particularly the conditions they're exposed to early in life. Therefore, if you want to improve society, children have to be raised in supportive, nurturing environments. And they need a good education, which should be provided by the community. He didn't think parents should have that responsibility once children reached the age of three.

Like other social reformers, who … many of whom felt that industrial societies were too competitive, well, Owen was like them in that he thought property should be shared. However, unlike those reformers who were repelled by all … by every aspect of industrialization, Owen was a big supporter of technology, of all science. He saw industrial advances as a way to work more efficiently, so that people would have more free time … better lives in general.

To implement his plan, Owen left England and went to the United States. He used some of his fortune to buy a small town

named New Harmony. Owen toured the United States promoting his planned community—inviting anyone and everyone to join. And his ideas attracted a wide range of participants—nearly a thousand people arrived in the spring of 1825 to get things rolling. Some were scientists and educators who were excited about his views on technology and school reform. Others were working families, or the unemployed, who were attracted to his commitment to equality through communal … through shared property.

Things went reasonably well for the first few months despite the fact that Owen was rarely present. He was back in England promoting his vision of the new social order. But, then, cracks … divisions started to develop among community members. As I indicated, Owen had recruited a very diverse, uh, combination of residents—and, even though he'd spent a lot of time promoting his ideas to potential participants before they joined, they … these people had different visions of what New Harmony should be once they got there. And Owen wasn't around to help reconcile … to help create some kind of consensus. When Owen did return to New Harmony in 1826, he wanted to push the community into an even more egalitarian economic arrangement. For many, this was just too much change, too fast—and the disagreements among community members became quite serious. I guess it's ironic that the town was called "New Harmony"—things were definitely not harmonious. Anyway, in an attempt to reduce dissension, the community decided not to adopt a new economic model, but it was too late. By mid-1827, tensions were running so high, the experiment was brought to an end. Owen went back to England and the town property was divided among some of the remaining residents.

So, was New Harmony a failure? Some certainly think so because it ended so quickly. Like many visionaries, Owen was a lot better at selling his ideas than he was at implementing them. And the arguments that arose over the economic arrangements undermined his case for the benefits of communal property. But I would argue that the educational reforms had a much greater … a much more lasting impact. New Harmony became the birthplace of a lot of "firsts" in the U.S.: the first infant school, the first trade school, the first public school, and the first free library. It turned out to be a laboratory for some educational ideals that would become standard practice by the end of the century. Significantly, the town didn't just die after Owen abandoned his experiment; in fact, it thrived as a cultural and scientific center up to the 1850s.

PAGE 245, LECTURE 2

Professor: OK, so we've been talking about the importance of promotions and advertising in making a company's products or services successful. You see a funny advertisement, you get a free sample, so you decide to try the product. These are very traditional and powerful ways of selling goods and services. But what else might work? For example, how many of you went to the movies last weekend? OK, I see a lot of hands. Ann, what did you go see?

Student A: I went to that new comedy, *Clowning Around*.

P: And why did you pick that movie?

SA: Well, uh, my roommate had seen it and said it was really good.

P: And, was it?

SA: Yeah, it was. But I was pretty sure it would be—we usually like the same things.

P: Did anyone else go see a movie based on someone's recommendation? Quite a few of you, I see. This is an example of what we call "word-of-mouth" marketing. Word-of-mouth marketing is any type of communication about products or services that comes from some source—maybe a person, or a review in the paper—some source that's *not* associated with the company that provides the product or service. How common is this type of marketing? Tom?

Student B: Uh, very, I think. I buy a lot of stuff—like music and video games—that my friends have tried—that they liked.

P: In fact, word-of-mouth marketing is very powerful for many types of products and services—and with people of all ages. So, why is that? Ann's already indicated one reason: she trusts her roommate's judgment because her roommate knows her, knows what she likes. So, this is a very focused … she's getting a highly customized recommendation.

SB: What I like … I mean the reason that I ask friends for advice is that they've already tried it … whatever it is that I'm thinking about buying … or doing …

P: And, that's another important element of word-of-mouth marketing. By talking to someone who's already had experience with that product—like someone who's already been to the movie—you're doing some very efficient information gathering, and you're reducing your risk of making an unsuccessful purchase. We've all seen ads for things that *sound* really attractive, but we usually wonder if we'll like it once we buy it. Knowing that someone else has already made that choice—and it worked out well—is very reassuring.

SA: You know what I don't like—it seems like everyone's always trying to sell me something. At least with advice from friends— well, they don't care if I buy something or not.

P: So, you're saying … when you turn to experts for advice, you want to know that their advice is completely independent. That they're not being paid by the company to promote their product. That you can trust them. Tom?

SB: I can see that word-of-mouth might be really effective but how, uh, how can a company control it?

P: Good question—and, of course, the answer is that they can't. But they can *influence* the process. They can bring their product or their service to the attention of people whose opinion is valued by others—whether it's experts in the media, or maybe the trendsetters in a particular target group. For example, we all have friends … we all know people who wear the coolest clothes. So, if you're a marketer and you can figure out who those style setters are … if you can get these trendsetters to try out your products— like your latest shoe design—well, you know that the shoe is much more likely to become a quick success.

SA: But what happens when the word-of-mouth is bad?

P: That's every marketer's nightmare—and I think that's why some of them avoid using this approach—they're afraid they'll generate bad publicity by mistake. And one thing studies have shown is that people are *three* times more likely to tell their friends about bad experiences than good ones. But bad word-of-mouth can happen anyway—so it's good for marketers to know when it's happening—and to try and fix it. Think about what happens when, for example, you get bad service at a restaurant.

SB: I tell my friends not to go there.

P: Exactly. But what if you complain to the manager about the service, and she not only apologizes very nicely, but she gives you some free dessert *and* some discount coupons for your next meal

there. You'd probably go back, and you'd probably tell your friends about the great manager there.

SB: You're right, I'd be pretty impressed.

P: It's too bad that more managers don't realize that doing this kind of thing well has an effect far beyond just that one customer. Now, let's talk about how technology affects this type of marketing—how much faster feedback spreads when you have e-mail and mobile phones.

Listen again to part of the lecture. Then answer question 6.

P: We've all seen ads for things that *sound* really attractive, but we usually wonder if we'll like it once we buy it. Knowing that someone else has already made that choice—and it worked out well—is very reassuring

SA: You know what I don't like?—it seems like everyone's always trying to sell me something.

Why does the student say this?

WRITING

INTEGRATED WRITING TASK 1

PAGE 256, LISTENING

Professor: The idea considered in the reading is not unreasonable in the abstract, but all the concrete evidence points to *internal* causes for the decline of Easter Island's culture 500 years ago. It's a sad story of a native culture that did not have the foresight to sustain itself.

In the centuries before 1500, the inhabitants of Easter Island were prosperous … so prosperous that they were able to invest extra time and energy in building giant statues, which became important signs of status. Different island communities began competing as to who could erect the most statues. Now here's where the problem for trees comes in: archaeological evidence shows that the islanders used tree logs to move the statues into position. So, as the number of statues increased, more and more trees had to be cut, until finally, 500 years ago, there were no more left.

Of course, once the trees were gone, the islanders could no longer build rafts to fish at sea, and so they could no longer catch big fish. As the necessities of life became harder and harder to get, the islanders no longer had the time and energy to create big statues. Without logs, of course, they couldn't move the statues anyway, so naturally the interest in making the statues declined.

Finally, it would not be surprising if the islanders lost confidence in their old gods when life on the island became a struggle for survival. I mean, the old gods wouldn't seem to be protecting them any more. So it would be natural for the islanders to have developed a different religious idea, hoping that the new god would ensure them a better life.

INTEGRATED WRITING TASK 2

PAGE 257, LISTENING

Professor: For some of the reasons presented in the reading, many companies have a policy of hiring outsiders to fill managerial positions. However, a closer examination will show that the policy is misguided.

First of all, the new perspective an outsider brings into the company's corporate structure often leads to conflict in the managerial team. Companies often have specific corporate philosophies … (for example, about how decisions are to be reached and how work is to be organized). So when outsiders bring with them a significantly different philosophy, this can create serious disagreement and conflict … and make it difficult for the managerial team as a whole to function smoothly and efficiently. An internal employee, by contrast, is more likely to know company tradition.

Another point to note is that hiring outsiders may entail an additional cost that perhaps isn't obvious. It's true that outside hires may come with required managerial skills and experience. But to become effective as managers in a new company, they also have to establish personal relationships with their new colleagues—get to know them and win their trust. This can often take more time than one would expect, and an uncomfortable settling-in period between a new boss and workers can also be more costly in lost productivity than on-the-job training for an internal employee.

Finally, suppose a company makes a point of hiring outsiders as managers instead of promoting insiders. Well, that company will soon find that its own best employees will have no choice but to look to advance their own careers outside the company. And when these key employees leave, they will also take their valuable business contacts away with them to their new employer.

SPEAKING

INTEGRATED SPEAKING TASK 1

PAGE 258, LISTENING

Student A: I don't think the professors are being unreasonable.

Student B: You can't be serious! We have a right to express our opinions.

SA: I see what you're getting at, but not in this case.

SB: What do you mean?

SA: Well, students who get high grades are going to say nice things about their professors. But if they don't get the grade they want, they'll say their professors are bad teachers.

SB: Yeah, but …

SA: Look, students here … we get to choose what classes we take, right?

SB: Right …

SA: And we get to pick our professors, right? Listen, I know one professor here who's a wonderful teacher. But she's a hard grader. You have to work hard to get a good grade in her class. So last year, a lot of students got low grades. And guess what?

SB: They wrote a lot of negative comments?

SA: Right, and that was bad for the students too, 'cause no one signed up for her course this year.

SB: No one?

SA: Well, hardly anyone. And the students who didn't sign up missed out on a great experience, 'cause like I said, she's a really great teacher, and they could have learned a lot from her.

INTEGRATED SPEAKING TASK 2

PAGE 259, LISTENING

Speaker: OK, so all citizens have the right to free speech. But can we talk anywhere and everywhere we want? Think about this example.

Remember last year, when our public school system decided to decrease the salaries of teacher's assistants? Needless to say, the teacher's assistants weren't happy about this, and many decided to protest the pay cuts.

To communicate their message, the teacher's assistants made signs to hold and pamphlets to distribute. They entered one of the public schools and began to speak out. But protesting there was disrupting classes … was preventing students from learning. School officials arrived and told protesters they had to leave.

The protesters left the school grounds and moved onto the sidewalk in front of it. They began protesting again; no one bothered them out there. And by the way, you might remember, they were successful.

Now obviously the government wouldn't allow a protest in a public school. No doubt about that. But on the sidewalk, a place where public expression is allowed, it's different. The government can't ban free expression there, because there the protesters wouldn't be preventing an essential government service, you see?

Answer Key

LISTENING

Conversation 1

1. C	**3.** A	**5.** C
2. A, D	**4.** B	

Conversation 2

1. B	**3.** A	**5.** D
2. C	**4.** C	

Lecture 1

1. C	**3.** A	**5.** C
2. B	**4.** A, C	**6.** D

Lecture 2

1. A
2. B
3. Benefit: B, C, E Not: A, D
4. B
5. D
6. C

READING

Reading 1

1. C
2. B
3. B
4. A
5. D
6. B
7. A
8. B
9. C
10. A
11. C
12. D
13. D
14. A, B, E

Reading 2

1. A
2. B
3. A
4. C
5. B
6. D
7. B
8. C
9. B
10. C
11. D
12. A
13. D
14. B, C, F

WRITING

Integrated Writing Task 1

<u>Key points</u>

Points made in the lecture counter claims made by points of the reading passage.

LECTURE POINT	READING PASSAGE POINT
The deforestation of Easter Island is most plausibly explained by overlogging by the native population who used the logs to transport their giant statues.	Easter Island was deforested by invaders who were unconcerned with sustaining its resources.
The making of giant statues stopped because economic difficulties left the Islanders without the energy to make them and because there were no logs left to transport the statues.	The cultural practices of Easter Island were disrupted by a foreign invasion.
It is likely that Easter Islanders adopted a new religion because they lost faith in their old gods.	The timing of the change in religion suggests a new practice introduced by outsiders.

Integrated Writing Task 2

<u>Key points</u>

Points made in the lecture counter claims made by points of the reading passage.

LECTURE POINT	READING PASSAGE POINT
Hiring outsiders as managers can create serious conflict within a company's managerial team.	Companies will benefit because outsiders can bring new perspectives that will reform inefficient practices.
Hiring outsiders can be costly because, unlike inside hires, outside hires require time to establish relationships with new colleagues during which there can be losses in productivity.	Hiring managers from the outside will be less expensive than promoting from within a company because outside hires will not require management training.
A policy of hiring outside managers will force inside employees seeking professional advancement to leave the company, taking valuable business contacts with them.	Companies will benefit from a policy of outside hiring because the outsiders will bring new business contacts with them.

SPEAKING

Integrated Speaking Task 1

Key points

1. The professors want the student association to stop publishing the Professor Ratings Survey.

2. The male student agrees with the professors, for several reasons:

   - In this case, he does not think the students have the right to express themselves because the ratings survey hurts both professors and students.

   - He thinks the survey is unfair to professors because students rate professors based on grades received in their classes.

   - He thinks the ratings survey hurts students because they might read negative comments about good professors and then decide not to take the professors' classes. If they do this, they would miss out on a positive experience.

Integrated Speaking Task 2

Key points

1. A nonpublic forum consists of government-owned property on which the government can ban free-speech activities because such activities could disrupt important government functions.

2. A traditional public forum such as a park or sidewalk is another type of government-owned property that is open for anyone to use. Free-speech activities are allowed in a traditional public forum.

3. The professor gives an example that uses both types of government-owned property.

   - Protesters tried to protest in a nonpublic forum.

   - When forced to leave, they moved to a traditional public forum in which free-speech activities are allowed.

Use the TOEFL iBT Scoring Rubrics on the following pages to assess responses to Integrated and Independent Tasks. For more detailed information and explanation of these rubrics, see the *NorthStar: Building Skills for the TOEFL iBT Teacher's Manual.*

TOEFL® iBT Test—Integrated Writing Rubrics

Score	Task Description
5	A response at this level successfully selects the important information from the lecture and coherently and accurately presents this information in relation to the relevant information presented in the reading. The response is well organized, and occasional language errors that are present do not result in inaccurate or imprecise presentation of content or connections.
4	A response at this level is generally good in selecting the important information from the lecture and in coherently and accurately presenting this information in relation to the relevant information in the reading, but it may have minor omission, inaccuracy, vagueness, or imprecision of some content from the lecture or in connection to points made in the reading. A response is also scored at this level if it has more frequent or noticeable minor language errors, as long as such usage and grammatical structures do not result in anything more than an occasional lapse of clarity or in the connection of ideas.
3	A response at this level contains some important information from the lecture and conveys some relevant connection to the reading, but it is marked by one or more of the following: • Although the overall response is definitely oriented to the task, it conveys only vague, global, unclear, or somewhat imprecise connection of the points made in the lecture to points made in the reading. • The response may omit one major key point made in the lecture. • Some key points made in the lecture or the reading, or connections between the two, may be incomplete, inaccurate, or imprecise. • Errors of usage and/or grammar may be more frequent or may result in noticeably vague expressions or obscured meanings in conveying ideas and connections.
2	A response at this level contains some relevant information from the lecture, but is marked by significant language difficulties or by significant omission or inaccuracy of important ideas from the lecture or in the connections between the lecture and the reading; a response at this level is marked by one or more of the following: • The response significantly misrepresents or completely omits the overall connection between the lecture and the reading. • The response significantly omits or significantly misrepresents important points made in the lecture. • The response contains language errors or expressions that largely obscure connections or meaning at key junctures, or that would likely obscure understanding of key ideas for a reader not already familiar with the reading and the lecture.
1	A response at this level is marked by one or more of the following: • The response provides little or no meaningful or relevant coherent content from the lecture. • The language level of the response is so low that it is difficult to derive meaning.
0	A response at this level merely copies sentences from the reading, rejects the topic or is otherwise not connected to the topic, is written in a foreign language, consists of keystroke characters, or is blank.

TOEFL® iBT Test—Independent Writing Rubrics

Score	Task Description
5	**An essay at this level largely accomplishes all of the following:** • effectively addresses the topic and task • is well organized and well developed, using clearly appropriate explanations, exemplifications, and/or details • displays unity, progression, and coherence • displays consistent facility in the use of language, demonstrating syntactic variety, appropriate word choice, and idiomaticity, though it may have minor lexical or grammatical errors
4	**An essay at this level largely accomplishes all of the following:** • addresses the topic and task well, though some points may not be fully elaborated • is generally well organized and well developed, using appropriate and sufficient explanations, exemplifications, and/or details • displays unity, progression, and coherence, though it may contain occasional redundancy, digression, or unclear connections • displays facility in the use of language, demonstrating syntactic variety and range of vocabulary, though it will probably have occasional noticeable minor errors in structure, word form, or use of idiomatic language that do not interfere with meaning
3	**An essay at this level is marked by one or more of the following:** • addresses the topic and task using somewhat developed explanations, exemplifications, and/or details • displays unity, progression, and coherence, though connection of ideas may be occasionally obscured • may demonstrate inconsistent facility in sentence formation and word choice that may result in lack of clarity and occasionally obscure meaning • may display accurate but limited range of syntactic structures and vocabulary
2	**An essay at this level may reveal one or more of the following weaknesses:** • limited development in response to the topic and task • inadequate organization or connection of ideas • inappropriate or insufficient exemplifications, explanations, or details to support or illustrate generalizations in response to the task • a noticeably inappropriate choice of words or word forms • an accumulation of errors in sentence structure and/or usage
1	**An essay at this level is seriously flawed by one or more of the following weaknesses:** • serious disorganization or underdevelopment • little or no detail, or irrelevant specifics, or questionable responsiveness to the task • serious and frequent errors in sentence structure or usage
0	**An essay at this level** merely copies words from the topic, rejects the topic, or is otherwise not connected to the topic, is written in a foreign language, consists of keystroke characters, or is blank.

TOEFL® iBT Test—Integrated Speaking Rubrics

Score	General Description	Delivery	Language Use	Topic Development
4	The response fulfills the demands of the task, with at most minor lapses in completeness. It is highly intelligible and exhibits sustained, coherent discourse. A response at this level is characterized by all of the following:	Speech is generally clear, fluid and sustained. It may include minor lapses or minor difficulties with pronunciation or intonation. Pace may vary at times as speaker attempts to recall information. Overall intelligibility remains high.	The response demonstrates good control of basic and complex grammatical structures that allow for coherent, efficient (automatic) expression of relevant ideas. Contains generally effective word choice. Though some minor (or systematic) errors or imprecise use may be noticeable, they do not require listener effort (or obscure meaning).	The response presents a clear progression of ideas and conveys the relevant information required by the task. It includes appropriate detail, though it may have minor errors or minor omissions.
3	The response addresses the task appropriately, but may fall short of being fully developed. It is generally intelligible and coherent, with some fluidity of expression, though it exhibits some noticeable lapses in the expression of ideas. A response at this level is characterized by at least two of the following:	Speech is generally clear, with some fluidity of expression, but it exhibits minor difficulties with pronunciation, intonation or pacing and may require some listener effort at times. Overall intelligibility remains good, however.	The response demonstrates fairly automatic and effective use of grammar and vocabulary, and fairly coherent expression of relevant ideas. Response may exhibit some imprecise or inaccurate use of vocabulary or grammatical structures or be somewhat limited in the range of structures used. Such limitations do not seriously interfere with the communication of the message.	The response is sustained and conveys relevant information required by the task. However, it exhibits some incompleteness, inaccuracy, lack of specificity with respect to content, or choppiness in the progression of ideas.
2	The response is connected to the task, though it may be missing some relevant information or contain inaccuracies. It contains some intelligible speech, but at times problems with intelligibility and/or overall coherence may obscure meaning. A response at this level is characterized by at least two of the following:	Speech is clear at times, though it exhibits problems with pronunciation, intonation or pacing and so may require significant listener effort. Speech may not be sustained at a consistent level throughout. Problems with intelligibility may obscure meaning in places (but not throughout).	The response is limited in the range and control of vocabulary and grammar demonstrated (some complex structures may be used, but typically contain errors). This results in limited or vague expression of relevant ideas and imprecise or inaccurate connections. Automaticity of expression may only be evident at the phrasal level.	The response conveys some relevant information but is clearly incomplete or inaccurate. It is incomplete if it omits key ideas, makes vague reference to key ideas, or demonstrates limited development of important information. An inaccurate response demonstrates misunderstanding of key ideas from the stimulus. Typically, ideas expressed may not be well connected or cohesive so that familiarity with the stimulus is necessary in order to follow what is being discussed.
1	The response is very limited in content or coherence or is only minimally connected to the task. Speech may be largely unintelligible. A response at this level is characterized by at least two of the following:	Consistent pronunciation and intonation problems cause considerable listener effort and frequently obscure meaning. Delivery is choppy, fragmented, or telegraphic. Speech contains frequent pauses and hesitations.	Range and control of grammar and vocabulary severely limits (or prevents) expression of ideas and connections among ideas. Some very low-level responses may rely on isolated words or short utterances to communicate ideas.	The response fails to provide much relevant content. Ideas that are expressed are often inaccurate, limited to vague utterances, or repetitions (including repetition of prompt).
0	Speaker makes no attempt to respond OR response is unrelated to the topic.			

TOEFL® iBT Test—Independent Speaking Rubrics

Score	General Description	Delivery	Language Use	Topic Development
4	The response fulfills the demands of the task, with at most minor lapses in completeness. It is highly intelligible and exhibits sustained, coherent discourse. A response at this level is characterized by all of the following:	Generally well-paced flow (fluid expression). Speech is clear. It may include minor lapses, or minor difficulties with pronunciation or intonation patterns, which do not affect overall intelligibility.	The response demonstrates effective use of grammar and vocabulary. It exhibits a fairly high degree of automaticity with good control of basic and complex structures (as appropriate). Some minor (or systematic) errors are noticeable but do not obscure meaning.	Response is sustained and sufficient to the task. It is generally well developed and coherent; relationships between ideas are clear (or clear progression of ideas).
3	The response addresses the task appropriately, but may fall short of being fully developed. It is generally intelligible and coherent, with some fluidity of expression though it exhibits some noticeable lapses in the expression of ideas. A response at this level is characterized by at least two of the following:	Speech is generally clear, with some fluidity of expression, though minor difficulties with pronunciation, intonation, or pacing are noticeable and may require listener effort at times (though overall intelligibility is not significantly affected).	The response demonstrates fairly automatic and effective use of grammar and vocabulary, and fairly coherent expression of relevant ideas. Response may exhibit some imprecise or inaccurate use of vocabulary or grammatical structures or be somewhat limited in the range of structures used. This may affect overall fluency, but it does not seriously interfere with the communication of the message.	Response is mostly coherent and sustained and conveys relevant ideas/information. Overall development is somewhat limited, usually lacks elaboration or specificity. Relationships between ideas may at times not be immediately clear.
2	The response addresses the task, but development of the topic is limited. It contains intelligible speech, although problems with delivery and/or overall coherence occur; meaning may be obscured in places. A response at this level is characterized by at least two of the following:	Speech is basically intelligible, though listener effort is needed because of unclear articulation, awkward intonation, or choppy rhythm/pace; meaning may be obscured in places.	The response demonstrates limited range and control of grammar and vocabulary. These limitations often prevent full expression of ideas. For the most part, only basic sentence structures are used successfully and spoken with fluidity. Structures and vocabulary may express mainly simple (short) and/or general propositions, with simple or unclear connections made among them (serial listing, conjunction, juxtaposition).	The response is connected to the task, though the number of ideas presented or the development of ideas is limited. Mostly basic ideas are expressed with limited elaboration (details and support). At times relevant substance may be vaguely expressed or repetitious. Connections of ideas may be unclear.
1	The response is very limited in content and/or coherence or is only minimally connected to the task, or speech is largely unintelligible. A response at this level is characterized by at least two of the following:	Consistent pronunciation, stress, and intonation difficulties cause considerable listener effort; delivery is choppy, fragmented, or telegraphic; frequent pauses and hesitations.	Range and control of grammar and vocabulary severely limits (or prevents) expression of ideas and connections among ideas. Some low level responses may rely heavily on practiced or formulaic expressions.	Limited relevant content is expressed. The response generally lacks substance beyond expression of very basic ideas. Speaker may be unable to sustain speech to complete task and may rely heavily on repetition of the prompt.
0	Speaker makes no attempt to respond OR response is unrelated to the topic.			

CD 1 TRACKING LIST

TRACK	ACTIVITY	PAGE
1	Introduction	
UNIT 1		
	Campus Conversation	
2	First Listening	3
	Second Listening	
3	Question 5	4
	Academic Listening	
4	First Listening	4
	Second Listening	
5	Question 4	5
6	Question 5	5
7	**Integrated Task, Listening**	11
UNIT 2		
	Campus Conversation	
8	First Listening	21
	Second Listening	
9	Question 3	22
10	Question 4	22
11	Question 5	22
	Academic Listening	
12	First Listening	23
	Second Listening	
13	Question 5	24
14	**Integrated Task, Listening**	30
UNIT 3		
	Campus Conversation	
15	First Listening	41
	Second Listening	
16	Question 3	42
17	Question 4	42
	Academic Listening	
18	First Listening	43
	Second Listening	
19	Question 3	44
20	Question 4	44
21	Question 5	44
22	**Integrated Task, Listening**	50
23	Examination, Item 2	53
24	Tips, Examples 1 and 2	55
25	Practice, Activity 1	55

TRACK	ACTIVITY	PAGE
UNIT 4		
	Campus Conversation	
26	First Listening	59
	Second Listening	
27	Question 2	60
28	Question 4	60
	Academic Listening	
29	First Listening	60
	Second Listening	
30	Question 2	61
31	Question 4	61
32	**Integrated Task, Listening**	69
UNIT 5		
	Campus Conversation	
33	First Listening	79
	Second Listening	
34	Question 3	80
	Academic Listening	
35	First Listening	80
	Second Listening	
36	Question 3	81
37	Question 4	81
38	**Integrated Task, Listening**	89
39	Practice, Activity 2	95
40	Question 1	96
41	Question 2	96
UNIT 6		
	Campus Conversation	
42	First Listening	99
	Second Listening	
43	Question 3	100
44	Question 5	101
	Academic Listening	
45	First Listening	101
	Second Listening	
46	Question 3	102
47	Question 4	102
48	**Integrated Task, Listening**	109
49	Practice, Activity 2	116

CD 2 TRACKING LIST

TRACK	ACTIVITY	PAGE
UNIT 7		
	Campus Conversation	
1	First Listening	119
	Second Listening	
2	Question 2	120
3	Question 4	120
	Academic Listening	
4	First Listening	120
	Second Listening	
5	Question 4	122
6	Question 5	122
7	Question 7	122
8	**Integrated Task, Listening**	129
UNIT 8		
	Campus Conversation	
9	First Listening	139
	Second Listening	
10	Question 2	140
11	Question 3	140
12	Question 4	140
	Academic Listening	
13	First Listening	141
	Second Listening	
14	Question 3	142
15	Question 4	142
16	**Integrated Task, Listening**	149
17	Practice, Activity 2	156
UNIT 9		
	Campus Conversation	
18	First Listening	162
	Second Listening	
19	Question 3	163
20	Question 5	163
21	Question 6	163
	Academic Listening	
22	First Listening	163
	Second Listening	
23	Question 3	164
24	Question 5	165
25	**Integrated Task, Listening**	172
26	Examination, Item 4	175

TRACK	ACTIVITY	PAGE
UNIT 10		
	Campus Conversation	
27	First Listening	182
	Second Listening	
28	Question 4	182
29	Question 5	183
	Academic Listening	
30	First Listening	183
	Second Listening	
31	Question 3	185
32	Question 4	185
33	**Integrated Task, Listening**	192
ETS PRACTICE SETS		
34	**Conversation 1**	242
35	Question 5	243
36	**Conversation 2**	243
37	Question 5	243
38	**Lecture 1**	243
39	**Lecture 2**	245
40	Question 6	246
41	Integrated Writing Task 1, Listening	256
42	Integrated Writing Task 2, Listening	257
43	Integrated Speaking Task 1, Listening	258
44	Integrated Speaking Task 2, Listening	259